The Artistry of Teaching i Higher Education

Introducing a fresh approach to conceptualising and actioning high-quality teaching in higher education, this essential volume fills a gap in current literature by expanding beyond the mere 'delivery' of teaching. Instead, it offers an evidence-based discussion of 'artistry' and demonstrates how this may be applied successfully within a higher education setting to enable better student learning. Key concepts such as improvisation, embodiment, knowing oneself and one's students, and a compassionate and relational approach to facilitating learning are unpacked throughout.

Filled with practical examples based on scholarship and experience from and applicable to a wide range of disciplines, *The Artistry of Teaching in Higher Education* is divided into three distinct parts which explore:

- Creativity, improvisation and context;
- Authenticity and professional identity;
- Developing the artistry of teaching.

An essential read for teachers, senior management, educational developers, and policy makers alike, this book acts as a call to action within higher education institutions to support and create space for learning, creativity and innovation, to the benefit of the development of their teachers' expertise.

Helen King is Professor and Director of Learning Innovation, Development & Skills at Bath Spa University, UK. Her career in educational development spans nearly three decades including leading roles within three UK universities and several UK-wide learning and teaching enhancement projects and organisations and as an independent consultant collaborating nationally and internationally.

The Staff and Educational Development Series
Series Editor: James Wisdom

Written by experienced and well-known practitioners and published in association with the Staff and Educational Development Association (SEDA), each book in the series contributes to the development of learning, teaching and training and assists in the professional development of staff. The books present new ideas for learning development and facilitate the exchange of information and good practice.

Titles in the series:

Developing Expertise for Teaching in Higher Education
Practical Ideas for Professional Learning and Development
Edited by Helen King

Advancing Student Engagement in Higher Education
Reflection, Critique and Challenge
Edited by Tom Lowe

Student Agency and Engagement
Shifting the Debate to Improve Assessment and Feedback
Tansy Jessop

Outdoor Learning in Higher Education
Educating Beyond the Seminar Room
Edited by Wendy Garnham and Paolo Oprandi

For more information about this series, please visit: https://www.routledge.com/SEDA-Series/book-series/SE0747

The Artistry of Teaching in Higher Education

Practical Ideas for Developing Creative Academic Practice

Edited by Helen King

with editorial contributions from Richard Bale, Erika Corradini, Peter Fossey, Deanne Gannaway, Leonardo Morantes-Africano, Shaun Mudd, and Jackie Potter

LONDON AND NEW YORK

Designed cover image: Getty Images

First published 2025
by Routledge
4 Park Square, Milton Park, Abingdon, Oxon OX14 4RN

and by Routledge
605 Third Avenue, New York, NY 10158

Routledge is an imprint of the Taylor & Francis Group, an informa business

© 2025 selection and editorial matter, Helen King; individual chapters, the contributors

The right of Helen King to be identified as the author of the editorial material, and of the authors for their individual chapters, has been asserted in accordance with sections 77 and 78 of the Copyright, Designs and Patents Act 1988.

All rights reserved. No part of this book may be reprinted or reproduced or utilised in any form or by any electronic, mechanical, or other means, now known or hereafter invented, including photocopying and recording, or in any information storage or retrieval system, without permission in writing from the publishers.

Trademark notice: Product or corporate names may be trademarks or registered trademarks, and are used only for identification and explanation without intent to infringe.

British Library Cataloguing-in-Publication Data
A catalogue record for this book is available from the British Library

ISBN: 978-1-032-56953-6 (hbk)
ISBN: 978-1-032-56952-9 (pbk)
ISBN: 978-1-003-43782-6 (ebk)

DOI: 10.4324/9781003437826

Typeset in Galliard
by SPi Technologies India Pvt Ltd (Straive)

To Carole and David Baume for their mentorship, inspiration and commitment to bettering learning in higher education.

Contents

Notes on the editor and contributors   x

Introduction: the artistry of teaching in higher education   1
HELEN KING, RICHARD BALE, ERIKA CORRADINI, PETER FOSSEY, DEANNE GANNAWAY, LEONARDO MORANTES-AFRICANO, SHAUN MUDD, AND JACKIE POTTER

PART I
Creativity, improvisation and context   15

1 Taking the "art" in "artistry" literally: an art-based theory of teaching expertise   17
MIKE BRYANT

2 Blackholes and revelations: understanding everyday creativity in higher education teacher practice   31
SAM ELKINGTON

3 The embodied realm of teaching   46
CURIE SCOTT

4 Expertise is ... never having to say you are sorry: academic development and the artistry of improvisation   62
JENNIE MILLS, JENNI CARR, NATASHA TAYLOR, AND CATRIONA CUNNINGHAM

5 The artistry of teaching as culturally self-aware, learning-centred, imaginative co-creation   74
ANNA SANTUCCI

PART II
Authenticity and professional identity   89

6 Authenticity in delivering contextual pedagogy and materials in cybersecurity   91
ABDULLAHI ARABO

7 Developing online communities of practice through relational pedagogy   106
JAMES LAYTON

8 The MIPA model of professional identities of dance teachers: negotiating professional identities in and across higher education   120
MICHELLE GROVES

9 From disciplinary expertise to academic artistry: the shifting professional identity, expertise, and artistry of the programme leader   135
JENNY LAWRENCE

10 The many identities of a learning technologist (and how to make the most of them)   149
EVAN DICKERSON

PART III
Developing the artistry of teaching   161

11 Developing the artistry of teaching and approaches to learning: what we can learn from those teaching theatre improvisation   163
PETIA PETROVA, SHAUN MUDD, IMOGEN PALMER, AND STEPHEN BROWN

12 The characteristics of expertise in online teaching in higher education   178
SARAH WILSON-MEDHURST AND MARK CHILDS

13 Developing the artistry of language teaching through
   practitioner research   193
   ANNA COSTANTINO

14 Facilitating in the moment: being ready for change   209
   LUCY NICHOLSON, RUTH SPENCER, AND KERSTIN WELLHÖFER

15 Professional development for artistry in higher education   224

   15.1 To 'toy with', 'think about' and 'experiment with': teacher
        development programmes as space for developing the artistry of
        teaching   224
        EMMA KENNEDY AND MARTIN COMPTON

   15.2 Developing teaching expertise for disciplinary contexts – building
        the bridges between institution and discipline perspectives   227
        JACKIE POTTER AND MOIRA LAFFERTY

   15.3 "What's in it for me?": professional services colleagues and
        teaching expertise   229
        SARAH FLOYD AND FIONA SMART

   15.4 Engaging in feedback dialogue to enhance expertise in
        healthcare teaching   232
        LUCY SPOWART AND TRISTAN PRICE

   15.5 Sketching new horizons: what does evaluation of staff
        development events tell us about developing expertise?   235
        CHARLOTTE STEVENS

   15.6 Building confidence through appreciative self-study   237
        CAITLIN KIGHT

Index   243

Notes on the editor and contributors

Editor

Helen King PhD NTF SFSEDA PFHEA is currently Professor and Director of Learning Innovation, Development & Skills at Bath Spa University, UK. Her career in educational development spans nearly three decades and has included leading roles in UK–wide learning and teaching enhancement projects and organisations (including Assistant Director of the Higher Education Academy Subject Centre for Geography, Earth & Environmental Sciences, Senior HE Policy Adviser for the Higher Education Funding Council for England, and current co-Chair of the Staff & Educational Development Association: SEDA), as an independent consultant collaborating with colleagues in the UK, USA, and Australia, and institutional roles (previously Head of Academic Staff Development at the University of Bath and Deputy Director of Academic Practice at the University of the West of England, Bristol). She has broad interests across a range of learning, teaching, and assessment themes, but her particular passion is supporting colleagues' professional learning and development. Her current research is exploring the characteristics of expertise for teaching in higher education. She is proud to hold a senior fellowship of the Staff & Educational Development Association (SFSEDA) and is a UK National Teaching Fellow (NTF), Principal Fellow of the Higher Education Academy (PFHEA), and Honorary Associate Professor at the University of Queensland. In her nonwork time, she thoroughly enjoys trail running and playing Bluegrass banjo (not necessarily at the same time), both of which feed into her research and educational development interests in various ways!

Co-Editors

Richard Bale is a Senior Teaching Fellow in Educational Development at Imperial College London, UK. He holds a PhD in corpus-based interpreter education, a Masters (MEd) in University Learning and Teaching, and is Senior Fellow of the Higher Education Academy (SFHEA). His first book,

Teaching with Confidence in Higher Education: Applying Strategies from the Performing Arts, was published in 2020 by Routledge.

Erika Corradini is a Principal Teaching Fellow in Academic Practice at the Centre for Higher Education Practice (CHEP) at the University of Southampton, UK. She leads Educator Development and the Scholarship of Teaching and Learning, nurturing early career academics. Her focus is on advancing learning and education through evaluating teaching practices and promoting SOTL. In her role, she provides professional development, contributing to a dynamic and innovative higher education environment.

Peter Fossey PhD SFHEA is an Associate Professor in the Academic Development Centre at the University of Warwick, UK. His interests include philosophy of emotions, philosophy of higher education, decolonisation, and academic integrity. He co-leads an AdvanceHE accredited teaching and learning development programme for new assistant professors at the university.

Deanne Gannaway has worked in academic development in the Australian higher education sector for over 20 years. Her teaching and scholarship focus on continuing professional learning for university teachers. She is currently Academic Lead (Professional Learning) in the Institute of Teaching and Learning Innovation (ITaLI) at the University of Queensland (UQ).

Leonardo Morantes-Africano EdD SFHEA currently works as curriculum lead and programme lead at the School of Education of Newcastle College University Centre, UK. Leo combines his passion as a practitioner in teacher education with research around social justice, moral philosophy, gender and identity studies, inclusion and belonging, and critical reflection.

Shaun Mudd PhD SFHEA is Head of Teaching Expertise Development at Bath Spa University, UK. He has previously worked in educational development at the University of the West of England (UWE Bristol) and University of Exeter, where he focussed especially on the initial professional development of new academic staff.

Jackie Potter is Dean of Academic Innovation at the University of Chester, UK and Professor of Learning and Development in HE. She is the Vice-Chair of the Heads of Educational Development Group and a Senior Fellow of the Staff and Educational Development Association. Tw/X: @Jac_Potter; LinkedIN Jacqueline Potter.

Contributors

Lucilene de Almeida is a doctoral student in Human Motricity—Dance Specialization at Faculty of Human Motricity, University of Lisbon, Portugal. She has a Master's in Artistic Performance (Dance) at Faculty of

Human Motricity—University Technical of Lisbon, and is a specialist in art education, Professor of Educational Dance at CENSUPEG and ballet at Cultural Center Theater Guaira. She holds a Bachelor's Degree in Dance and Physiotherapy.

Abdullahi Arabo PhD SFHEA, is Associate Professor at the University of the West of England (UWE) excelling in cyber science and network security. He has received awards for his dedication in cyber professional development, induction into UWE's Black Hall of Fame, and a National Teaching Fellowship in 2022. His leadership and funding contributions led to UWE's recognition as a Centre of Excellence in Cyber Security.

Laura Ashcroft is a lecturer in counselling, teaching on both the MSc Counselling and PGDip Counselling Children and Young People programmes at Bangor University, UK. She also works as a sessional counsellor both for the NHS Primary Care Mental Health Counselling Service and a local private practice.

Monica Biagioli is Senior Lecturer Design Innovation at London College of Communication, UK. She contributes art and design approaches to support understanding and reflection, with special attention to the role that informal spaces play in communication. Her projects include curation, project development, and the use of arts-based methods to develop understanding.

Stephen Brown is a professional coach, business psychologist and senior facilitator and trainer for the NHS based in Bristol, UK. He has been performing improv since 2014 and has been working with the Bristol Improv Theatre on their Applied Improv workshops since 2019.

Mike Bryant MA PGCE SFHEA is Project Director in the Division of Learning and Teaching, Charles Sturt University, Australia; a sessional academic at Monash University; and a research degree candidate at UCL. He specialises in the leadership of curriculum and digital education initiatives in tertiary education and researches teaching expertise in digital environments.

Jenni Carr PhD is Senior Academic Developer at The London School of Economics and Political Science, UK. She is Programme Director for the PGCertHE. Jenni also leads projects promoting the use of creative pedagogies in the social sciences, with a particular interest in using simulations to support authentic learning.

Mark Childs is a senior learning designer at Durham University, UK. He has a PhD in Education from the University of Warwick and was awarded a National Teaching Fellowship in 2021 for his research and teaching using virtual reality and videoconferencing. He is one of the co-hosts of the podcast Pedagodzilla.

Notes on the editor and contributors xiii

Martin Compton PhD PFHEA SCMALT has been an educator for over 30 years, working in schools, colleges, and universities in the UK and overseas. He is currently College Lead for Programme, Module and Assessment Design at King's College London, UK, leading on pedagogical responses to generative AI (and broader technological changes).

Modesto Corderi Novoa is a Chinese language teacher and researcher/teacher trainer in the use of drama in the language classroom. He holds a PhD in Language Acquisition in Multilingual Settings from the University of the Basque Country in Spain, a BA in Chinese, and a Master's MTCSOL from Beijing Language and Culture University in China.

Anna Costantino is an applied linguist and language educator at the University of Greenwich and Regent's University London, UK. She is a practitioner-researcher and member of the Centre for Research in Language and Heritage at the University of Greenwich. Her research interests include teacher and learner development and participatory practitioner research.

Catriona Cunningham is Professor and Head of the Department of Learning & Teaching Enhancement at the University of Edinburgh Napier in Scotland where she leads on strategic learning and teaching priorities across the institution. She is passionate about higher education and is particularly interested in interculturalism in higher education, student engagement, and academic identities.

Evan Dickerson SFHEA is the Learning Technologist at Guildhall School of Music & Drama, UK. He has been Head of E-Learning at Bloomsbury Institute and Queen Mary University of London, after various roles at other higher education institutions. When a Jisc HE Adviser, he provided digital learning support to over 60 UK universities and colleges and has been a consultant to universities in Australia, Cyprus, Denmark, Malta, Romania, and Spain. He is also an internationally published writer on classical music and opera.

Sam Elkington PhD is Professor of Learning and Teaching at Teesside University, UK, where he leads on the University's learning and teaching enhancement portfolio. Sam is a PFHEA, National Teaching Fellow (NTF, 2021), and is also an executive committee member and pedagogic research lead for the Association of National Teaching Fellows.

Sarah Floyd PhD is a Reader in Higher Education Practice at Ulster University, Northern Ireland, and a Principal Fellow. She leads Ulster's Advance HE–accredited provision and Education Excellence Awards. She has a keen commitment to ensure that all who impact on student learning have opportunities to be valued and recognised.

Michelle Groves is a dance educator and researcher who has worked in higher education for over 30 years. Her interests focus on professional identity formation in higher and professional education. As Director of Education for the Royal Academy of Dance, UK, Michelle is passionate about raising the professional standing of dance teaching.

Laura Heels PhD is a Lecturer in computer science at Newcastle University, UK, specialising in education practice with a particular focus on inclusivity of CS education. Part of Laura's role in the Department of Computing is EDI director, which involves reviewing policies and creating an environment which is inclusive and fair for everyone.

Clive Holtham is Professor of Information Management at Bayes Business School, City, University of London, UK. He was made a UK National Teaching Fellow in 2003. He combines a professional background in accounting and technology with active development of arts-based initiatives in management and research.

Mary Jacob is a lecturer at Aberystwyth University, UK, leading the Postgraduate Certificate in Teaching in Higher Education. She curates the Weekly Resource Roundup of events and publications about learning and teaching. She holds SFSEDA, SFHEA, PGCTHE, and CMALT. She posts on Twitter as Mary Jacob L&T.

Emma Kennedy PhD SFHEA has been working in educational development since 2015. She currently works at the University of Greenwich, UK, leading the Postgraduate Certificate in Higher Education and the Academic Professional Apprenticeship as well as leading on staff development in inclusivity. She is also co-editor of the SEDA Blog.

Caitlin Kight PhD is an educator specialising in pedagogies of liberation, self-study, and creativity. Originally an ecologist, Caitlin maintains an interest in science communication; she is a Dakshin Foundation fellow and editor/writer for *Current Conservation* and *CC Kids*. Her daily webcomic, Doodlewax, is posted on Twitter and Instagram at @specialagentCK.

Moira Lafferty is Head of Psychology at the University of Chester, UK, and is a Health and Care Professions Council–registered Sport and Exercise Psychologist as well as an Associate Fellow of the British Psychological Society. Tw/X: @ProfMoiraL; LinkedIN Moira Lafferty

Jenny Lawrence PFHEA, NTF, CATE is Director of the Oxford Centre for Academic Enhancement and Development at Oxford Brookes University, UK.

James Layton is a Lecturer in performance at the University of the West of Scotland. He has published in areas including time and performance, arts and health, and digital performance. His recent monograph, *Bergson and*

Notes on the editor and contributors   xv

Durational Performance: (Re)Ma(r)king Time, is published by Intellect Books / University of Chicago Press.

Lindsay Marshall PhD is Emeritus Professor of Educational Practice in Computer Science at Newcastle University School of Computing, UK. He is a National Teaching Fellow and plays the mandolin.

Jennie Mills PhD is Associate Professor at the Academic Development Centre at the University of Warwick, UK. Her research explores the arts-based and post-qualitative pedagogies and practices within academic development and higher education research.

Lucy Nicholson is a dance artist and senior lecturer with the University of Central Lancashire, UK. She specialises in embodied facilitation and The Laban/Bartenieff Movement System. She has worked internationally as a community dance artist and has extensive experience of developing projects within criminal justice and recovery settings. She uses dance and movement to empower and support people to discover something new about themselves and their environment.

Imogen Palmer is Applied Improv Lead of Bristol Improv Theatre and Artistic Director of theatre company The Delight Collective, UK. She/they has over a decade's experience as a performer, director, and facilitator and will soon complete an MA in Dramatherapy at the University of Roehampton.

Petia Petrova PhD SFHEA is Associate Director of Academic Practice at the University of the West of England (UWE Bristol), and in her spare time – an improvisor. She has a particular interest in how we offer deep and meaningful, as well as practical and applied, professional development for university staff.

Tristan Price PhD is Programme Lead and Lecturer in Clinical Education at the Peninsula Medical School, University of Plymouth, UK. Tristan's research focusses on areas related to workforce sustainability, with a particular focus on doctor performance and regulation. Tristan also researches and practices innovative pedagogies in clinical education.

Julia Reeve is a National Teaching Fellow, educational consultant, and LEGO® Serious Play® facilitator, specialising in playful, multisensory learning with an emphasis on compassion, well-being, and inclusion. She works across disciplines and in diverse settings including prison education. Julia shares her practice at https://www.juliareeve.co.uk/.

Charlie Reis FHEA, is Director of the Educational Development Unit at Xi'an Jiaotong–Liverpool University, China, and the founder of the China-based Association for Partnership in Educational Development. His research includes expertise in teaching, Chinese philosophy, and contemporary pedagogy and artificial intelligence in learning and teaching.

Anna Santucci PhD is Senior Lecturer in the Centre for Integration of Research, Teaching and Learning at University College Cork (Ireland), chair of POD Network's Professional Development Committee, and editor of its *POD Speaks*. Her transdisciplinary scholarship critically promotes interculturality and equity in higher education via co-creation, reflection, and dialogue.

Curie Scott is an education / arts & health consultant. An award-winning teacher, she bridges scientific and creative communities as a medical doctor with a doctorate in drawing for thinking. Curie is convinced that well-being is improved when art and medicine work together and has featured on radio and television.

Fay Short is Professor of Psychology at Bangor University, UK, and a Chartered Psychologist with the British Psychological Society. She is also a qualified therapist and a registered member of the British Association for Counselling and Psychotherapy. Her current roles include Course Director for the MSc in Counselling and Associate Pro-Vice Chancellor for Employability.

Fiona Smart, PhD, PFHEA is a professor and learning and teaching enhancement consultant who works internationally and within the UK. Fiona is the Deputy Lead of the Scottish Principal Fellow Network and was one of three creators of the Intangibles Methodology. Together with Associate Professor Celia Popovic, York University, Toronto, Fiona is the co-creator of EDTA and the instigator of its bi-monthly speakeasies.

Ruth Spencer FHEA is an independent dance artist and senior lecturer whose practice is rooted in education and community settings. Ruth encourages individuals to discover and explore movement in relationship to self and other. She has vast experience of working as a dance artist and educator, in mainstream and SEND schools and colleges, delivering creative arts programmes, research projects, INSET training, and mentoring programmes independently and in partnership with national and international arts organisations.

Lucy Spowart is a higher education consultant, executive coach, and honorary professor in educational enhancement at the University of Plymouth, UK. Lucy was awarded a Principal Fellow in 2018 and a National Teaching Fellowship in 2020. Her research interests include continual professional development, teaching accreditation, and impact evaluation.

Charlotte Stevens PhD FSEDA SFHEA is Assistant Professor (Digital Education) in the Academic Development Centre at the University of Warwick, UK. Previously, she spent 18 years at the Open University UK, where she led on evaluation of staff development events for associate lecturers. Her research interests include evidencing impacts of professional development, understanding the digital learning experience, and creative approaches to reflection.

Natasha Taylor PhD is a teacher and researcher with interests in creative arts pedagogies, reflective practice, and the scholarship of teaching and learning. She is Head of Educational Development at COLLARTS (in Melbourne, Australia), where she leads the Staff Development Programme and the Graduate Certificate in Higher Education (Creative Arts).

Carys Watts PhD is Senior Lecturer in Enterprise (biosciences) at Newcastle University, UK. Her education specialism includes innovation, creativity, entrepreneurship, laboratory and digital skills development, and molecular biosciences. Values-led, she champions EDI, global cultural competence, the UN SDGs, and cross-disciplinary co-creativity. She holds Fellowship of Enterprise Educators UK and SF HEA status.

Kerstin Wellhöfer works creatively, educationally, and therapeutically with people of all ages, addressing health, expression and joy. She focusses on inclusion and neurodivergent ways of navigating life trauma, nervous system regulating, and co-creating presence through embodied creative explorations. She delivered somatic dance education for UCLan on BA Dance Performance & Teaching and MA, Dance & Somatic Wellbeing.

Sarah Wilson-Medhurst is an independent HE consultant and researcher with extensive experience of academic and curriculum development, strategic leadership, mentoring, pedagogic research, and evaluation. Sarah is Principal Fellow of HEA, Associate of Advance HE, Member of British Computer Society, and School Governor chairing the Curriculum and Data Committee.

Nia Young PhD is Director of Teaching and Learning for the School of Education at Bangor University, UK, a lecturer in childhood and youth studies, and in counselling. Nia is a keen advocate of children's well-being and participation rights and is now the Course Director for a Post-Graduate Diploma in Counselling Children and Young People.

Introduction

The artistry of teaching in higher education

Helen King, Richard Bale, Erika Corradini, Peter Fossey, Deanne Gannaway, Leonardo Morantes-Africano, Shaun Mudd, and Jackie Potter

Excellence and expertise

The notion of excellence is pre-eminent in many sectors including higher education (HE). In England, the government introduced the Teaching Excellence Framework (TEF) to recognise the quality of HE above a baseline standard. In the UK and internationally there are individual and team excellence awards for teaching, and many HE institutions cite "striving for excellence", or equivalent, in their mission statements and strategies. The importance of high-quality learning and teaching is a key issue for HE institutions (HEIs) and their stakeholders, particularly within those HE systems requiring tuition fees to be paid by their students, as well as the moral imperative towards learners. However, excellence is poorly defined in terms of the characteristics of an individual teacher. Criteria for excellence, for example, in national teaching awards offer an indication but they are based on experience and assumptions rather than empirical evidence (King, 2022). The concept of expertise, on the other hand, has a deep and broad theoretical and empirical foundation which offers a fresh approach to considering the characteristics of high-performing practitioners (e.g. Ericsson et al., 2006; Hambrick et al., 2018).

Excellence in any field can be recognised by the high-quality outcomes achieved in that activity. In England, the quality of teaching in HEIs is measured by the regulator (the Office for Students) through outcomes including graduating students' satisfaction (through the National Student Survey, NSS) and their later achievement of good employment or further study (Graduate Outcomes Survey, GOS). However, these outcomes reveal little about the nature of the inputs, of the elements required to enable good student learning. In England, the Teaching Excellence Framework digs a little deeper into HE quality to explore and judge the nature of the students' learning experience through qualitative statements written by the HEIs and their students. Internationally, many institutions utilise digital surveys, peer observation, and other techniques to evaluate the quality of their teachers through review of their outputs. And national awards for teaching excellence, such as Canada's

3M National Teaching Fellowships, similarly include output criteria based on leadership, excellence, and innovation.

Looking at these various frameworks and awards can provide a sense of how good teaching is experienced by the learner and the positive outcomes resulting from it. However, they offer few insights into the process of teaching and of becoming an excellent teacher. The UK's National Teaching Fellowship (NTF) and Collaborative Award for Teaching Excellence (CATE) hint at these through their criteria "Developing Excellence" and "Collaborative Approach" respectively. The process of developing teaching practice is also an important component of the Professional Standards Framework (PSF: Advance HE, 2023) which emphasises evidence-informed practice and continuing professional development.

Teaching excellence, therefore, as described through quality, award, and recognition criteria, is not a particularly useful concept. As outlined previously, the criteria for excellence do not provide sufficient insights to understand the nature of high-quality teaching practice from the teacher perspective. In addition, the term suggests a static point to be reached. *Excellence* is something we can strive for but is, ultimately, unattainable as, by definition, we can't all be above average, let alone outstanding. The concept of *expertise*, however, offers an approach for considering the "inputs" to high-quality teaching, provides insights into the diversity of knowledge and skills required "to fulfil academic work in the contemporary academy", and emphasises "the need to [develop] across a whole career path" (Gannaway, 2022, p.65). The extensive research and literature on expertise in a variety of professions and activities including music, sport, medicine, business, taxi driving, and taxidermy (e.g. Kneebone, 2021), to name but a few, suggests some common components which can be categorised as follows (King, 2022):

1) A foundation of **knowledge** (facts, underpinning concepts, and theories) and **skills** (practical application of this knowledge) acquired through learning and experience.
2) **Intentional and ongoing reflection**: experience alone does not necessarily enable optimum development of knowledge, skills, and wisdom (e.g. Di Stefano et al., 2023). To most effectively improve and develop, one must reflect on and learn from that experience. Hence, professional activities require some type of self-determined learning and development which might be manifest in ways such as deliberate practice (Ericsson et al., 1993) or progressive problem solving (Bereiter & Scardamalia, 1993);
3) Particular **ways of thinking and practising** (Hounsell & Anderson, 2005) or a "wisdom of practice" (van Heerden, 2005) that transcends the competent application of knowledge and skills and brings about characteristics that we recognise as expertise and, ultimately, enables high-quality outcomes.

For the profession of teaching in HE, these characteristics of expertise might be considered as (King, 2022) (Figure I.1):

- **Pedagogical Content Knowledge** (PCK: Shulman, 1986): the weaving together of knowledge and skills relating to teaching (pedagogy) and those relating to the subject being taught;
- **Professional Learning**: an intentional and evidence-informed approach to continually developing one's practice (King, 2019) founded on an inquisitive and scholarly approach to teaching (Corradini, 2022; Healey, 2023), and including a critical approach to reflection in order to make sense of one's own experience and to inform future practice (Morantes-Africano, 2022);
- **Artistry of Teaching**: the ways of thinking and practising as a teacher that particularly sets apart the expert from the experienced non-expert.

Ways of thinking and practising in teaching

Effective ways of thinking and practising which lead to consistently high-quality outcomes go beyond a transactional relationship between the practitioner and their subject. Mechanical following of procedures can only be effective in a perfectly predictable world, and this is not the world of teaching and learning. "Because of the multidimensionality, simultaneity, immediacy, and unpredictability of the classroom, teachers need to be able to attend to multiple events simultaneously" (Tsui, 2003, p.30). The persistent following of a procedure in this type of environment is unlikely to result in the desired outcome for the teacher or their student. An expertise-led approach to a novel or unexpected situation has the potential to be transformational and the

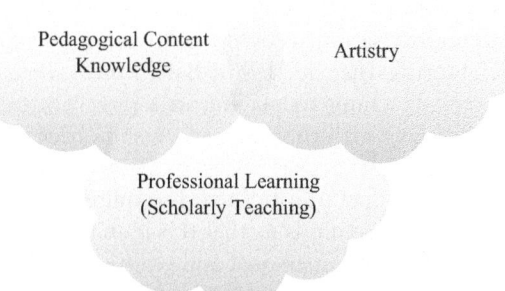

Figure I.1 A model of expertise for teaching in higher education
Adapted from King, 2022 p.19

outcome will be the product of the practitioner's unique adaptation to the specific situation. Teaching is not merely a case of delivering lesson plans but is a complex task that involves "the moral and the technical, the cognitive and affective, the intellectual and conative, mind and body" (Humphreys & Hyland, 2002). Hence, ways of thinking and practising in teaching are "the starting point of the process for collecting, reflecting, reasoning, understanding, and accumulating practical wisdom" (Huang, 2015).

If expertise in teaching requires something beyond pedagogic competency that can be particularly recognised in the response to unpredictable events, then when seeking to characterise expertise "… let us search, instead, for an epistemology of practice implicit in the artistic, intuitive processes which some practitioners bring to situations of uncertainty, instability, uniqueness and value conflict" (Schön, 1982, p.49).

The Artistry of Teaching in Higher Education

Ways of thinking and practising in the disciplines have been a valuable perspective in higher education to consider the development of curricula (e.g. Barradell et al., 2018), but the concept of "teacher thinking" has mostly only been explored at other educational levels, particularly in relation to initial teacher education (Huang, 2015). Schön (1987, p.13) suggests that "Inherent in the practice of the professionals we recognize as unusually competent is a core of artistry. Artistry is … a kind of knowing, … an art of problem framing, an art of implementation, and an art of improvisation". Emerging from her model on expertise in teaching in higher education, Helen King (2022) characterises the epistemology for teachers in HE as the "Artistry of Teaching", this being "a way of describing impromptu and idiosyncratic behaviours that elevate teaching beyond the formulaic or routine" (Bryant, 2024, this volume p. XX). Effective teaching in any educational context is a complex dance on an uneven surface. Based on foundational skills and knowledge, it requires almost instantaneous reflection-in-action (Schön, 1982), rapid reaction, and improvisation, as described through the concept of "adaptive expertise" (Hatano & Inagaki, 1986; Bale, 2022). In a similar analogy, Eisner (2002) likened teaching to playing in a jazz band with the need to collaborate and interweave with the other players in order to create harmony from dissonance.

However, it is not just "fleet of foot" that is required for effective teaching. The concept of artistry also reminds us that this is an expertise of engagement with other humans and that the personal and emotional elements of teaching and of learning are an integral part of the process (Fossey, 2022).

> At root, teaching, especially in higher education, is about authenticity.… To be authentic demands courage on the part of the teacher as well as the student; to try to teach in different ways that promote dialogue, to be honest

about their own ideological or theoretical perspectives and to engage with students as co-learners.... It is about building a relationship with students based on trust and respect.

(Macfarlane, 2007 p.59)

As summarised by King (2022, p.9), artistry is

a substantial and critical element of teaching practice that is rarely explicitly addressed in higher education. The artistry of teaching, as a named dimension of the model, is a powerful reminder of the need for a conception of expertise that is dynamic and socially constructed

(Tennant et al., 2010)

Artistry includes acknowledging our own limitations and the expertise of others (and in this way expertise has more humility than 'excellence' has), the importance of care and empathy (McCune, 2019), and the importance of community and collaboration, both with our students and with other teachers (Shulman, 1993; Collins & Evans, 2018). The concept of expertise necessarily shifts the focus from teacher as didact to the teacher and learners as communal players where everyone has a valid perspective to share. It also recognises that expertise in teaching is not simply about practised routines but requires creativity, improvisation and curiosity for what is going on in the learning space. Expertise is characterised theoretically and illustrated empirically as an ongoing journey motivated by our curiosity as teacher-evaluators (Hattie, 2015) and our care for effective student learning.

These ideas are not new for the teaching profession in general; in 1978 Gage noted: "As a practical art, teaching must be recognised as a process that calls for intuition, creativity, improvisation, and expressiveness" (p. 15) and Eisner expressed the concept of artistry of teaching over 20 years ago (2002). One's artistry as a teacher develops over a period of time through experience, practice, learning, and reflection. Artistry is authentic and idiosyncratic; we each develop our own ways of thinking and practising to suit the complexities of our own teaching experiences. This development of our personal artistry and expertise can also be supported and enhanced (potentially even accelerated) through formal professional learning opportunities from early in one's career. Until recently, professional development opportunities for teaching in higher education have tended to focus on PCK and, in particular, the theory and practice of pedagogy. However, as illustrated in this book, there is now emerging in the literature and educational development practice in HE an increasing interest in improvisation, creativity, play, collaboration, and compassionate and relational pedagogies which go beyond theoretical underpinnings to explore more deeply the application of an authentic PCK in real-life teaching.

As learning institutions, higher education providers need to offer strategically aligned and integrated professional development that supports its teachers to make meaning of pedagogy for themselves and their students, so that they can extend beyond competency-based pedagogy (how to teach) towards authentic artistry (how to enable learning) "because it is learning that matters most" (Baume, 2023 p.7).

Structure of the book

An inaugural "Expertise Symposium" was held in October 2020, from which arose the book *Developing Expertise for Teaching in Higher Education* (King, 2022). The symposium and book explored the concept of expertise and unpacked further ideas on pedagogical content knowledge, professional learning, and artistry. A key theme arising from the symposium and book was the importance of the relational nature of teaching. As noted in the introductory chapter (p. 9), "The artistry of teaching, as a named dimension of the model, is a powerful reminder of the need for a conception of expertise that engages with humans – teachers and students – rather than with objects such as chess pieces". As an under-researched and under-utilised element of teacher expertise, artistry was calling out for more discussion, interpretation, and application.

The contributions in this book arose from presentations at the second Expertise Symposium, which had the specific theme of Artistry of Teaching. This event in October 2022 was convened by the editor and supported and hosted by the co-editors including colleagues at the University of Warwick. Although the majority of the contributions are from the UK, others from Australia, China, Ireland, Portugal, and Spain provide a rich and diverse perspective.

Part I: Creativity, improvisation and context

The first part of this book explores the notion of "adaptive expertise" in the context of teaching and how it is manifest through creativity, improvisation, and awareness of self, students, and institutional context. In Chapter 1, Mike Bryant introduces the concept of "artistry" through exploring its roots in occupational expertise where someone is considered highly skilled and successful in their particular, specialised domain. He notes the connections made in the philosophical, psychological, and cognitive neuroscience literature between this type of skill and art, with the caveat that this "performance" focus on artistry neglects the moral and social impact of the expert and has, therefore, limitations when considering the expertise of teaching. Drawing on art theory and hermeneutic philosophy, Mike suggests the idea of "responsible enquiry" as an art-based theory of teaching which shifts the focus from what the "artist does" to what the "art does". Separately within this chapter, Clive Holtham and Monica Biagioli share a practical example of an "indisciplinary" collaborative approach which can enable this shift in focus and mindset. When applied to the HE teacher, the "responsible enquiry" model highlights the teacher's social impact and why a teacher does what they do, embracing the relational, moral, and ethical considerations of the HE context.

In Chapter 2, Sam Elkington describes research he has undertaken to explore everyday creative practices and the personal meaning attached to the micro-behaviours of educators he interviewed from a wide range of disciplines. Through his meticulous exposure of the detail and nuance of creative practice, Sam reveals "everyday creative praxis" as intentionally focused on process, as innovative and new and set within a context of personal understanding that embraces the possibilities of both failure and success in endeavours. The need to accept these possibilities as opportunities for learning is also recommended by Fay Short and colleagues in their short piece on "imposter syndrome", embedded within the chapter.

The affective influences on the artistry of teaching are further explored in Chapter 3 where Curie Scott discusses the importance of embodied thinking in teaching. She argues that embodiment tools are useful both for novice teachers who may experience performance anxiety and also for more experienced teachers who may draw on routine expertise to perform their teaching role. Curie presents some of her doctoral research and shares drawing models with the aim of emphasising self-awareness and self-regulation in teaching. Curie proposes that drawing is one way of developing and catalysing embodied thinking, and she offers three drawing activities with which teachers can experiment in their own practice. This concept of embodiment is further explored within the chapter by Lucilene Almeida who emphasises the importance of the holistic context and that "both teacher and student engagement occurs within cognitive-affective patterns that take into account the environment" (p.X). Ideas around context and embodiment are picked up by Jennie Mills and co-writers in Chapter 4 using the theoretical lenses of Bourdieu's embodied and institutionalised capital to explore their own relationship with expertise and improvisation as academic developers working in the Academy. Through close attention to four extracts from handwritten letters exchanged between the authors, the idea of *illusio*, of understanding the rules of the game, is explored to elucidate the ways academic developers do and can promote both orthodox and heterodox positions through their work.

Anna Santucci continues with the theme of embodiment and self-awareness in the final chapter of this section, arguing that, through the development of cultural self-awareness, teachers can hone their expertise in the artistry of teaching. In particular, she explores how understanding and reflecting on our identity can help us to creatively co-create learning-centred practices. Anna discusses three interrelated concepts, proposing that the artistry of teaching is: culturally self-aware, foregrounding the importance of understanding who we are as educators; learning-centred, focusing in on the very essence of what it means for humans to learn; and imaginative co-creation, emphasising the importance of being open to possibilities and transformative learning in "safely brave enough" learning and teaching spaces. She concludes by offering several stimulus

8 Helen King et al.

questions for reflection to help readers to develop cultural self-awareness, learning centredness, and imaginative co-creation. Within this chapter, Monica Ward reflects on her experience of teaching using a challenge-based learning approach, emphasising aspects of artistry such as developing the ability to adapt, to improvise, and to become comfortable with releasing control.

Part II: Authenticity and professional identity

The second part continues the theme of self-awareness and context to further explore aspects of personal and professional identity, and how these interweave and influence one's approach to teaching. Practical examples and ideas for bringing authenticity to any classroom are provided by Abdullahi Arabo in the context of teaching cybersecurity. He illustrates how using methods such as current real-life case studies and interactive technology with timely feedback can have a positive impact on inclusivity and student engagement. In addition to making authentic connections with the professional practice of the discipline, Mary Jacob complements this chapter with ideas on relational pedagogy and how to be one's authentic self in the classroom in order to nurture a communal learning environment.

An approach to developing a community of learners within a solely online learning environment is explored in Chapter 7 by James Layton, who reflects on the experience of teaching drama during the COVID-19 pandemic. Emphasising that collaborative learning is important to all subjects, he shows how it is not necessarily limited to a physical co-presence and that online communities of practice, dialogue, and enquiry can enhance relational learning experiences and encourage deep learning. In contrast, Jennifer Savage presents a short reflective case of teaching ceramics during the COVID-19 pandemic, highlighting the difficulties and obstructions to learning when students' ability to interact physically with clay and materials was removed, which reduced their opportunity to express their artistic intentions.

The remaining three chapters in this part look at professional identity from the perspective of three different roles in higher education: the (dance and fashion) teacher (Chapter 8 – Michelle Groves and Julia Reeve), the programme leader (Chapter 9 – Jenny Lawrence), and the learning technologist (Chapter 10 – Evan Dickerson). Whilst these are different types of roles, there are many similarities in terms of their complexity, requiring synergy with multiple others and multiple selves. It is suggested that a dynamic personal construction of identity in this complex environment might be mediated through collaboration, communication, and reflection and that it is as important to have knowledge of one's (evolving) professional identity as it is to understand one's professional role. To aid the development of this knowledge, Michelle Groves' MIPA (Materialist/Idealist positioning and Passive/Active agency) Model of Professional Identities of Dance Teachers offers a tool to help HE professionals reflect on and elucidate their multiple identities.

Part III: Developing the artistry of teaching

The final section considers different ways to support the development and enhancement of this facet of teaching which appears to be so important for enabling good student learning. Building on the ideas of adaptive expertise introduced in Part I, Chapter 11 discusses the design and facilitation of an innovative professional development programme: Improvisation Skills for Teachers. The authors present an evaluation of the programme, highlighting several benefits of developing improvisational skills for teachers. The chapter is written collaboratively by educational developers Petia Petrova and Shaun Mudd and improvisers and applied improv teachers Imogen Palmer and Stephen Brown, providing unique insights from higher education and theatre arts perspectives. Delving further into performative approaches to teaching, Modesto Corderi Novoa presents a contribution in this chapter about the use of performance and embodiment to teach complex, sometimes untranslatable, intercultural concepts. Taking the example of *Yuánfèn* – a concept in Chinese translated as "serendipity in a relationship", Modesto discusses how the use of dramatic expression, beyond speaking and writing in words, can help learners to understand and embody such complex intercultural concepts.

In Chapter 12, Sarah Wilson-Medhurst and Mark Childs suggest that some teachers' hostility to online learning may be due in part to a loss of artistry. They explore reflections of online teaching during the COVID-19 pandemic which exemplify some challenging experiences. Many teachers would previously have experienced a sense of artistry and flow in their in-person teaching before the pandemic, but the rapid shift to online (an unfamiliar method for most participants in their qualitative survey) meant that many suddenly lost this feeling. This then exacerbated some colleagues' negative attitudes and beliefs regarding educational technology, forming a self-sustaining cycle by making them ever more reluctant to develop their practice in this area. Sarah and Mark echo James Layton's (Chapter 7) sentiments on the communal learning benefits of online teaching and argue that it can be both useful and inclusive. To support professional development, they propose a model to help staff surface their attitudes and beliefs, identity, and artistry regarding online teaching.

In Chapter 13, Anna Costantino offers her perspective on a "progressive problem-solving" model of professional learning (Bereiter & Scardamalia, 1993). Her experience of practitioner research in the context of language teaching illustrates the importance of opportunities for professional development that emphasise collaboration, curiosity, creativity, and innovation. Within this chapter and emphasising the argument for this teacher-led and creative approach to professional development, Leonardo Morantes-Africano and colleagues contend that teacher autonomy should be an underpinning principle of artistry.

Chapter 14 revisits the concept of embodiment introduced in Part I. Lucy Nicholson, Ruth Spencer, and Kerstin Wellhöfer share their experiences and self-explorations as both dancers and lecturers in dance performance and teaching. By unpacking their professional experience and training they identify ways to attend to and support themselves before, during, and after teaching experiences. This attention to self then enables them to be more responsive and available to those they are teaching. This need for responsivity is also important for students themselves, and within this chapter Charlie Reis offers a short contribution arguing the importance of spontaneity as a crucial component in developing artistry in the curriculum.

To finish, Chapter 15 offers a selection of six examples of approaches to professional development for artistry in teaching in higher education. Emma Kennedy and Martin Compton begin the chapter with an evidence-informed discussion on the positive impact of Postgraduate Certificate (PGCert) programmes for new lecturers which offer space for learning about teaching, experimentation, feedback, and sharing. The value of the peer observation element of the PGCert expressed by participants is also highlighted in Section 15.4, where Lucy Spowart and Tristan Price discuss their "Review of Educational Practice" approach as a model of evidence-informed development and as an example of a relational pedagogy.

The challenge for these types of programmes is ubiquitous – time – and the authors call on the community of educational developers to challenge institutions who claim to be supportive of professional development to match this with action on workload allocations. The importance of strategic connections between institutions and educational development is discussed by Jackie Potter and Moira Lafferty in the second example. They illustrate this through the concept of building bridges between teachers' disciplinary contexts (physically located within their academic departments) and learning and teaching development often offered through centrally located functions ('Educational Development Units'). Artistry and authentic teacher identity is developed through communities of practice that bring together teachers from across the institution. However, it is when they "cross the bridge" back to their academic department that they are able to implement their pedagogic learning. An institutional and academic departmental culture of support for and valuing of professional development is required to enable a frequent crossing of the bridge by teachers at all stages in their careers. In Section 15.3, Sarah Floyd and Fiona Smart surfaces the key role that many professional services' staff have in relation to teaching and/or supporting learning but which is often undermined through a dichotomous culture with academics. Allowing such staff to participate in schemes to gain a Fellowship of the Higher Education Academy (HEA) will not only appropriately recognise the breadth of expertise located across the institution but may also encourage a more inclusive and collaborative culture for the enhancement of learning and teaching.

A wide range of approaches to "professional learning" or "scholarly teaching" are shared throughout this book including practitioner research, formal learning through PGCerts, development programmes, recognition through

HEA Fellowships, peer observation, and communities of practice. The benefits of these are manifest through opportunities for collaboration and shared experience, and for self-reflection and self-awareness. Sections 15.5 and 15.6 echo these respectively with a demonstration of the impact of development events (Charlotte Stevens) and a model of "appreciative self-study" (Caitlin Kight).

Conclusion: enabling the artistry of teaching in higher education

As illustrated by the varied contributions in this book, the artistry of teaching in higher education is about improvisation, embodiment, knowing oneself and one's students, and a compassionate and relational approach to facilitating learning. This artistry might be developed through experience and it can also be supported through professional development. But expertise in teaching is also highly influenced by the environmental context (Berliner, 2001); not all teachers in higher education feel that they have the time, space, or even permission to focus on their teaching and to engage in the continuous learning, progressive problem solving, and creative conversations required to develop expertise (Elkington, 2024 and Kennedy & Compton, 2024, this volume; McVitty, 2023).

As noted by King (2022, p.10): "If higher education institutions are to achieve their missions of excellence in education, then they must also foster and enable a culture of professional learning for teaching.... Without this active institutional-level commitment, expertise in teaching will only ever be a subculture of the few." To better enable the development of expertise, a cross-institution, strategic, and integrated approach is required (Gannaway, 2022) that builds bridges between academic structures and professional services provision (Potter & Lafferty, 2024, this volume). It is positive to see that "support for staff professional development and excellent academic practice is embedded across the provider" featured as a "student experience" criterion in the most recent Teaching Excellence Framework exercise in England (OfS, 2022, p.74), but there is still a considerable culture change required in HE for institutions to truly become "institutions that learn" and provide sufficient space for all teachers to develop their artistry and expertise to their full potential.

The complexity of the learning environment suggests that there may not be a definitive model of "good teaching" but that it's important to recognise, value, and support the different dimensions of teaching expertise that can impact on student learning. It is similarly important to equitably recognise the value that all higher education practitioners bring to the student learning experience, whether located in academic departments or central professional services. Teachers in higher education bring a rich and diverse expertise developed from their knowledge and understanding of their discipline and of pedagogy in order to competently teach and support learning. Some teachers, however, continue to develop beyond competency and towards expertise, embodying a sense of professional identity, continuing to learn and enhance their craft, and taking a curiosity-driven, evidence-informed and authentic approach with the potential to offer a transformational learning experience for all. The intention of this book is to provide a starting point for conversations about the hitherto less-discussed "artistry" dimension of expertise and the ways of thinking and practising as a teacher and to promote opportunities for its development through a strategic approach to professional learning, collaboration, scholarly teaching, creativity, and innovation.

Key take-aways

- Expertise for teaching in higher education comprises three interacting dimensions: pedagogical content knowledge, professional learning (scholarly teaching), and artistry.
- The idea of "artistry of teaching" recognises the complexity of the learning environment and that expertise in teaching requires an understanding of one's professional identity, creativity, improvisation, curiosity, and care for learners and learning.
- In order to provide a consistently high-quality learning experience, higher education institutions should seek to develop a strategic and integrated approach to supporting learning, creativity, innovation, and the development of expertise.

References

Advance HE (2023). *Professional Standards Framework (PSF 2023)*. https://www.advance-he.ac.uk/teaching-and-learning/psf

Bale, R. (2022). Developing adaptive expertise: what can we learn from improvisation and the performing arts? In: King, H. (ed.) *Developing Expertise for Teaching in Higher Education: Practical Ideas for Professional Learning and Development*, Routledge, Abingdon. pp. 203–217 .DOI:10.4324/9781003198772-19

Barradell, S., Barrie, S. & Peseta, T. (2018). Ways of thinking and practising: Highlighting the complexities of higher education curriculum, *Innovations in Education and Teaching International*, 55(3), 266–275, DOI:10.1080/14703297.2017.1372299

Baume, D. (2023). My obituary for SEDA. *Educational Developments*, 243 5–7 https://www.seda.ac.uk/seda-publishing/educational-developments/educational-developments-issue-24-3-2023/

Bereiter, C. & Scardamalia, M. (1993). *Surpassing Ourselves: An Enquiry into the Nature and Implications of Expertise*. Open Court, Illinois.

Berliner, D.C. (2001). Learning about and learning from expert teachers. *International Journal of Educational Research*, 35, 463–482.

Bryant, M. (2024 this volume). Taking the "art" in "artistry" literally: an art-based theory of teaching expertise. In: King, H., Bale, R., Corradini, E., Fossey, P., Gannaway, D., Morantes-Africano, L., Mudd, S. & Potter, J. (eds.) *The Artistry of Teaching in Higher Education: A Practical Guide to Supporting Creative Academic Practice*. Routledge, Abingdon.

Collins, H. & Evans, R. (2018). A sociological/philosophical perspective on expertise: the acquisition of expertise through socialization. In: Ericsson, K.A., Hoffmann, R.R., Kozbelt, A. & Williams, A.M. (eds.) *The Cambridge Handbook of Expertise and Expert Performance*. (2nd edn). Cambridge University Press, Cambridge. DOI:10.1017/9781316480748.002

Corradini, E. (2022). Developing pedagogical content knowledge through the integration of education research and practice in higher education. In: King, H. (ed.) *Developing Expertise for Teaching in Higher Education: Practical Ideas for Professional Learning and Development*, Routledge, Abingdon. pp. 142–154. DOI:10.4324/9781003198772-13

Di Stefano, G., Francesca, G., Pisano, G. & Staats, B. R. (2023). *Learning by Thinking: How Reflection Can Spur Progress Along the Learning Curve*. Harvard Business School NOM Unit Working Paper No. 14-093, Kenan Institute of Private Enterprise Research Paper No. 2414478. DOI:10.2139/ssrn.2414478

Eisner, E.W. (2002). From episteme to phronesis to artistry in the study and improvement of teaching. *Teaching and Teacher Education*, 18, 375–385.

Elkington, S. (2024 this volume). Blackholes and revelations: exploring everyday creative praxis in higher education teacher practice. In: King, H., Bale, R., Corradini, E., Fossey, P., Gannaway, D., Morantes-Africano, L., Potter, J. & Mudd, S. (eds.) *The Artistry of Teaching in Higher Education: A Practical Guide to Supporting Creative Academic Practice*. Routledge, Abingdon.

Ericsson, K.A., Charness, N., Feltovich, P.J. & Hoffman, R.R. (2006). *The Cambridge Handbook of Expertise and Expert Performance*. Cambridge University Press, New York.

Ericsson, K.A., Krampe, R.T. & Tesch-Romer, C. (1993). The role of deliberate practice in the acquisition of expert performance. *Psychological Review*, 100(3), 363–406.

Fossey, P. (2022). Emotion work and the artistry of teaching. In: King, H. (ed.) *Developing Expertise for Teaching in Higher Education: Practical Ideas for Professional Learning and Development*. Routledge, Abingdon. pp. 231–244 DOI:10.4324/9781003198772-21

Gage, N.L. (1978). *The Scientific Basis of the Art of Teaching*. Teachers College Press, New York.

Gannaway, D. (2022). A whole-university approach to building expertise in higher education teaching. In: King, H. (ed.) *Developing Expertise for Teaching in Higher Education: Practical Ideas for Professional Learning and Development*, Routledge, Abingdon. pp. 57–68. DOI:10.4324/9781003198772-6

Hattie, J. (2015). The applicability of visible learning to higher education. *Scholarship of Teaching and Learning in Psychology*, 1(1), 79–91. DOI:10.1037/stl0000021

Healey, M. (2023). *Reflections on Developing the Scholarship of Teaching and Learning*. https://www.healeyheconsultants.co.uk/resource

Hambrick, D.Z., Campitelli, G. & Mcnamara, B.N. (2018) *The Science of Expertise: Behavioral, Neural and Genetic Approaches to Complex Skill*. Routledge, New York.

Hatano, G. & Inagaki, K. (1986). Two courses of expertise. In: Stevenson, H., Azuma, H. & Hakuta, K. (eds.) *Child Development and Education in Japan*. Freeman, New York. pp. 262–272.

Hounsell, D. & Anderson, C. (2005). Ways of Thinking and Practising in Biology and History: Disciplinary Aspects of Teaching and Learning Environments. *Paper presented at Higher Education Colloquium, Centre for Teaching, Learning and Assessment, Teaching and Learning within the Disciplines. University of Edinburgh* http://www.etl.tla.ed.ac.uk/docs/BioHistWTP.pdf

Huang, J.L. (2015). Cultivating teacher thinking: ideas and practice. *Educational Research for Policy & Practice*, 14, 247–257. DOI:10.1007/s10671-015-9184-1

Humphreys, M. & Hyland, T. (2002) Theory, practice and performance in teaching: professionalism, intuition, and jazz. *Educational Studies*, 28(1), 5–15. DOI:10.1080/03055690120090343

Kennedy, E. & Compton, M. (2024 this volume). To 'toy with', 'think about' and 'experiment with': teacher development programmes as space for developing the artistry of teaching. In: King, H., Bale, R., Corradini, E., Fossey, P., Gannaway, D., Morantes-Africano, L., Mudd, S. & Potter, J. (eds.) *The Artistry of Teaching in Higher Education: A Practical Guide to Supporting Creative Academic Practice.* Routledge, Abingdon.

King, H. (2019). Continuing Professional Development: what do award-winning academics do? *Educational Developments*, 20(2) 1–4.

King, H. (2022). The characteristics of expertise for teaching in higher education. In: King (ed.) *Developing Expertise for Teaching in Higher Education*, Routledge, Abingdon.

Kneebone, R. (2021). *Expert: Understanding the Path to Mastery.* Penguin

Macfarlane, B. (2007). Beyond performance in teaching excellence. In: Skelton, A. (ed.) *International Perspectives on Teaching Excellence in Higher Education*, Routledge, Abingdon, pp. 48–59.

McCune, V. (2019). Academic identities in contemporary higher education: sustaining identities that value teaching. *Teaching in Higher Education*, 26, 1–17. DOI:13562517.2019.1632826

McVitty, D. (2023). In: King, H., Saunders, C. & Pinny, K. *SEDA/ALT's 30th Birthday Celebration Summit. SEDA blog December 20, 2023.* https://thesedablog.wordpress.com/

Morantes-Africano, L. (2022). Critical reflection as a tool to develop expertise in teaching in higher education. In: King, H. (ed.) *Developing Expertise for Teaching in Higher Education: Practical Ideas for Professional Learning and Development*, Routledge, Abingdon. pp. 29–43. DOI:10.4324/9781003198772-4

OfS (2022). *Regulatory advice 22 Guidance on the Teaching Excellence Framework (TEF) 2023*, Office for Students https://www.officeforstudents.org.uk/publications/regulatory-advice-22-guidance-on-the-teaching-excellence-framework-2023/

Potter, J. & Lafferty, M. (2024 this volume). Developing teaching expertise for disciplinary contexts – building the bridges between institution and discipline perspectives. In: King, H., Bale, R., Corradini, E., Fossey, P., Gannaway, D., Morantes-Africano, L., Mudd, S. & Potter, J. (eds.) *The Artistry of Teaching In Higher Education: A Practical Guide To Supporting Creative Academic Practice.* Routledge, Abingdon.

Schön, D.A. (1982). *The Reflective Practitioner: How Professionals Think in Action.* Basic Books, New York.

Schön, D.A. (1987). *Educating the Reflective Practitioner.* Jossey-Bass, San Francisco.

Shulman, L.S. (1986). Those who understand: Knowledge growth in teaching. *Educational Researcher*, 15(2) 4–31.

Shulman, L.S. (1993). Forum: teaching as community property. *Change: The Magazine of Higher Learning*, 25(6), 6–7. DOI:10.1080/00091383.1993.9938465

Tsui, A.B.M. (2003). *Understanding Expertise in Teaching: Case Studies of Second Language Teachers.* Cambridge University Press, New York

Tennant, M., McMullen, C. & Kaczynski, D. (2010). University Teaching Expertise. In: Tennant, M., McMullen, C. & Kaczynski, D., *Teaching, Learning and Research in Higher Education*. Routledge

van Heerden, A. (2005). Articulating the processes at the heart of Chemistry. In: Riordan, T. & Roth, J., (eds.), *Disciplines as Frameworks for Learning: Teaching the Practice of the Disciplines.* Sterling, VA, Stylus. pp. 95–120.

Part I

Creativity, improvisation and context

Chapter 1

Taking the "art" in "artistry" literally

An art-based theory of teaching expertise

Mike Bryant

Introduction

What if teaching were not artistry, but art? This chapter proposes a theoretical model of teaching expertise based on the role of art in society as another way to think about the artistry of teaching in higher education. Artistry, in the sense of acquired fluency in thinking and skilled task performance, is often identified as a feature of occupational expertise. Although the concept of expert artistry can be valuable, I will argue it also warrants critical scrutiny. Accordingly, I first discuss the origins of this concept and consider some of its limitations when applied to learning and teaching. In the course of the chapter, I suggest a complementary art-based theoretical model of teaching expertise, which I call *responsible enquiry*. Finally, I outline the relevance of this model for practice, in the light of digitisation and the increasing importance of artificial intelligence.

Expert teacher artistry has been proposed as a way of describing impromptu and idiosyncratic behaviours that elevate teaching beyond the formulaic or routine. For its advocates, the concept conveys the experienced and successful teacher's "intuitive, improvisatory and existentialist spontaneity" (Humphreys & Hyland, 2002, p. 5). Some theorists of teacher artistry, such as Colman (1967), focus on experienced teachers' ability to draw on multiple forms of knowledge in an intuitive way. Others, like Delamont (1995), stress the role of experimentation and willingness to depart from formal plans. Still others emphasise reciprocal self-expression and rapport between expert teacher and student, a typical metaphor being the teacher as orchestral conductor (Eisner, 1983). The introduction to this volume brings together these different strands in the literature, defining teacher artistry as a series of characteristic ways of thinking and practising associated with expertise in teaching.

A general criticism of approaches to professional learning that focus on teacher skill or behaviour, such as expert teacher artistry, is that they tend to neglect the efficacy and impact of the teacher's work (Timperley et al., 2007). A more specific criticism of teacher artistry theories, grounded in cognitive and biographic teacher development studies, is that such theories presuppose precisely those forms of autonomy and agency that teachers most often lack (Kelchtermans, 2009). In higher education, it can be argued that learning and teaching is primarily about the ability of the curriculum as a whole to create positive change in the professions and broader society; an individual teacher's in-situ actions play a relatively small part. More prosaically, the spontaneity and intuitive decision-making associated with theories of teacher artistry are constrained by many factors over which individual members of staff have little influence day to day. These include the timetable, student evaluations of teaching, subject content, and assessment. A related point is that theories of teacher artistry in higher education are always, to an extent, political moves (Jarvis, 2019, p. 17), pushing back, for example, against audit cultures (Clegg, 2009); sector-wide regulation (King, 2022); or standardisation of curriculum (Lupton, 2013). As such, they may say more about aspirations for the sector than the actual conditions under which people in occupational learning and teaching roles operate.

In the light of these criticisms, this chapter will begin by assessing the continued relevance of expert teacher artistry in higher education alongside possible alternatives. In the first section, I ask what *kind* of theory expert teacher artistry is and what theories of art have informed it, looking in depth at the origins of expert artistry as a developmental theory of work.

What kind of theory is expert teacher artistry?

We often ascribe artistic qualities to the occupational behaviour of experts, where an expert is someone highly skilled and successful in a specialised field. A case in point is the project, a central feature of contemporary work (Lundin et al., 2015). The concept of the project as a work methodology is artistic in origin, deriving from the art theory of Friedrich Schlegel (Osborne, 2013, pp. 58–59). The popularisation of project methods in industry, government, and the public sector has been accompanied by a heightened emphasis on spontaneity and creativity. Acting on impulse, rapid changes in direction, and using imagination to anticipate future conditions have all become part of what it means to work effectively in a project setting (Boutinet, 2012, pp. 238–239). Meanwhile, a vocabulary of artistic composition has come to be associated with workplace projects; witness the "epics" and "stories" of agile software development (Dimitrijević et al, 2015). The belief that expert performance has artistic qualities has spilled over into daily language. We might say a skateboarder, a surfer, or a chef possesses artistry if they show the right mix of flair, versatility, and exceptional skill.

Alongside business practice and everyday language, there is a substantial literature in the fields of philosophy of mind, psychology, and cognitive neuroscience that connects skilled performance with art. For instance, the philosopher Barbara Gail Montero (2016) has argued that certain common features of expert behaviour – apparent effortlessness, "breakthrough" moments, and exceptionally rapid, accurate appraisals of domain-relevant events – are underpinned by complex patterns of alertness and motion-sense. For Montero, the characteristics of expert behaviour and their underlying cognitive patterns are artistic in two senses: they feature heavily in creative occupations, and they are also identical to some of the ways we appreciate beauty. Her work draws on observation and first-person accounts of accomplished people in action: golfers, nurses, body artists, classical cellists, eighteenth-century poets, and rock musicians, among others.

Arguments like Montero's (2016) rely on an underlying premise. To take them seriously, we must accept that virtuoso performers from different fields go about their work in fundamentally similar ways. When we call someone an expert, according to Montero (pp. 64–67), we're primarily describing *how* they carry out domain-relevant tasks. Montero's account assumes that because experts are likely to have performed such tasks on many previous occasions, their task performance will exhibit certain typical features that are impossible for a novice – or a machine – to replicate. Winch (2010, p. 138) calls this the "fluency" view of expertise.

Though influential, Winch argues, "fluency" theories have multiple shortcomings. They fail to give a satisfactory account of the ethical dimension of expertise; is a skilled defence counsel who unnecessarily subjects a complainant to harmful questioning validly described as an expert? Also, they often substitute the virtuoso for the artist, conflating task performance and role performance, although the two are not the same. For example, a schoolteacher might be highly skilled in giving feedback to students as a result of prolonged practical experience. Whilst this proficiency in giving feedback might set them apart from others with less experience it would not necessarily indicate they were an expert in other aspects of their role.

John Dewey: the "arts of life"

For a fuller understanding of the concept of expert artistry, we can look to the work of the 20th-century philosopher John Dewey, one of its most influential proponents. According to Dewey ([1932] 1989), all experience is artistry. As Dewey defines it, experience means being absorbed in the flow of an activity, balancing intuitive action with receptivity to one's own body and the external environment. For Dewey, this kind of thoughtful absorption – which he regards as essential to any true experience – is inherently artistic. All human occupations have an artistry that must be acquired, he suggests; "the intelligent mechanic … is artistically engaged" (p. 11). Like his contemporaries Virginia Woolf and Henri Matisse, Dewey draws no firm distinction between fine art and the "arts of life" (p. 339). Indeed, if we were prepared to give the dignity and beauty of everyday work the same recognition as sculpture or painting, he argues, we could radically transform society.

As a source for his argument, Dewey ([1932] 1989, pp. 38–39) cites the Romantic poet John Keats ([1819] 2002, p. 270), who wrote that most people "make their way with the same instinctiveness, the same unwandering eye from their purposes ... as the Hawk". Implicitly, Dewey draws on Kant's ([1790] 1952, §46) definition of genius as non-replicable and Hegel's ([1840] 1986, p. 44) theory that all human beings have a fundamental vocation. Beyond literary and philosophical influences, another factor that swayed Dewey and his Modernist peers to make the case for expert artistry was alarm that soul-destroying routine and constant distraction were becoming workplace norms as automation took hold (Howarth, 2019, p. 264). Much the same apprehension is expressed, via comedy, in Charlie Chaplin's *Modern Times* (1936).

In an early essay, Dewey ([1904] 1977) gives more specific hints about what expert artistry means for teacher development. He claims that teachers are too often encouraged to learn in a mechanical way; they are schooled in the habit of copying methods and instructional designs that seem to bring about desired student behaviours. Ultimately, these teachers harm their own intellectual growth, Dewey warns. Because their focus is on doing what works, rather than understanding why it works, they have no theoretical basis for ongoing learning. Likewise, their students quickly work out that giving the appearance of being engaged is all that matters. By contrast, genuine teaching development means a here-and-now interaction between a teacher and their environment, he argues. A teacher must be "saturated" (p. 256) with knowledge about fundamental concepts of their subject as they relate to their students' thinking, so that they can apply and refine this knowledge intuitively. Teachers also need to develop imagination and spontaneity, he suggests, or "insight into soul-action" (p. 254); this helps them anticipate the cognitive paths their students will take in real time, constantly adjusting their own behaviour in response.

By themselves, Dewey's ideas are not "fluency" theories. He argues that expertise is ultimately about the well-being of the society that experts live in, not just how they think or what they do. However, present-day "fluency" views of expertise are steeped in his work. Consider widely promoted ideas like Schön's (1987) concept of reflective practice; the "masterful coping" of Dreyfus and Dreyfus's (1991, pp. 235–236) five-stage expertise model; Argyris and Schön's (1996) theory of organisational learning; and "pedagogical content knowledge", the theory that expert teaching requires special ways of knowing and reasoning about subject matter (Deng, 2007). All treat specific forms of cognition and action as primary characteristics of expertise; all were influenced by Dewey. Because of its currency in fields like workplace learning and organisational development, the "fluency" view of expertise has shaped the ways in which we understand work situations (Winch, 2010). At the same time, socio-economic developments such as the rise of "project society" (Lundin et al., 2015) have reinforced its plausibility to the extent that Dewey's ideas might sound self-evident when repeated more than a century later. To borrow a phrase from Midgley (2003), expert artistry has become a "myth we live by".

Theoretical implications

Because of its familiarity, revisiting the Deweyan roots of the idea of occupational artistry is essential groundwork, I would argue, if we are to understand its scope and limitations. Three points in particular follow from the preceding discussion. Firstly, Dewey's ([1932] 1989) theory is a cinematic celebration of the fine detail of everyday occupations: "the fire-engine rushing by; the machines excavating enormous holes in the earth; the human-fly climbing the steeple-side" (p. 11). It therefore makes sense as a basis for exploring how apparently mundane aspects of the work of teaching – responding to discussion forum posts, say – embody complex forms of judgement and merit their own status and recognition.

Secondly, Dewey's theory is, to an extent, a reaction to the automation of manual labour before World War II. His writing treads a fine line between the drabness of mechanisation and the joy of being immersed in a routine task. In our own time, when automation of thought and language is a pressing concern, the idea of expert teacher artistry might therefore valuably highlight aspects of teaching that machines cannot do. However, it is less likely to help us understand learning and teaching in settings where there is a high degree of interdependence between humans and computers.

Lastly, Dewey ([1904] 1977, p. 254) defines teaching as an ability to imagine a student's future mental power. A teacher is, as in Shelley's ([1840] 1965, p. 140) famous definition of a poet, "a mirror of the gigantic shadows which futurity casts on the present". Implicit in this definition is an assumption that teacher and student have common goals and that a student might wish to be so empowered by their teacher's imagination. Dewey's theory is therefore likely to have limited explanatory power in teaching situations whose purposes are not settled or where students validly interpret subject matter in novel ways.

A theoretical alternative?

So influential has the idea of occupational artistry become that it is easy to forget that there are other ways to think about expertise in work contexts. Perhaps the most obvious of these is the study of how credible sources of information make a contribution to knowledge in broader society. In Western and some Asian philosophical traditions, this study and the practices it describes are known as hermeneutics.

Many cultural traditions have also considered expertise primarily in terms of what it adds to social understanding. For example, there is the epistemic role of country and shared narrative for many Australian Aboriginal and Torres Strait Islander people (Harrison & Greenfield, 2011); the Classical Islamic *adab* tradition of literature that provides exemplars and guidance for good conduct (Sha'ar, 2016); and the concept of the public intellectual in the Arab world and mainland Europe (Said, 2002).

Alternative concepts of expertise are found in Western educational research, too. Although the psychologist Lee Shulman is often identified with the theory of "pedagogical content knowledge" discussed earlier, Shulman (1986, 2008), drawing on the model of Jewish scholarship of the Torah and Talmud, considered such knowledge to be part of a shared body of practical wisdom to which all teachers contribute.

It is notable that all these traditions view expertise as a matter of collective as well as individual agency. It is also notable that they are prepared to consider as sources of expertise not just people, but places, objects like books, institutions, and public personae. This broader concept of what an expert can be is evident in the history of the English word "teacher", from the Old English word *tǣcan*, which until relatively recently had the meaning of "something that shows or points out". Only in the later industrial period did it come to stand, as it does in expert teacher artistry, for a person in a specific occupational role (Oxford English Dictionary, 1989).

Likewise, there is more to art than a way of thinking and practising. As we have seen, expert artistry theories define art as a kind of skilled performance characterised by thoughtful absorption found both in culturally prestigious art forms like orchestral music and in everyday occupations. By contrast, recent art theory tends to emphasise the role of the arts in social movements, digital environments, and urban spaces (Osborne, 2013) whereas contemporary arts like street art and network art cross established formal categories, blurring the boundaries between creator or performer, technology, and audience (Welch, 1995).

In the next section, I will suggest an alternative theoretical model to expert teacher artistry. Drawing from art theory and hermeneutic philosophy, I will ask what it would mean for contemporary higher education if we were to see the teacher as a contributor to social knowledge rather than a creator or performer.

Responsible enquiry: an art-based theory of teaching expertise

This section outlines an art-based theory of teaching expertise and discusses its implications for learning and teaching in higher education. I will refer to the work of the philosopher of hermeneutics Hans-Georg Gadamer, beginning by sketching out Gadamer's philosophy of expertise, in which art plays a major role.

Art can help us understand how expertise works in society, Gadamer ([1960] 1989) argues. For Gadamer, works of art change our sense of ourselves and the world; often, as in the case of a tragic novel or film, causing us to contemplate things we find uncomfortable or disturbing. Artworks have an experiential quality, Gadamer claims. We can encounter the same work many times, he points out; our perceptions of a work often mature or progress in the course of our interactions with it. Also, in Gadamer's account, works of art have a relevance and timeliness that goes beyond the intentions of the artist. A good example is that we can still find artworks compelling when we know they have been created via generative artificial intelligence; or, as is true of some ancient works, when we are unsure who created them and why.

Sources of expertise like an academic paper or an expert legal opinion have similar properties to works of art, Gadamer ([1960] 1989) suggests. They prompt us to think differently about how we act. They can be interpreted in different ways, superseded, or overridden. Also, when we make a judgement about whether they are worth listening to, we do not just consider who has authored them; it matters to us whether they have characteristics we associate with truth and relate to something we care about.

According to Gadamer ([1931] 1991; [1960] 1989), the fundamentals that apply to expert scientific and legal sources also apply to learning and teaching. He defines teachers and students as contributors to social knowledge, or participants in a truthful conversation, and argues that there is much we can learn from the role of art in society about how such a conversation should be held.

A theory of teaching expertise based on Gadamer's ideas would have three principles, I suggest. First would come the principle of *friendship* (Gadamer [1960] 1989, pp. 332–33). Here, friendship does not mean personal attachment; it means self-knowledge and moral sympathy with others, putting our own needs to one side. Recalling that universities were complicit in the Holocaust, Gadamer ([1947] 1992) argues that expertise of any kind is dangerous if it is not grounded in friendship. As with works of art, we can only benefit from an encounter with knowledge if we are open to what it might reveal about ourselves and our relationships.

There is a tendency in higher education to think about self- and interpersonal awareness and cooperation as competencies to be taught (Clarke, 2018, p. 1927). In contrast, Gadamer encourages us to understand the curriculum as a series of existing relationships – between methodologies, points of view, departments, or institutions – which students must join and navigate. Contemporary higher education increasingly emphasises learning and teaching across institutions and in workplace and public settings; however, the question of what is meant by a "teacher" is complex, with technical systems playing a growing instructional role. In these circumstances, following Gadamer's principle means teaching via professional relationships, creating opportunities for students to form their own, and being honest about the relational difficulties and dilemmas that accompany learning and teaching (see Arabo, this volume). There is little point in seeking to teach, say, interpersonal skills to students while glossing over disagreements among staff and institutional partners about what the curriculum is and what it should do.

A second principle would be *nurturing moral sense*. The idea of moral sense is an old one, figuring, in Western traditions, in the work of the Roman Stoics and the Enlightenment philosophers Vico and Shaftesbury. Moral sense is about how people reach practical judgements, at work and in everyday life; how they know what to do. For Gadamer ([1960] 1989, pp. 20–1), moral sense is not an art or skill but a disposition, like tact or courage; it allows people to theorise what truth and integrity mean in a given situation.

Some theories of "authentic learning" hold that people learn best when the social conditions under which they learn correspond most closely to those in which learning will be applied (Wald & Harland, 2017, p. 753). Gadamer ([1960] 1989) has the opposite view. Moral sense is "not nourished on the true but on the probable, the verisimilar" (p. 19); we develop it when the conditions of everyday life are suspended, he argues. An example would be a health science simulation of a pandemic, which allows students to learn about practical judgements in a public health context precisely *because* what they do has no real impact on health outcomes. Rather than a real-world experience, Gadamer (p. 63) suggests, this kind of "verisimilar" learning is an adventure, similar to the experience of art:

> An adventure ... interrupts the customary course of events, but is positively and significantly related to the context which it interrupts. Thus an adventure lets life be felt as a whole, in its breadth and in its strength. Here lies the fascination of an adventure. It removes the conditions and obligations of everyday life. It ventures out into the uncertain.

Aside from simulations, something else educators can do to venture "out into the uncertain" is to give artworks a role within the curriculum (Bleakley, 2015). Recent novels that explore the implications of artificial intelligence (for example Ravn, 2020), or the growing number of video games with artistic qualities (Hayot, 2021), offer a possible way of nurturing students' disposition to act with integrity. In Box 1.1, Clive Holtham and Monica Biagioli summarise their "indisciplinary" exploration that showed that "professionals in any discipline, even without any skill in fine art practice, can infuse their professional practice with mindsets evolved in the fine arts".

Lastly, *data as self-giving*. As discussed by Williamson, Bayne, and Shay (2020), some researchers have investigated whether analytics-based insights offer new value for teaching and student learning. Such work is misdirected, according to Gadamer ([1960] 1989). It is meaningless to speak of practice being driven or informed by data, Gadamer argues, since data are an intrinsic part of all human experience. Our habit of thinking of systematically collected data as a separate informational category is, for Gadamer, no more than a symptom of uncritical faith in scientific methods; it ignores both the social practices that give rise to such data and their interconnectedness with language. As Rosenberg (2013, p. 18) has written, "false data is data nonetheless". Consequently, data in the scientific or technical sense are not "given" or definitive, Gadamer ([1960] 1989, p. 59) maintains, but "self-giving"

Box 1.1 In search of indisciplinary artistry: teachers collaborating across disciplinary chasms

Clive Holtham and Monica Biagioli

Many universities are emphasising the importance of multidisciplinary collaboration in both teaching and research, but in most of higher education, reward and reputation is wholly geared towards discipline-based parameters. Although extreme collaboration is sometimes called transdisciplinary or "beyond all discipline" (Nicolescu, 2018), there are even advocates for indisciplinarity: "transgression of organisational boundaries" (Mitchell, 1995).

This summary outlines how two colleagues from apparently unrelated disciplines collaborated actively over several years to co-create, evolve, and refine an arts-based reflective learning method, namely the creation and use of "zines" – small booklets handmade by paper folding (Kyle & Warchol, 2018). The method was initiated in a school of art and design. Zines have been used with undergraduates and postgraduates, in executive education up to and including chief executives, and within organisational change initiatives. In parallel, a business school had been evolving partly preprinted reflective workbooks and journals to encourage reflection both by students of management and by professional managers (Holtham et al., 2021).

Low-key collaboration within a large EU project connected two teachers across the apparently wide chasm between business and art/design. It was not until 2019 that explicit effort was put into the collaboration leading to joint production not only of customised zines, but also of learning processes that would aim to maximise the value of the pedagogic method, primarily in disciplines other than art and design. Key distinctions were needed between:

- Art-based methods: non-artists drawing on tools and methods originating in the fine arts;
- Artistic expertise: skilled in the practice of the fine arts;
- Artful mindset: ingenuity and lateral thinking in creative problem solving in any discipline.

For business learners, the priority was achieving the intersection of art-based and artful but not requiring or assuming artistic expertise (Adler, 2006; Barry, 1996). Neither the concept of artfulness, as used in the collaboration, nor of pedagogic artistry as emphasised in this book, necessitates artistic expertise. But one conclusion from the case study is that professionals in any discipline, even without any skill in fine art practice, can infuse their professional practice with mindsets evolved in the

> fine arts, including imagination, ambiguity (Weil, 1986), negative space (Ou, 2009), playfulness, and embodiment (Tyson, 2016). This infusion applies as much to teachers in any discipline, not just those in or related to the fine arts.
>
> The two collaborators reviewed:
>
> (a) The importance of the art-based/artful/artistic triad in the context of both educational artistry and professional excellence.
> (b) Factors promoting the trajectory towards indisciplinary thinking and practice
>
> What began as a multidisciplinary undertaking evolved into transdisciplinary and now has elements of indisciplinarity. The shared focus of both academics has been developing methods for teaching, learning, and executing everyday reflective practice (Schön, 1987). The most recent paper-folded zine arising from the collaboration (Biagioli and Holtham, 2022) has involved two zines folded from initially octagonal shapes, and sets out to document the evolution of the zine method itself. This zine was explicitly designed as a limited-edition risograph printed artwork, designed to showcase the value of indisciplinarity.

(p. 588). Like artworks, they give more of themselves away the more we interact with them, helping us ask better questions.

In the light of the digitisation of higher education, this principle suggests that students need practical experience of the specific characteristics and limitations of different types of data; also, that they need to consider whether the goals that data support are worthwhile. It would therefore be important for educators and course designers to give students some degree of responsibility for negotiating ethical, commercial, and practical challenges associated with the use of data and technical systems, avoiding reliance on example data sets generated or accessed in isolation. The difficulty of finding useful data should not be underestimated (Borgman, 2015); however, exposure to these challenges can be a helpful way for students to learn (Bell et al., 2016).

These three principles – friendship, nurturing moral sense, and data as self-giving – can be summed up with the term *responsible enquiry*. Here, "responsible" has the multiple meanings of acting with integrity or behaving responsibly; being responsive to situations; and also being answerable, or able to account, for our practice and judgements. Higham, Freathy and Wegerif (2010) suggest a comparable use of "responsible" in the context of leadership theory.

I would argue that this theoretical framework offers a promising alternative to theories of expert teacher artistry. That's because it acknowledges that learning and teaching often has the goal of contributing to professional practice, not simply preparing students for future careers. It recognises staff and students working across institutions; interrelationships between people and technical systems; and specific practices associated with digitisation. It also asks *why* those people do what they do, not just what's in their repertoire; foregrounding questions of professional ethics that are of signal importance in digital education and 21st-century work.

Conclusion

This chapter has considered the idea of expert teacher artistry in contemporary higher education, arguing that it is primarily a theory about the value of skilled occupational task performance. While it can help to elevate the status of pedagogic work by highlighting its complexity, I have argued, it is limited by its inattention to potential constraints on teacher autonomy, as well as its neglect of the possibility that curriculum might have contested goals and interpretations. Changing the theoretical focus from what the artist does to what art does, I have outlined a theory of teaching as responsible enquiry, influenced by the role of art in society, with three principles:

- Friendship;
- Nurturing moral sense;
- Approaching data as "self-giving".

Key take-aways

- Teaching through professional relationships, and allowing students to form them, is critical in contemporary higher education;
- We should allow students to step away from real-world conditions to help them develop moral judgement. Simulations, and including art in the curriculum, are both excellent ways to do this;
- Giving students experience of ethical and practical considerations related to data and digitisation is important whenever possible.

References

Adler, N.J. (2006). The arts and leadership: now that we can do anything, what will we do? *Academy of Management Learning and Education*, 5(4), pp. 466–499. DOI:10.1016/S1475-9152(07)00211-6

Argyris, C. & Schön, D.A. (1996). *Organizational Learning II: Theory, Method, and Practice*. Reading, MA: Addison-Wesley.

Barry, D. (1996). Artful inquiry: a symbolic constructivist approach to social science research. *Qualitative Inquiry*, 2(4), pp. 411–438. DOI:10.1177/107780049600200403

Bell, J., Carland, R., Fraser, P. & Thomson, A. (2016). "History is a conversation": teaching student historians through making digital histories. *History Australia*, 13(3), pp. 415–430. DOI:10.1080/14490854.2016.1202373

Biagioli, M. & Holtham, C. (2022). *Unfold, Risograph.* London College of Communication, ISBN 978-1-906908-80-5

Bleakley, A. (2015). *Medical Humanities and Medical Education: How the Medical Humanities Can Shape Better Doctors.* Abingdon: Routledge. DOI:10.4324/9781315771724

Borgman, C. L. (2015). *Big Data, Little Data, No Data: Scholarship in the Networked World.* Cambridge, MA: MIT Press. DOI:10.7551/mitpress/9963.001.0001

Boutinet, J.-P. (2012). *Anthropologie du projet.* 2nd edn. Paris: Quadrige, Presses Universitaires de France. DOI:10.3917/puf.bouti.2012.01

Clarke, M. (2018). Rethinking graduate employability: the role of capital, individual attributes, and context. *Studies in Higher Education,* 43(11), pp. 1923–1937. DOI:10.1080/03075079.2017.1294152

Clegg, S. (2009). Forms of knowing and academic development practice. *Studies in Higher Education,* 34(4), pp. 403–416. DOI:10.1080/03075070902771937

Colman, J. E. (1967). *The Master Teachers and the Art of Teaching.* New York: Pitman.

Delamont, S. (1995). Teachers as artists, in Anderson, L.W. (ed.) *International Encyclopedia of Teaching and Teacher Education.* 2nd edn. Oxford: Pergamon, pp. 6–8.

Deng, Z. (2007). Transforming the subject matter: examining the intellectual roots of pedagogical content knowledge. *Curriculum Inquiry,* 37(3), pp. 279–295. DOI:10.1111/j.1467-873X.2007.00386.x

Dewey, J. ([1904] 1977). The relation of theory to practice in education, in Boydston, J.A. (ed.) *The Middle Works, 1899-1924. Volume 3: 1903-1906.* Carbondale, IL: Southern Illinois University Press, pp. 249–272.

Dewey, J. ([1932] 1989). *The Later Works, 1925–1953. Volume 10: Art as Experience.* in Boydston, J.A. (ed.) Carbondale, IL: Southern Illinois University Press.

Dimitrijević, S., Jovanović, J. & Devedžić, V. (2015). A comparative study of software tools for user story management. *Information and Software Technology,* 57, pp. 352–368. DOI:10.1016/j.infsof.2014.05.012.

Dreyfus, H.L. & Dreyfus, S.E. (1991). Towards a phenomenology of ethical expertise. *Human Studies,* 14(4), pp. 229–250. DOI:10.1007/BF02205607

Eisner, E.W. (1983). The art and craft of teaching. *Educational Leadership,* 40(4), pp. 4–13. Available at: https://www.ascd.org/el/articles/the-art-and-craft-of-teaching

Gadamer, H.-G. ([1960] 1989). *Truth and Method.* 2nd edn. Originally translated by W. Glen-Doepel; translation revised by J. Weinsheimer & D.G. Marshall. Reprint, London: Bloomsbury Academic, 2013.

Gadamer, H.-G. ([1931] 1991). *Plato's dialectical ethics: phenomenological interpretations relating to the 'Philebus'.* Translated by R.M. Wallace. New Haven, CT: Yale University Press.

Gadamer, H.-G. ([1947] 1992). On the primordiality of science: a rectoral address. in Misgeld, D. & Nicholson, G. (eds.) *Hans-Georg Gadamer on Education, Poetry, and History: Applied Hermeneutics.* Translated by L. Schmidt & M. Reuss. Albany: State University of New York Press, pp. 15–21.

Harrison, N. & Greenfield, M. (2011). Relationship to place: positioning Aboriginal knowledge and perspectives in classroom pedagogies. *Critical Studies in Education,* 52(1), pp. 65–76. DOI:10.1080/17508487.2011.536513

Hayot, E. (2021). Video games and the novel. *Daedalus,* 150(1), pp. 178–187. https://www.jstor.org/stable/10.2307/48609832 DOI:10.1162/daed_a_01841

Hegel, G.W.F. ([1840] 1986). *The Philosophical Propaedeutic.* in George, M. & Vincent, A.; translated by A.V. Miller. Oxford: Basil Blackwell.

Higham, R., Freathy, R. & Wegerif, R. (2010). Developing responsible leadership through a "pedagogy of challenge": an investigation into the impact of leadership education on teenagers. *School Leadership and Management,* 30(5), pp. 419–434. DOI:10.1080/13632434.2010.525229

Holtham, C., Biagioli, M., Owens, A. & Pässilä, A. (2021). Crafting strategic thinking: creative pedagogy for management studies. *Innovative Practice in Higher Education*, 4 (2).

Howarth, P. (2019). Introduction: modernism and/as pedagogy, *Modernist Cultures*, 14(3), pp. 261–290. DOI:10.3366/mod.2019.0256

Humphreys, M. & Hyland, T. (2002). Theory, practice and performance in teaching: professionalism, intuition, and jazz. *Educational Studies*, 28(1), pp. 5–15. DOI:10.1080/03055690120090343

Jarvis, C. (2019). The art of freedom in HE teacher development. *Teaching in Higher Education: Critical Perspectives*, 24(1), pp. 17–31. DOI:10.1080/13562517.2018.1456422

Kant, I. ([1790] 1952). *The critique of judgement*. Translated by J.C. Meredith. Oxford: Clarendon.

Keats, J. ([1819] 2002). John Keats to George & Georgiana Keats, March 19th, in Scott, G.F. (ed.) *Selected Letters of John Keats*. Rev. edn. Cambridge, MA: Harvard University Press, p. 270. DOI:10.4159/9780674039391

Kelchtermans, G. (2009). Who I am in how I teach is the message: self-understanding, vulnerability and reflection. *Teachers and Teaching: Theory and Practice*, 15(2), pp. 257–272. DOI:10.1080/13540600902875332

King, H. (2022). Introduction: developing expertise for teaching in higher education. in King, H. (ed.) *Developing Expertise for Teaching in Higher Education: Practical Ideas for Professional Learning and Development*. Abingdon: Routledge, pp. 1–12. DOI:10.4324/9781003198772-1

Kyle, H. & Warchol, U. (2018). *The Art of the Fold: How to Make Innovative Books and Paper Structures*. Illustrated edition. London: Laurence King Publishing.

Lundin, R.A., Arvidsson, N., Brady, T., Ekstedt, E., Midler, C. & Sydow, J. (2015). *Managing and Working in Project Society: Institutional Challenges of Temporary Organizations*. Cambridge: Cambridge University Press. DOI:10.1017/CBO9781139939454

Lupton, M. (2013). Reclaiming the art of teaching. *Teaching in Higher Education: Critical Perspectives*, 18(2), pp. 156–166. DOI:10.1080/13562517.2012.694098

Midgley, M. (2003). *The Myths We Live By*. London: Routledge. DOI:10.4324/9780203828328

Mitchell, W. J. T. (1995). Interdisciplinarity and visual culture. *The Art Bulletin*, 77(4), pp. 540–544

Modern Times (1936). Directed by C. Chaplin [Feature Film]. Beverley Hills: United Artists.

Montero, B.G. (2016). *Thought in Action: Expertise and the Conscious Mind*. Oxford: Oxford University Press. DOI:10.1093/acprof:oso/9780199596775.001.0001

Nicolescu, B. (2018). The transdisciplinary evolution of the university condition for sustainable development. in Fam, D., Neuhauser, L., & Gibbs, P. (eds.) *Transdisciplinary Theory, Practice and Education: The Art of Collaborative Research and Collective Learning*. Cham: Springer International Publishing, pp. 73–81. DOI:10.1007/978-3-319-93743-4_6

Osborne, P. (2013). *Anywhere or Not At All: Philosophy of Contemporary Art*. London: Verso.

Ou, L. (2009). *Keats and Negative Capability*. Illustrated edition. London; New York: Continuum.

Ravn, O. (2020). *The Employees*. Translated by M. Aitken. London: Lolli.

Rosenberg, D. (2013). Data before the fact. in Gitelman, L. (ed.) *"Raw data" is an Oxymoron*. Cambridge, MA: MIT Press, pp. 15–40. DOI:10.7551/mitpress/9302.003.0003

Said, E.W. (2002). The public role of writers and intellectuals. in Small, H. (ed.) *The Public Intellectual*. Oxford: Blackwell, pp. 19–39. DOI:10.1002/9780470775967.ch1

Schön, D.A. (1987). *Educating the Reflective Practitioner: Toward a New Design for Teaching and Learning in the Professions*. San Francisco, CA, US: Jossey-Bass.

Sha'ar, N. (ed.) (2016). *The Qur'an and* adab*: The Shaping of Literary Traditions in Classical Islam*. Oxford: Oxford University Press.

Shelley, P.B. ([1840] 1965). A defence of poetry. in Ingpen, R. & Peck, W.E. (eds.) *The Complete Works. Volume 7: Prose*. London: Ernest Benn.

Shulman, L.S. (1986). Those who understand: knowledge growth in teaching. *Educational Researcher*, 15(2), pp. 4–14. DOI:10.2307/1175860

Shulman, L.S. (2008). Pedagogies of interpretation, argumentation, and formation: from understanding to identity in Jewish education. *Journal of Jewish Education*, 74(S1), pp. 5–15. DOI:10.1080/15244110802493289

Oxford English Dictionary (1989). Teacher in *Oxford English Dictionary*. 2nd edn. Oxford: Clarendon Press. DOI:10.1093/OED/1093605645

Timperley, H., Wilson, A., Barrar, H. & Fung, I. (2007). *Teacher Professional Learning and Development: Best Evidence Synthesis Iteration*. Wellington: New Zealand Ministry of Education. https://www.educationcounts.govt.nz/publications/series/2515/15341

Tyson, R. (2016). Pedagogical imagination and practical wisdom: the role of success-narratives in teacher education and professional development. *Reflective Practice*, 17(4), pp. 456–471. doi:10.1080/14623943.2016.1172479

Wald, N. & Harland, T. (2017). A framework for authenticity in designing a research-based curriculum. *Teaching in Higher Education: Critical Perspectives*, 22(7), pp. 751–765. DOI:10.1080/13562517.2017.1289509

Weil, J. (1986). The role of ambiguity in the arts. *ETC: A Review of General Semantics*, 43(1), pp. 83–89.

Welch, C. (ed.) (1995). *Eternal Network: A Mail Art Anthology*. Calgary: University of Calgary Press.

Williamson, B., Bayne, S. & Shay, S. (2020). Introduction: the datafication of teaching in higher education, critical issues and perspectives. *Teaching in Higher Education: Critical Perspectives*, 25(4), pp. 351–365. DOI:10.1080/13562517.2020.1748811

Winch, C. (2010). *Dimensions of Expertise: A Conceptual Exploration of Vocational Knowledge*. London: Continuum. DOI:10.5040/9781472541093

Chapter 2

Blackholes and revelations

Understanding everyday creativity in higher education teacher practice

Sam Elkington

Introduction

So much of the higher education (HE) teacher's role is focussed on objective performance and maintaining high levels of achievement with comparatively little attention given to the role of creativity in their own professional learning strategies. This is because normative conceptualisations of creativity in HE discourse tend to bias breakthrough thinking, cutting-edge practice, and large-scale innovation (Elkington et al., 2019). In truth, we know relatively little about the mechanisms underlying everyday creative behaviours in the context of professional practice strategies of educators. This chapter captures and examines productive inquiry research aimed at developing a more informed understanding of the personal meaning(s) HE teachers from different disciplines ascribe to creativity in their day-to-day practice. The chapter draws upon key research findings to provide insight into how creativity comes to frame the thinking and actions of HE teachers as they reflect on and learn from certain everyday experiences; how the nature of the interplay between such activities and the structure of practice cultures impacts on practitioners' everyday creative behaviours; and how such "everyday creative praxis" allows them to navigate challenge, express their individuality, and occasionally make significant contributions in their own practice domains.

Creativity or creativities?

In HE settings, creativity is core to realising a vibrant learning environment and is the context for many of the wider capabilities and complex learning educators seek to develop through their courses and modules. While different disciplines in HE may recognise and value different forms of creativity, pedagogically speaking, the ability to think and work creatively is widely recognised as a catalyst for innovation, adaption, and resilience in HE teacher practice (Jackson, 2016).

Creativity is perhaps still most often used to refer to a generalised ability to generate new concepts and artefacts. Such "product-oriented" conceptualisations of creativity tend to favour innovative, cutting-edge practice and assume that creativity should be defined as the production of original work that has value – it

DOI: 10.4324/9781003437826-4

satisfies a certain need or aim (Boden, 2010). In contrast, "process-oriented' conceptualisations of creativity introduce a range of perspectives beyond the contribution of a singular individual to focus on mental processes and strategies and the potential of creativity to generate new ideas and solutions to complex problems (McWilliams, 2009). From a process orientation, creativity is not the result of one person or even a set of people, but of intersecting and interacting relationships between them and others (Csikszentmihalyi, 1997). To stimulate a productive creative process, it is not enough to simply engage the individual; individual creativity will only thrive when people are part of a larger creative "system" through which different ideas, attitudes, and perspectives can come together in new and interesting ways (Jahnke, 2011). In the context of HE, the curriculum, and, by extension, related teacher practice strategies, combine to form such a system.

Richards (2010) suggests that when creativity is seen as part of everyday processes it can offer a dynamic way of thinking, of experiencing the world around us, and for understanding how our actions come to affect it. According to Richards, this everyday form of creativity includes the ability to generate novel and useful ideas or solutions in everyday life situations. It involves using one's imagination, curiosity, and problem-solving skills to create something new and valuable. A key feature of everyday creativity is that it often occurs in response to challenges, constraints, or limitations, such as scarcity of resources or increasing time pressures. People use their creativity to find innovative solutions within these constraints; for instance, educators devising new ways to organize themselves around different modalities of work and practice both during and post-pandemic.

Another important aspect of everyday creativity is that it is often collaborative and social. People bounce ideas off one another and build on each other's creative contributions to come up with new and better solutions to problems. When viewed from this perspective, creativity can also be seen as a way of learning and exploration. Through experimentation and trial and error, people can develop new skills, expand their knowledge, and discover new possibilities in practice. This chapter presents the findings of productive inquiry research aimed at developing a more informed understanding of the personal meaning HE teachers from different disciplines ascribe to creativity in their day-to-day practice.

A productive inquiry

Productive inquiry aims to deliberately engage in ways of participating in the technical and social exchanges that comprise teacher practice to gain insight into the experiences, sensibilities, beliefs, and idiosyncrasies of practice settings. In the context of the present research, the goal was to utilise productive inquiry as a way of gaining access to an informed understanding of the actions participants take when they experience creativity in their day-to-day practice. Methodologically, this required an attitude of open inquiry and an associated mode of interaction that enabled the author (as researcher) to enter into exchanges with groups of different teaching staff with an authentic desire for discovery. Such an approach is based upon establishing trust and providing space for open dialogue to take place. Initially, this took the form of a workshop series facilitated (both in person and online) by the author designed to bring teachers from different HE disciplines together to specifically explore and discuss creativity in everyday practice settings.

Spanning a period of nine months, the workshop series was part of an open call offered at three different post-92 institutions in the UK for HE teachers to engage in a process of exploration and discovery with regards to the role of creativity in their teaching practice. By bringing together teaching staff from a range of disciplines, the intention was to create an environment wherein participants felt comfortable and willing to discuss their experiences and collaboratively in that moment work with the author (as facilitator) to tease out, share, and consider different perspectives on creativity-in-practice. Drawing on the work of Belluigi (2013), the workshop was structured on the basis of two prepositions of creativity-in-practice: 1) that we all create our own meanings and understandings of creativity based on our individual experiences and values and the contexts in which we live and work; and 2) that we can contextualise apparently abstract notions of creativity in particular practice settings by positioning intentional interaction and discussion as a generative means of calling attention to and giving meaning to our own creativity in the contexts in which we work.

Workshop participants were invited to sketch out, using images and words, a first-person account of their experiences of creativity-in-practice by responding to two prompts: 1) What role does creativity play in your day-to-day work practice(s)?; and 2) When do you feel at your most creative in your practice? When responding to each prompt, participants were encouraged to reflect on, discuss, and share their interpretations and observations on the range of individual sketches of creativity-in-practice generated before collectively drawing out the apparent similarities and differences in the experiences described. This structure enabled the collection of participants' specific views concerning creativity in their own practice, as well as their general perspectives upon the role of creativity in their discipline and institutional contexts, including the barriers and enablers to its expression. This exploratory workshop structure acted as the foundation on which to identify and engage a purposeful sample of individual teachers to participate in a subsequent phase of interpretative phenomenological analysis as a means of obtaining a level of "descriptive insight" that would allow the author to get as close to the participants' views of everyday creative practice as possible.

Interpretive phenomenological analysis (IPA) of everyday creative experience

IPA is a contemporary qualitative methodology committed to the systematic exploration of how individuals make sense of their personal and social worlds through experience (Smith et al., 2009). Crucially for the present research with its focus on creativity in HE teacher practice, IPA is idiographic in that it emphasises the in-depth examination of how individuals in their unique contexts make sense of a given phenomenon (i.e., everyday creativity); it seeks to learn from each participant's individual story, and through intentional analysis, generate an informative understanding of participants' thoughts, beliefs, and behaviours. The workshop series provided the means through which to approach those participants who had demonstrated an ability to clearly articulate personal accounts of creativity in their everyday practice experiences during in-workshop exchanges. In the end, 12 workshop participants were invited to take part in a series of semi-structured interviews with a final sample of 11 teachers from a range of disciplines completing the interview process.

An interview schedule containing open-ended, non-directive questions was developed and structured around the same prompts used in the workshop series to build in a level of continuity for participants between their workshop experience and the interview process. Participants were given considerable leeway to discuss themes or issues they considered to be pertinent to their experiences of everyday creative practice. Researcher prompts were used sparingly as participants were generally highly articulate and were able to perorate. All interviews were recorded and a verbatim transcript produced for each ready for analysis.

IPA boasts a flexible set of guidelines for analysis, which can be adapted by investigators in accordance with their research objective (Smith and Osborn, 2008), characterised by a set of common principles based on a process of thematic analysis consisting of six distinct stages:

1. The transcript data was read and re-read to become familiar with the content and gain a sense of the participants' experiences.
2. An initial round of coding was completed to identify meaningful units of text that capture the essence of the participants' experiences.
3. Throughout, a process of constant comparison was completed to identify emergent patterns and themes emphasising the commonalities and variations in participants' experiences.
4. Emergent themes were then refined and organized into more specific categories, gradually providing a range of detailed insights into participants' experiences.
5. An interpretative description capturing the essence of participants' experiences was then developed that represented a deeper understanding of the underlying meanings and significance attached to the experiences.
6. These interpretative descriptions were then shared with participants to ensure accuracy and validity, with feedback and clarification on any misinterpretations used to hone a final narrative account.

As is accepted practice in IPA (Smith et al., 2009), the research findings for the present study are collated and presented as a joint 'results and discussion' and are loosely structured around the two prompts used to structure both workshops and interviews; each prompt acts as a linguistic tag for emergent themes derived from participants' experiences of everyday creative practice. Quotes from participants are utilised in the sections that follow to be illustrative of a range of features inherent to the variety of everyday creative practice experiences described.

What role does creativity play in your day-to-day work practice(s)?

Everyday creativity can be supported and nurtured, as well as weakened and suffocated through educators' working environments – revealed in the data in the form of a range of constraining and liberating factors. For example, participants discussed how working in a culture that emphasises conformity and discourages risk-taking can stifle personal creativity through a lack of support for new ideas and cause hesitation to express their creative thoughts:

> There are certainly no guarantees. There is so much of what I have to do in my role that actually [...] well, actively gets in the way of me being able to think and work creatively.
>
> [Participant 7]

Fearing negative judgement from colleagues was a clear inhibiting factor for participants when expressing their creative ideas, often leading to self-censorship and conformity:

> It very much depends on what I'm doing and who I'm doing it with. But a lot of the time I feel like I'm pushing against the environment and those I'm working with [...] which isn't necessarily set up to encourage my creativity.
>
> [Participant 3]

This is illustrative of the negative potential of social influence in relation to creative expression for those who might choose to deviate from the norm or take risks in their practice. More crucially, where creativity was experienced, participants reported they needed to feel they had time and space for reflection, experimentation, and exploration:

> We have a very supportive working environment that really tries to get out of the way of staff and allows them to explore their practice, to express themselves creatively. I mean, we're an arts-based department, so I guess you would expect that.
>
> [Participant 2]

A perceived lack of autonomy over work processes and decisions impeded many participants' ability to explore creative solutions, discouraging independent thinking and restricting their motivation to be innovative in their practice:

> When I do experience creativity in my practice, it is often when I've found myself outside the usual confines of my work routine, which can be stifling and difficult to let go of.
>
> [Participant 9]

For many participants, creativity thrived best in diverse environments that fostered the exchange of different perspectives and ideas:

> I know I can pull on the experience and input of my colleagues and they know they can seek that from me too. That sense of shared practice is important when faced with new teaching challenges, especially when they are shared challenges [...] it's a collective working out of things.
>
> [Participant 3]

In situations where working environments or teams lack diversity or collaboration is discouraged, individuals can find it challenging to engage in creative dialogue and generate novel solutions, for example:

> It can be difficult when there's a feeling that you're not supported to try new things and knowing that you don't necessarily have access to different views and opinions which are important in seeing and doing differently.
>
> [Participant 6]

Almost without exception, participants described professional settings that prioritised efficiency and productivity over creative thinking and action, features that are symptomatic of a broader HE context where performativity, surveillance, and regulation have been intensified via digital technologies (Gourlay, 2022). Indeed, this focus on performative measures and standardised processes dissuaded many from exploring unconventional or untested approaches:

> We're constantly being told to think about the wider impact of what we do. Thinking differently about your practice is fine, but can you demonstrate the impact and value for others beyond that situation?
>
> [Participant 8]

Perhaps most crucially, the descriptive experiences of participants revealed that rather than being an individual trait or characteristic, personal experiences of creative practice emerged from the dynamic interactions between individuals and their environment. This fits with Csikszentmihalyi's (1997) view that an individual's creative engagement is relational; it is situated as part of a broader system that includes rules and practices and a social dimension. From this perspective, creative practice is the result of intersecting and interacting relationships between an individual and others as part of a broader system of practice that includes the particular social and cultural conditions of HE. This presents a view of creative practice as a complex, largely unpredictable, and multidimensional process that can only thrive as part of a larger system of engagement.

When do you feel at your most creative in your practice?

Participants' accounts of everyday creativity rendered explicit the diversity of ways in which educators come to perceive and understand creative practice, how they use such practice to navigate challenges across different environments and action contexts, and how they are motivated to express their individual creativity therein. This was demonstrated through practitioners' ability to effectively communicate about themselves and their creative ideas, being open to new insights, and confidently putting new learning to work in ways that enable them to adapt to and thrive in different situations and scenarios.

Openness

Openness emerged as a general capacity relevant to educators' everyday creative practice evidenced through exploratory and self-reflective behaviour and a receptivity to new or different knowledge and ideas, as well as new roles, and relationships with peers and their students. For some educators this took the form of experimenting with different practice options to navigate unfamiliar and/or challenging encounters:

> I try to be open to different ways of working [...] I've gotten more adept at dealing with tasks or situations that are challenging [...] not being wedded to one routine or one strategy when faced with a teaching problem.
> [Participant 9]

For other educators, they felt most creative in their practice when they were able to involve themselves in a deliberate process of networking and working collaboratively, for example:

> I feel I'm most creative when sharing a new problem or task [...] focusing on working through a problem with others who might have their own ideas and be willing to try different things out.
> [Participant 8]

The absence of such receptivity in practice tended to lead to feelings of frustration, anxiety, and overwhelm for educators who often aligned themselves with a sense of "lack" in their capacity for openness – the idea that there is not enough time, or not enough space. In the words of one participant:

> I often find myself in situations where I just don't have the capacity to be as creative as I'd like. Either I am constantly task-switching and moving from one thing to another, or time is so tight that I'm just going through the motions.
>
> [Participant 3]

Being able to connect with a sense of openness and receptivity in their practice allowed educators to shift perspective without forcing or needing to control an outcome or situation:

> I try to be open to different ways of thinking and working [...] I've gotten more adept at dealing with challenging tasks or situations, not being wedded to one approach or strategy when faced with a problem.
>
> [Participant 10]

When educators were able to align themselves with a sense of openness it afforded a break from the struggle of pushing to make something happen to meet some outcome and instead offered the opportunity to generate new insights and energy from and through intentional practice.

Perseverance

To continue experiencing the energy and sense of fulfillment felt in moments of creative expression and action, participants were quick to note there was also the occasional need to persevere, to meet and navigate challenges inherent to a particular action context. This was evidenced through adaptive behaviours, the capacity to leverage learning and utilise individual and collective skills and knowledge to cope with (often unanticipated) problems and challenges. In this sense, the need to persevere resembled the broader idea of resilience as a response to overcoming obstacles and dealing with uncertain situations and outcomes. When describing occasions when they felt most creative in their practice, participants articulated the need for perseverance aligned to a positive motivational outlook when trying to make sense of problems, modelling and reasoning about them, and monitoring or changing direction:

> It can certainly be a case of blackholes one minute and revelations the next [...] not knowing how it's going to play out. So much of my own creativity

comes down to just having a go. Things might not work out, but then sometimes things click.

[Participant 5]

For some participants, perseverance included actively seeking out and gathering more and/or different information and perspectives on which to make decisions. Indeed, seeking out and considering alternative scenarios aligned to shared teaching issues or challenges provided opportunities for participants to think about the plausibility of outcomes across different practice settings. Crucially, for many participants such perseverance was experienced as a collective enterprise as they checked-in with peers and engaged in their own rudimental forms of productive inquiry; modelling or representing ideas to others, considering the explanations of peers, or monitoring and considering their problem-solving strategies against their own:

> I might try out a new approach or ask a colleague if they can model for some aspect of practice I want to become more proficient in.
>
> [Participant 6]

This emphasis on perseverance as an attitude and disposition towards group dynamics, rather than as an individual trait, is important in helping to understand how the context (task, peers, and resources) shapes the emergence of everyday creative practice in collaborative settings like education, over time.

Curiosity

Whilst in some circumstances it can seem necessary or even preferable to simplify or restrict what is experienced, it can put a limit on thinking and the willingness to seek out and explore new perspectives on practice. Maintaining an attitude of curiosity emerged as another general capacity core to educators' experiences of everyday creative practice evidenced through inquiry and information-seeking behaviour and the ability to elicit, evaluate, and refine existing knowledge. For some educators, their experiences of creative practice were most strongly associated with seeking out new perspectives to learn or acquire particular sorts of information helpful to them in the moment:

> I'm most creative when I'm practically wrestling with a new or interesting topic or problem [...] really focused on working through a problem and trying different things out.
>
> [Participant 8]

Several educators spoke of enacting such curiosity as a means of actively approaching familiar tasks in novel ways. Applying an attitude of curiosity in day-to-day work practices provided these educators with a basis on which to challenge assumptions about what they believed to know to be effective or expected behaviour:

> Often my first thought is whether in that situation there's opportunity to work through new ideas with students. It could be a very small thing, a gesture, but there's still an opportunity to do something differently.
> [Participant 4]

For other educators, enacting such curiosity and personal flexibility was born out of an awareness of what is intrinsically challenging alongside their personal limitations to act creatively in particular contexts, for example:

> It's about figuring out the fit between the challenge in that situation, for me, and how I can still have a positive impact on my students in practice.
> [Participant 2]

The ability to be able to seek out and then use knowledge, skills, and behaviours developed in one context and apply these in another context was an important ingredient in the kinds of work educators described as encouraging their most creative efforts.

Proactivity

For many of the educators, 'being creative' in practice terms was closely linked to the extent to which they felt they were able to cope with changes in their immediate circumstances and think about and respond to problems and tasks in novel and creative ways. On occasion this might proceed from small, easily accomplished activities; on other occasions circumstances might require that they make things happen for themselves, coming up with practical and pragmatic solutions, evidenced through self-initiated, anticipatory, and generative behaviours:

> For me, it can be a bit like living by bricolage [...] you might be faced with a problem which you know you don't quite have the right tools for, but it's a matter of using what you've got [...] you repurpose what you do have to find a way forward.
> [Participant 10]

Such behaviours approximate Runco's (2006) core features of 'personal creativity' which require 'discretion' (deciding when to construct an original course of action and when to conform instead), 'intentions' (enacting the values that motivate creative effort), and the 'capacity' to construct new ways of thinking and working. Relatedly, how creative practice was experienced varied between educators in part based on whether individuals felt they were able to exercise their discretion when initiating solutions:

> Sometimes not overthinking what you're doing or trying to plan everything to within an inch of its life can mean giving yourself the space to be creative in that moment.
>
> [Participant 1]

Enacting discretion and autonomy in practice is fundamentally about making decisions to invest or not in certain courses of action (Sternberg, 2012). Though such investments appeared to be a necessary feature of creative practice, there are always opportunity costs, as to invest in one course of action means an individual is kept from investing time and energy in another. Certainly, motivation plays a role in determining the relevant investment and subsequent value attributed to creative achievement which tended, at least initially, to be intrinsic to the individual:

> Having an open working dynamic can help to energize and develop new ideas all at the same time when I'm teaching [...] but you have to be willing to take that risk.
>
> [Participant 6]

This intrinsic value is recognised in the theory of personal creativity under the label of "intentions" with people exercising discretion by selecting a course of action based on what is valuable from a personal development perspective (Runco, 2006). A key challenge to creativity, curiosity and risk-taking might be a sense of "imposter syndrome" as described by Fay Short et al. in Box 2.1.

Everyday creativity – more than an occasional reprieve?

Based on the insights presented in this chapter, finding creativity in day-to-day practice often meant pushing beyond tried and tested routines, requiring educators to act with a certain degree of openness, curiosity, proactivity, and, at times, the need to persevere. This might mean coming up with solutions to everyday problems, solutions that are novel and useful in the moment. At other times solutions may need to be more practical and pragmatic, and often forgotten when they have served their purpose. This presents a view of creativity as a path, not an outcome, constructed from attainable and ordinary actions that inhabit and emerge from activities that, in time, can grow to hold significance in the practice repertoires of educators.

Though such everyday creative acts can be assembled from small-scale, personal systems and routines that are completely mechanistic in practical terms,

Box 2.1 Shifting identities and authenticity of teachers and learners in education

Fay Short, Nia Young, and Laura Ashcroft

The role of an educator is multifaceted and constantly evolving. Academics must be lifelong learners, continuously absorbing new knowledge and insights from their own subject and the field of pedagogy, either through reading and conferences or formal programmes of study. This constant pressure to upskill alongside the shifting experience of being a teacher and learner can significantly impact on our professional identity.

Imposter syndrome (Clance & Imes, 1978) is one of the greatest threats to our authentic sense of identity. One systematic review of 62 peer-reviewed studies from across the world found that it affects individuals regardless of gender, age, or culture, with a prevalence rate as high as 82% (Bravata et al., 2020). In higher education, both students and teachers can experience the fear of being exposed as imposters who achieved success through luck rather than ability. This fear intensifies when educators are pushed out of their comfort zones, which often happens when transitioning between teacher and student identities.

Teacher to student ...

Nia, an experienced lecturer, completed a master's qualification in her own academic department. Despite her reputation as a respected academic, she was convinced that she would be 'found out' as 'not good enough' when colleagues graded her essays. At least peer review has some distance and anonymity!

Student to teacher ...

Laura, a high-achieving student with a teaching background, secured a lectureship in the same programme immediately after completing her master's. However, she began questioning her abilities as she started working alongside the tutors she had previously admired as 'superior'.

Teaching the teacher ...

Fay did not switch roles formally, but her position as lecturer on the master's completed by Nia and Laura meant she had to switch between working with them as colleagues and as students. She had won national teaching awards, yet she feared being exposed as a 'poor teacher' when colleague Nia sat in her class and as a "fraud" when student Laura joined her teaching team.

> Reflecting on these experiences highlights three insights for managing imposter syndrome:
>
> 1. **Imposter syndrome does not discriminate on the basis of experience, knowledge, or skill.** Even those who seem confident in their expertise can be battling an inner voice telling them they are not good enough. Knowing that these feelings are shared by those we respect and admire can help us recognise our own fears as invalid.
> 2. **Communication helps defeat negativity and quash fear.** The divide between student and lecturer can become a gulf when communication is poor, but self-disclosure and honesty can close that divide to enable shifts across the roles to occur more freely. In this way, teachers can learn from students and students can educate teachers, even when there are no formal role changes.
> 3. **Everything is grist for the mill.** Whether we succeed or fail, we can learn from all experiences. Once we accept this as part of our lives, we shift permanently into the role of learner as our job title becomes less important than our state of mind.
>
> By understanding these key points, educators can better manage imposter syndrome and foster a more authentic professional identity.

they go far towards describing how educators work with the subtle details of their day-to-day experiences to bring about larger, lasting, changes in practice. Despite their economy, these micro-practices are not simplistic; as has been demonstrated, they embody how the everyday practical realities of educators can emerge into something tangibly innovative. This transformation from the relatively mundane and subtle to the novel and useful has implications for defining what it means to be creative in everyday practice terms, defined here by the author as comprising:

> ... an individual's dynamic acquaintance with a set of behaviours not directly related to any one specific activity, but rather to an individual's ability to generate, understand, and act upon new ideas to bring about personal change that enriches their day-to-day practice.

In time, the interactions and aggregations of these smaller creative acts can come together to form larger assemblages of practice that are, technically speaking, complex. This presents a view of everyday creativity as something approximate and contextual, whilst at the same time being necessarily reflexive and emergent. As such, these heuristic procedures lack the guarantee of a favourable outcome but nevertheless provide the basis for an everyday creative praxis, comprising the opportunities and methods for everyday creative expression.

Untangling everyday creative praxis

If as educators we take seriously the in-practice sensitivity essential to such everyday creative praxis, we might be more likely to approach our day-to-day activities in very different ways. We might, for instance, enter into situations of uncertainty (and even conflict) with curiosity about how such circumstances emerged and what purpose(s) it was serving, rather than from the perspective of why it was occurring and who or what was at fault. Seeking to develop creativity-in-practice is to seek a greater sense of authorship and authenticity day to day that, in turn, shifts focus from knowledge and 'knowing' (existing understandings of professional settings) on to a sense of 'coming-to-know' and 'becoming' – characterised by a willingness to engage, to have a go, and learn; a preparedness to listen and explore; and an openness to new experiences and perspectives, as well as a determination to keep improving and moving forwards. This process of coming-to-know highlights a developing 'sense of being' as a cornerstone of everyday creativity as it mediates the ways in which staff engage with various aspects of their educational work, from the practical to the ongoing development of emerging and worthwhile forms of doing and acting that are inherently relational.

Expanding on the work of Richards (2010), a consideration of this 'relational domain' in creative engagement necessarily includes not only the environment in which such practice occurs, but also enactment of a 'tolerance for uncertainty' where the educator can develop their reflexive capacity for working productively within uncertain conditions. At the level of praxis, this is about recognising the discomfort that can arise in the face of uncertainty and the development of the sort of dispositions, abilities, and strategies to deal with the unknown and the ambiguous and learning how to persevere and navigate such conditions in productive and meaningful ways.

In summary, far from being trivial or constrained to less serious domains of professional life or being of intermittent relevance, everyday creativity as it has been presented in this chapter represents a pervasive and dynamic way of knowing, doing, and being that offers an often-overlooked source of insight and innovation for educators, at the same time as being a source of enjoyment, learning, purpose, and personal growth.

Key take-aways

- Enacting everyday creativity represents a shift in focus from product-focussed modes of practice to an intentional focus on process and in-the-moment strategies for generating new ideas and solutions to problems.
- The acceptance of uncertainty and failure as much as the reward for success plays a key part in realising everyday creativity in practice.

- Realising the conditions for everyday creativity requires a broader practice outlook that is facilitative, enabling, proactive, and open to the possibilities of collaboration and experimentation.

References

Belluigi, D. Z. (2013). A proposed schema for the conditions of creativity in fine art studio practice. *International Journal of Education and the Arts*, 14(19), pp. 1–22. https://www.ijea.org/v14n9/

Boden, M. A. (2010). *Creativity and Art: Three Roads to Surprise*. Oxford: Oxford University Press.

Bravata, D. M., Watts, S. A., Keefer, A. L., Madhusudhan, D. K., Taylor, K. T., Clark, D. M., & Hagg, H. K. (2020). Prevalence, predictors, and treatment of impostor syndrome: a systematic review. *Journal of General Internal Medicine*, 35, pp. 1252–1275. DOI:10.1007/s11606-019-05364-1

Clance, P. R., & Imes, S. A. (1978). The imposter phenomenon in high achieving women: dynamics and therapeutic intervention. *Psychotherapy: Theory, Research & Practice*, 15(3), p. 241. DOI:10.1037/h0086006

Csikszentmihalyi, M. (1997). *Creativity: Flow and the Psychology of Discovery and Invention*. New York: Harper Collins.

Elkington, S., Westwood, D. & Nerantzi, C. (2019). Creativity for student engagement: Purpose, process, product. *Student Engagement in Higher Education Journal*, 2(3), pp. 1–6. https://sehej.raise-network.com/raise/article/view/1008

Gourlay, L. (2022). Surveillance and Datafication in Higher Education: Documentation of the Human. *Postdigital Science Education*. DOI:10.1007/s42438-022-00352-x

Jackson, N. (2016). *Exploring Learning Ecologies*. London: Chalk Mountain.

Jahnke, I. (2011). How to Foster Creativity in Technology Enhanced Learning. In White, B., King, I. & Tsang, P. (Eds.), *Social Media Tools and Platforms in Learning Environments: Present and Future*. Springer. pp. 95–116. DOI:10.1007/978-3-642-20392-3_6

McWilliam, E. (2009). Teaching for creativity: from sage to guide to meddler. *Asia Pacific Journal of Education*, 29(3), pp. 281–293. DOI:10.1080/02188790903092787

Richards, R. (2010). Everyday creativity: Process and way of life—Four key issues. In J. C. Kaufman & R. J. Sternberg (Eds.), *The Cambridge Handbook of Creativity*. Cambridge: Cambridge University Press. pp. 189–215.

Runco, M. A. (2006). Reasoning and personal creativity. In J.C. Kaufman & J. Baer (Eds). *Creativity and Reason in Cognitive Development*. Cambridge: Cambridge University Press, pp. 99–116.

Smith, J. A., & Osborn, M. (2008). Interpretative phenomenological analysis. In J. A. Smith (Ed.) *Qualitative Psychology: A Practical Guide to Research Methods*. London: Sage, pp. 53–81.

Smith, J. A., Flowers, P., & Larkin, M. (2009). *Interpretative Phenomenological Analysis: Theory, Method, and Research*. London: Sage.

Sternberg, R. J. (2012). The assessment of creativity: An investment-based approach. *Creativity Research Journal*, 24(1), pp. 3–12. DOI:10.1080/10400419.2012.652925

Chapter 3

The embodied realm of teaching

Curie Scott

Introduction

As teachers, we may be uncomfortable thinking about teaching as performance. However, those with expertise in the artistry of teaching are excellent at performing the role, both preparing and leaving gaps to improvise in the moment when teaching (Humphreys & Hyland, 2002). The learning space is a wide-awake dynamic "lived" curriculum where:

> You've got to improvise – it's like a performance in a way. One in which the audience can heckle and change the ending [...] you just have to prepare as best you can and then cope.
> (Edwards et al., 2006, p. 60)

The teacher's role is not primarily about our subject discipline, but about what we carry and share with our students about the discipline and the philosophy of learning. The more self-aware we are of our embodiment the more adept we become in our teaching performance.

This chapter considers the embodied 'realm' of teaching, which has performative, relational, and transactional dimensions. It draws upon my personal narrative as an educator with two decades experience as both a teacher and coach in higher education (HE) and draws upon newer work, driven by my PhD, as an embodiment facilitator.

What is embodiment?

Definitions of embodiment abound (see Ziemke, 2003). Here, embodiment is defined as a 'Self' who is regulated or boundaried in their transactional relationships with others and within their surrounding environment. Scholarly work on embodiment within education includes recent primers edited by Jennifer Leigh (2019) and Steven Stolz (2022). This body-mind interconnectedness along with socioemotional connection with others are evident in education (Lave & Wenger, 1991; Heron, 1992; Mezirow, 2009; Jarvis, 2012).

DOI: 10.4324/9781003437826-5

The embodied realm of teaching 47

This chapter uses Walsh's embodied intelligence model (2020, p. 25), a 2 × 2 cube exploring (a) awareness and (b) regulation of self and others. There is an added depth dimension encompassing one's state or pattern.

> We are all unconsciously embodied, meaning we have a certain semi-permanent set of habits kept in place by our bodily being.
>
> (Walsh, 2020, p. 24)

Embodiment includes our longer-term habitual set of patterns and also temporary states which we all bring to our work (see Figure 3.1). If you are unsure of your patterns, you can ask others how they see you or complete strengths or personality inventories. My patterns include helping people; I am detail orientated, organised, enthusiastic, and usually over-prepared. This differs from my shifting, temporary states in response to the surrounding context.

Embodied teaching involves the educator's being or self. This comprises the brain, body, and bodily interactions, which includes language, feelings, and sensations (Lakoff & Johnson, 1999). An educator is also embedded as a "body-in-space, the body as it interacts with the physical and social environment ... born into social and cultural milieus which transcend our individual

EMBODIED INTELLIGENCE

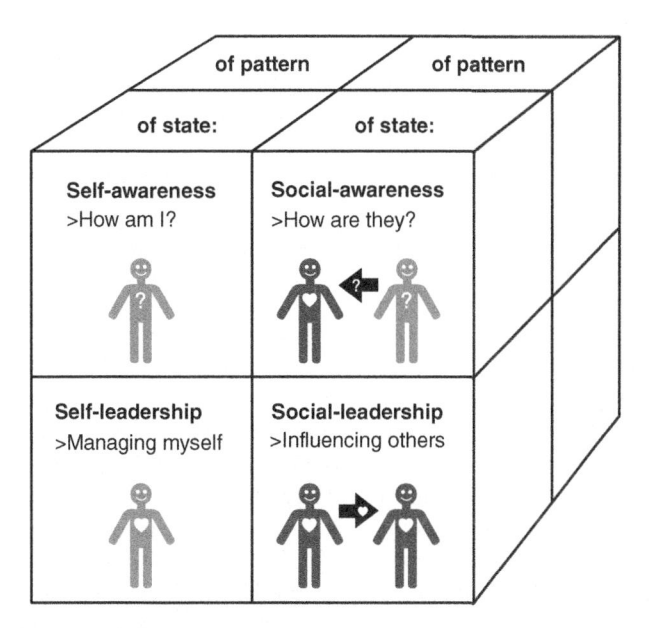

	of pattern of state: **Self-awareness** >How am I?	of pattern of state: **Social-awareness** >How are they?
	Self-leadership >Managing myself	**Social-leadership** >Influencing others

Figure 3.1 Embodied Cognition

Walsh, 2020, p. 25; used with permission

bodies in time" (Rohrer, 2007, p. 345). In other words, as educators, we are infused with values from our own socio-historical context but also develop our learning philosophy and education practices from various cultures, which include our academic discipline(s) and any education-based training and development. These occupation-based cultures are also known as academic tribes (Becher & Trowler, 2001) or communities of practice (Wenger, 1998).

Embodiment tools improve self-awareness, which can lead to improved self-regulation as well as improving working relationships with others due to social-awareness insight and influencing others. I suggest the embodied realm of teaching comprises:

- The personal realm: teacher-self persona or embodiment
- The curricular realm: respective philosophies of learning, expectations of roles of teachers and students, relationship with their students and the learning space (either physical or digital), and the academic discipline
- The students' realm: students' learner-self personas or embodiment
- The wider realm of education: includes communities of practice (see Scott, 2024) and the HEI culture

The more comfortable a teacher is inhabiting the aforementioned realms authentically, the more others might describe them as a 'natural teacher'.

How does drawing relate to embodiment?

My doctorate was on the types of thinking that participants experienced from a Drawing Programme (DP) to explore perceptions of future ageing (Scott, 2018). Embodied cognition helped explain the PhD research findings. As my awareness, understanding, and integration with the embodiment field continues, I can see that embodied cognition threads through my work.

The interdisciplinary doctorate was pedagogically inclined. University students from different health professional pathways and local people over 60 years old were invited to a DP. Participants drew individually and shared their resultant drawing and their in-the-moment understanding of it to the group. Anyone could offer insights, interpretations, or questions. Each week, participants took their own drawings home and displayed them, sending in evolving understandings to me as they reflected on their drawings. At the end of the three months the group reconvened to discuss the impact.

The drawing or mark-making that interested me related to exploratory or experiential drawing where one mark led to another without being 'correctly' placed for a desired drawing outcome. We are all likely to be familiar with this scribbling, doodling, or sketching done whilst figuring out how to redesign room layouts, or mind mapping ideas for writing or just making marks whilst in a meeting. These forms of drawing help to generate ideas on the page (Fish & Scrivener, 1990; Ferguson, 1992; Tversky & Suwa, 2009). Drawing the "known, not-yet-known and the unknowable ..." (Rosenberg, 2012, p. 122) is jumbled together inconsequentially on the page which acts as "a thinking space – not a space in which thought is re-presented but rather a space where thinking is presenced" (Rosenberg, 2012, p. 109).

I defined **generative drawing** as mark-making for enactive, emergent non-propositional thinking to be presenced, accepting indeterminate marks as holders of potential meaning (Scott, 2018). Analysis centred on five drawing reflection activities linked to thinking about their future ageing. There were three variations of how drawing was experienced:

1. Habituated thinking
2. Embodied thinking
3. Transformational thinking

Habituated thinking, or patterned thinking, refers to the propositional knowledge and related behaviours based on cultural dominant normalised 'truths' implicitly held without conscious critique. In terms of teaching and learning, this may be traditionally held beliefs within disciplines on 'the way things are' ontologically, which will influence our held philosophy of learning and thereby inform how we teach our disciplines.

As they partnered with the generative drawing process in the DP, discussions, and reflection over three months, participants' emerging thoughts, glimmers, or understandings on both ageing and drawing evolved. Generative drawing caused "disjunctures" (Jarvis, 2012) or "disorienting dilemmas" (Mezirow, 2009) making participants "question myths they had unthinkingly absorbed" (Scott, 2018, p. 307), resulting in 'embodied thinking'.

I accidentally muted the audio during video analyses. I noticed 'drawings in-the-air' as participants made bodily gestures as they spoke. The metaphors in the drawings and language about ageing leant an added dimension. Participants also spoke of recursive 'conversations' which I called 'interlogues' where "... [their] capacity to think, conceptualise, understand, reason and to know about ageing connected with the individual's story (both past and current); their body (the sensory, affective and motor aspects); language (metaphors are of special interest here); the passage of time; and their social relationships" (Scott, 2018, p. 248). In Box 3.1, Lucilene Almeida explores the relationship between sensory, affective, and motor aspects of learning in the context of dance.

Through the refining process of embodied thinking emerged **transformational thinking**. Over the three months participants became more open to interrogating their own thinking, testing this out in a group setting, and "rather than continuing unthinkingly along the same patterned way of doing things, swayed unknowingly by the stereotypes and myths in their culture, they encountered a branching point where some of them described choosing a new way of being" (Scott, 2018, p. 265).

Box 3.1 Cognitive-affective interrelationships in meaningful body experiences in classical dance teaching and learning

Lucilene Almeida

One of the main challenges in the beginning of the 21st century is to rethink teaching-learning models. In ballet, as in all motor learning, this reflection emerges in order to prepare students for a scenario that is very different from that of the last century.

Hopper et al. (2018) propose that we need to reflect on how each individual person develops their own body schema, how they embody and individualize these body schemas for teaching and learning sensory-motor skills according to their own physical and cognitive conditions. Within the framework of Ausubel's Meaningful Learning Theory (1963), with the contributions of the perception-action approaches of Gibson's ecological psychology (1979) and neuroscience studies, teacher-student interaction enables connections to arise during the process of sensory-motor development, with special attention on the apprehension of dance movements and on cognitive-affective construction.

The act of learning and teaching is mediated by a specific field of representations about the same knowledge provided by both teacher and student, and by the teaching material (Lemos, 2011; Moreira, 2012), in which teacher and student co-evolve through the simultaneous construction of interactions and experiences in relation to the apprehension of the teaching material (Agra et al., 2019). According to the Coevolution Theory (Lewin & Volberda, 1999), the result is an intentional relationship where one person predisposes self to helping the other to learn something.

Bastos and Alves (2013) state that "o afeto é a fonte de energia de que a cognição necessita para o seu pleno funcionamento [affect is the source of energy that cognition needs for its full functioning]" (p. 43) and remind us that both teacher and student engagement occurs within cognitive-affective patterns that take into account the environment. For student engagement with the teaching material, we need to understand motor development as directly relating to the individual's biology, motor activities required for survival, and environmental conditions (Gallahue, Ozmun, and Goodway, 2013). Additionally, this process should be understood as continuous throughout life, from conception to death. Therefore, it is important for the ballet teacher to encourage students to find a meaningful experience.

The teacher's action could be understood as a facilitator of the individual perception process to stimulate students in the embodiment (re) knowledge from their own interests, experiences, and knowledge towards the perception of themselves and their own movement

> (Marques, 2012; Baldi, 2016). Accordingly, when the teacher selects strategies, they should have the sensitivity and the care for motor learning, respecting the body by attending to the student's performance, and thus encouraging an embodied and meaningful experience. Highlighting the importance of a co-construction knowledge enables both teacher and student realize and perform in a relational manner, incorporating both self and the other's intervention, resulting in a willingness to affect and be affected by the experience environment-context, as well as to accomplish the embodied knowledge of dance (Ribeiro, 2015).

Generative drawing afforded a way of exploring a subject (one's future ageing) with indefinite boundaries and "... opened up alternative routes, perhaps more forgiving than words alone, to externalise and reason their thinking" (Scott, 2018, p. 250). It is this potential of generative drawing for metacognition that I think is crucial to HE learning environments. Across our disciplines, it is valuable for staff and students to engage in practices that help us become aware of our socio-culturally conditioned beliefs and assumptions (Hofstede, 2011), the dominant narratives that no longer serve us. Generative drawing helped people explore and externalise their thoughts, which then led to them being able to identify, interrogate, and critically appraise their thinking.

The teaching pendulum of performance

In the corporate sector, performance is explicitly part of the system, including performance reviews and financial remuneration for performance. In HE, performance is also key, but more implicit with ill-defined success metrics. I propose a pendulum of performance in teaching practice. This correlates well to Csíkszentmihályi's (1997) flow theory, further developed into the nine-channel flow model of subjective experience (see Reese, 2015). In Figure 3.2, intrinsic motivation is predicted when skill and challenge are balanced, but low. When skill and challenge are balanced and high, the flow channel supersedes. Intrinsic motivation may remain bounded by the apathy channel, or it may supersede the other six channels where they overlap. For the context of this chapter an educator's temporary state alters depending on how their level of skill or ability (x-axis) matches the challenges they face (y-axis).

The central equilibrium point, when the role is most satisfying, and teaching practice is embodied, aligns with the flow "channel" on the diagonal. The educator's temporary state can pendulum or swing through all nine segments depending on their level of skill and their current challenge. The pendulum arc covers different "performances" of teaching. For example, novice teachers often experience "anxiety" (top left; low skill/high challenge) if contractually obliged to successfully gain a teaching qualification in their first year of

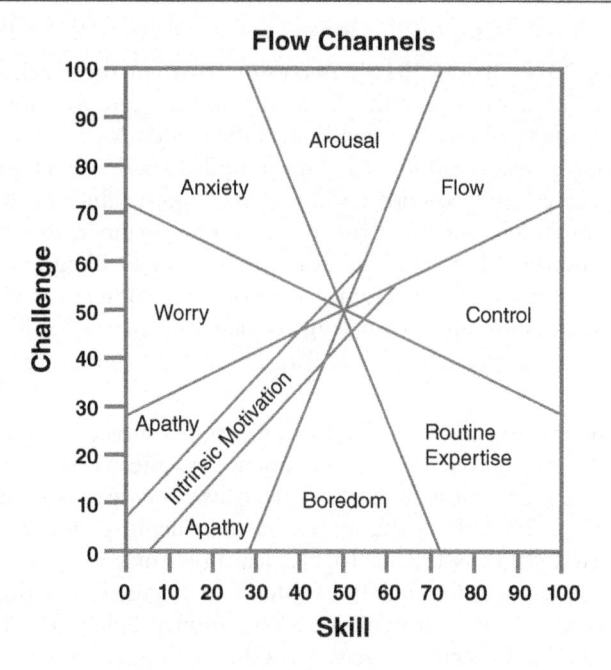

Figure 3.2 The nine-channel flow model of subjective experience

See Reese, 2015; copyright 2014 by Debbie Denise Reese, used with permission

teaching practice. Conversely, highly adept educators may experience "boredom" or perform their "routine expertise" (middle and bottom right; high skills/low challenge). These experienced teachers utilise their now tacit knowledge (Polanyi, 1966), which is integrated into their Self to perform the role of teacher mechanistically.

Educators may get overwhelmed trying to balance their various responsibilities and meet expectations. An educator's response to daily challenges or stressors may cause them to cycle through states such as anxiety, worry, boredom, or apathy (Figure 3.2). There are physiological changes in their body during these states. During anxiety and arousal, the activated sympathetic nervous system causes a high respiratory rate or breath-holding, increased heart rate, a sense of alertness and focus, and held tension in the body (notably the jaw, shoulders and lower abdomen).

We perceive these internal bodily signals, and others such as hunger or tiredness, through our 'interoceptive' sensory awareness. Interoception offers early warning signals that something is wrong. We may ignore and 'push through', disregarding basic needs such as having a drink, eating, or taking a break. I regularly did not eat till I finished a pile of marking. It may work in short bursts and give the impression of diligent dedication but is unsustainable in the long term.

Dependent on a person's coping mechanisms, colleagues start to notice the impact when internal stress responses are externalised and become visible as a change in behaviour. Short term irritation or abruptness may escalate. Signs of health impairment at work include distress, absenteeism, withdrawal, extreme behaviours (e.g., sudden outbursts of crying or angry retorts), and decrease in work performance (Dimoff & Kelloway, 2019). Other core needs such as sleep or the health of family relationships are likely to be impacted too, and the spiral continues downwards into ill health.

You may recognise yourself or colleagues in this description.

Reclaiming self-regulation

Embodiment practices improve self-awareness and self-regulation. By ignoring and overriding our interoceptive awareness, we become desensitised and can no longer perceive clear bodily indicators that something is wrong. That is, we cannot regulate ourselves as we cannot sense being out of equilibrium. It requires conscious effort to reclaim and reconnect to our internal state. The practice of embodiment comprises three interconnected processes which build sequentially through (1) awareness, (2) attention, and (3) intention (Walsh, 2021). That is, we need to first become aware of, or simply notice or tune into, our bodily sensations. For example, stop now and tune into your breath, either in the nostrils or the sensation of your chest moving.

I was startled to notice, during the daily practice of five one-minute bodily 'check-ins' for a coaching embodiment certification, that I held my breath and clenched my jaw whilst working. Slowly, I realised breath-holding was the beginning of a stress state (a temporary state) which stemmed from me doggedly continuing, despite my hunger or the need to stretch, to 'get the job done!' Once I became aware of this, I then could attend to it and make a change by taking a breath in and exhaling for longer and releasing jaw tension. As I have become more aware of my bodily senses and state, I can change the ratios of work to rest periods by being intentional. This conscious slowing down activates the parasympathetic nervous system and can be accelerated through polyvagal practices (see Porges, 2011).

Embodiment practices involving awareness-attention-intention have improved my ability for deep scholarly work (Berg & Seeber, 2016; Newport, 2016). As well as these one-minute bodily check-ins, another technique to attune to interoception (the felt sense in the body) is to bring conscious focussed 'awareness' and 'attention' to different parts of the body. For example, wherever you are, bring your internal awareness to whatever surface your hands are on (the temperature, texture, or surface) and then each fingertip. Further techniques such as active breathwork or posing in physical postures help bring a sense of ease and rest and improve confidence (Loncar, 2021). The cross-fertilisation of techniques from improvisation and theatre disciplines into courses for new lecturers (see Bale [2022] and work by Petrova et al. and Mills et al. in Chapters 3 and 5 in this book) are encouraging.

Drawing for embodiment practices

Embodiment tools are particularly helpful at times when feeling overwhelmed. No special equipment is needed apart from gentle guided instructions assisting the person to shift their awareness and attention to other sensations such as sound, touch, or the breath, or using distraction techniques such as colouring books, fidget toys, or the warm comforting sensation of holding a hot drink.

Low-pressure generative drawing (Scott, 2018) also facilitates embodiment. The examples in this chapter have, in practice, provided a route for slowing down and helped develop a sense of awareness of the present moment and a shift into a more restful, calm state. After initial nervousness about drawing, which is readily dealt with (see Scott, 2021), people start getting absorbed in their drawing. They exclaim how quickly time has passed and about the subjective awareness of feeling soothed or focussed. An academic said "I feel guilty about feeling calm". As an embodiment practice, drawing has the potential to shift us from frenzied, reactive work states to rested, proactive work slowed-down states necessary for deep thought (Berg & Seeber, 2016).

I bring, as we all do, my own set of values to my work. This includes a regard for embodiment or the interconnectedness of head-heart-hand knowledge (the humanising framework in Devis-Rozental & Clarke, 2020). I like 'finding the gold', looking for the best in people, and working with them to develop their potential. This corresponds to the **heliotropic effect**: that all living systems naturally incline towards the light (or positivity) and away from the dark (or negativity) (Cooperrider, 1990), which can be leveraged to promote positive collaboration (Scott, 2024). The way you might use these drawing tools can be adapted to fit with your values.

I start sessions with a short, quick centring practice (Walsh, 2017 is an excellent resource) to settle attention and focus on our time together. These centring tools are beneficial in HE (McColl, 2016; Clughen, 2023) and provide strategies for future use. Drawing activities, though nominally 'easy' with cheap, accessible materials can be emotionally provoking, so sensitivity and ethical considerations are paramount. This includes enough time for a debrief on how to engage people with drawing as most adults are highly self-conscious; they 'can't draw', and there can be potential for triggering trauma so an awareness in how to manage these situations is useful (see Scott, 2021).

For those new to teaching practice a personalised "Landscape of Life" (Scott, 2020) creates undulating 'hills' and 'valleys' of our personal narratives to identify what informs our philosophy of learning.

This chapter considers drawings to bring conscious awareness and re-engage with the present moment. As these drawing activities stem from doctoral research and scholarship, I welcome feedback on how you adapt and use them further.

A mindfulness hand-doodle

Embodiment has a broader scope than mindfulness (Walsh, 2020), but sometimes attuning to the present moment, to regather attention and the subsequent activation of the parasympathetic nervous system helps teachers settle (Collins, 2019). Mindfulness is purposeful awareness and attention to the present moment with openness, without labelling and judging the moment (Kabat-Zinn, 1994). A hand-doodle (Figure 3.3) drawing embraces zero expectation of aesthetic quality and can be with individuals or groups, for example, during an assessment preparation seminar. With groups, I ask people to tune into the 'sense' or 'atmosphere' in the room before the drawing and then draw their attention to the atmosphere during drawing. White copier paper and a thick pen (e.g., a Sharpie) works well. Instructions are given out steadily one by one.

Figure 3.3 A doodled hand

Author's own image

Participants are asked to draw around their hand as a template. If people seem nervous about their drawing skills, I lightheartedly point out that "There! You've drawn a hand!" They then divide the palm of the hand into sections with curved lines. In each section they are asked to repeat a single symbol or mark to fill one section before moving to the next. Doodling can last as long as you choose. Doodling, a familiar process, improves memory recall (Andrade, 2009) and reduces psychological distress (Crawford & Crawford, 2021). I tend to use a single colour to limit cognitive dissonance on choosing the 'right' colour.

Drawing a collage to navigate uncertainty

A collaged drawing is easy to create but the materials are more extensive: A4 card, magazine images, glue, felt tips/marker pens. A larger space to move around tables works best and takes 15–40 minutes with additional time for discussion in small groups. I spread out collage materials and use an open-ended prompt such as, What is learning? Where are you at with your research? What is hope? I ask people to collect a pile of images they feel drawn to or that somehow resonate but not to actively think about finding a particular image. I use the phrase: "let the images choose you!" After 5–10 minutes, they arrange the images in a way that interests them on A4 card. These are glued and drawings can be created on top. Collage promotes a "trompe l'esprit – a kind of ontological strangeness" (Vaughan, 2005, p. 5). Various metaphors arise and there is a richness in discussion. People are keen to share their emerging thoughts provoked by the process. Figure 3.4, my first research collage, was on the prompt "Where am I at with my research?" This 15-minute collage during a research session with other postgraduates was pivotal as I was struggling to navigate doctoral work.

My immediate reflexive commentary demonstrated that all the images were ambiguous. I kept being drawn to the image of the candles (top right) and something 'clicked'. I note that "As a PhD student in my first six months, I felt like an uninitiated acolyte in a hallowed sacred space ... I felt like a visitor to a religious space such as a temple, a church or mosque full of candles ... I was allowed to light a candle as a visitor but did not belong in the space. As a PhD student, I needed to pass through various initiation rites to prove my worth in order to be admitted as a priest into this sacred academic realm" (Scott, 2018, p. 282). Finally, as I glued the image of random chalkboard marks, I accidentally saw the reverse, an origami dinosaur, "a humorous visual interpolation: whilst I felt daunted by the 'initiation' rites described above, I could hold to the fact that I had advanced skills in various arenas such as origami" (Scott, 2018, p. 282).

Drawing out barriers and vulnerabilities

For those new to teaching, information overload, excessive choice, lack of flexibility, and fear of technology are common factors that can be unsettling and are not conducive to learning or flourishing (Collins, 2019). Of course,

Figure 3.4 A collage on the prompt: Where are you at with your research?
Author's own image

worry and anxiety will happen whenever the challenges faced are beyond someone's capabilities (Csíkszentmihályi, 1997). Calibrated exposure, or scaffolded learning (Bruner, 1975) through formative or summative presentations, for instance a micro-teach or group presentation, may help. Ongoing peer review such as critique on videoed or live teaching also improves performance. For example, once we become aware of our distracting body language, we can use techniques such as clasping our hands together to reduce large arm gestures, or not carrying a pen to prevent clicking it incessantly. The scaffolding provided for presentation is usually routine, procedural 'how to' knowledge, but I think this could be improved by integrated embodiment techniques.

Anxiety reduces when fears are openly acknowledged as *shared* fears through drawing. A resultant camaraderie arises. A Footnotes grid (West, 2007; Figure 3.5) drawn on copier paper with a pen takes approximately 5–10 minutes. A page is folded in half, consecutively, four times to create a small grid. People are asked to create a ten-second drawing on the prompt such as: What stops you writing? What worries you about this course? Drawings are basic stick figures, shapes, and cartoons. After completing one grid, another drawing is done in a blank grid. The page is unfolded and refolded to expose a different blank grid each time. In discussions, their fears, barriers, or modes of procrastination then need to be sensitively handled, ideally in a lighthearted way, to demonstrate that others are also held back by similar concerns.

Figure 3.5 A footnotes grid on the prompt: What concerns do you have about this course?

Author's own image

The simple drawing activities occupy enough attention to concentrate on the task at hand. Generally, people share they feel more settled or rested afterwards with a deepening of socioemotional connection (Devis-Rozental, 2018). These drawings are enabling and can help harness thinking and assist intention setting or action planning.

Key take-aways

This chapter explored the embodied realm of teaching. It embraced that teaching has performative components and that drawing contributes to embodied thinking, and it offered three drawing activities to help teachers consider the present moment.

- **Embodied education has performative components**: whether online or physically, our bodily presence communicates volumes. The pendulum of performance of teacher embodiment swings between the novice teacher suffering from performance anxiety to the experienced teacher who performs their routine expertise.

- **Generative drawing promotes embodied thinking**: generative drawing developed for doctoral research appears to shift people's thinking from habit-driven uncritiqued thinking to embodied thinking followed by a deep level of transformational thinking. I have taken drawing practices into education, leadership, and organisational settings.
- **Three drawing activities** that contribute to embodiment are offered for teachers to use and adapt. They include a drawing for centring, a Footnotes grid for drawing out barriers and vulnerabilities, and a collage to navigate uncertainty.

References

Agra, G., Formiga, N.S., Oliveira, P.S., Costa, M.M. L., Fernandes, M.D.G.M., & Nóbrega, M.M.L.D. (2019). Analysis of the concept of meaningful learning in light of the Ausubel's Theory. *Revista Brasileira de Enfermagem*, 72(1), pp. 248–255. DOI:10.1590/0034-7167-2017-0691

Andrade, J. (2009). What does doodling do? *Applied Cognitive Psychology*, 24, pp. 100–106. DOI:10.1002/acp.1561

Ausubel, D.P. (1963). *The Psychology of Meaningful Verbal Learning*. Grune & Stratton.

Baldi, N.C. (2016). Educação somática e construtivismo: revendo a pedagogia da dança. *OuvirOUver*, 12(2), pp. 256–269. https://seer.ufu.br/index.php/ouvirouver/article/view/31205/19493

Bale, R. (2022). Developing adaptive expertise: what can we learn from improvisation and the performing arts? In King, H. (ed.), *Developing Expertise for Teaching in Higher Education: Practical Ideas for Professional Learning and Development*. Routledge, pp. 203–217. DOI:10.4324/9781003198772

Bastos, L.S. & Alves, M. (2013). As influências de Vygotsky e Luria à neurociência contemporânea e à compreensão do processo de aprendizagem. ISSN online: 2176-9230. ISSN press: pp. 1984-4239. DOI: 10.25119/praxis-5-10-580

Becher, T. & Trowler, P.R. (2001). *Academic Tribes and Territories: Intellectual Inquiry and the Cultures of Disciplines*. (2nd edition). Society for Research into Higher Education/Open University Press.

Berg, M. & Seeber, B.K. (2016). *The Slow Professor: Challenging the Culture of Speed in the Academy*. University of Toronto Press.

Bruner, J.S. (1975). From communication to language: A psychological perspective. *Cognition* 3, pp. 255–287. DOI:10.1016/0010-0277(74)90012-2

Clughen, L. (2023). 'Embodiment is the future': What is embodiment and is it the future paradigm for learning and teaching in higher education? *Innovations in Education and Teaching International*. DOI:10.1080/14703297.2023.2215226

Collins, S. (2019). *Neuroscience for Learning and Development: How to Apply Neuroscience and Psychology for Improved Learning and Training*. (2nd edition). Kogan Page.

Cooperrider, D.L. (1990). Positive image, positive action: The affirmative basis of organizing. In Srivastva, S. & Cooperrider, D.L. (eds.), *Appreciative Management and Leadership: The Power of Positive Thought And Action in Organizations*, Jossey Bass, pp. 91–125.

Crawford, P. & Crawford, J.O. (2021). *Cabin Fever: Surviving Lockdown in the Coronavirus Pandemic*. Emerald Press.

Csíkszentmihályi, M., (1997). *Finding Flow: The Psychology of Engagement With Everyday Life*. Rider.

Devis-Rozental, C. (2018). *Developing Socio-Emotional Intelligence in Higher Education Scholars*. Palgrave Macmillan.

Devis-Rozental, C. & Clarke, S. (2020). *Humanising Higher Education: A Positive Approach to Enhancing Wellbeing*. Palgrave Macmillan.

Dimoff, J.K. & Kelloway, E.K. (2019). Signs of struggle (SOS): The development and validation of a behavioural mental health checklist for the workplace. *Work & Stress*, 33(3), pp. 295–313. DOI:10.1080/02678373.2018.1503359

Edwards, M., McGoldrick, C. & Oliver, M. (2006). Creativity and curricula in higher education: academics perspectives. In Jackson, N. (ed.), *Developing Creativity in Higher Education: An Imaginative Curriculum*. Routledge. pp. 59–73.

Ferguson, E.S., (1992). *Engineering and the Mind's Eye*. MIT Press.

Fish, J. & Scrivener, S. (1990). Amplifying the mind's eye: sketching and visual cognition. *Leonardo*, 23(1), pp. 117–126. DOI:10.2307/1578475

Gallahue, D., Ozmun, J.C. & Goodway, J.D. (2013). *Compreendendo o desenvolvimento motor: bebês, crianças, adolescentes e adultos*. (7a. ed). McGraw Hill, Artmed e AMGH Editora.

Gibson, J.J. (1979). *The Ecological Approach to Visual Perception*. Mifflin & Company.

Heron, J. (1992). *Feeling and Personhood: Psychology in Another Key*. Sage.

Hofstede, G. (2011). National cultures, organizational cultures, and the role of management. In González, F. (ed.), *Values and Ethics for the 21st Century*. BBVA Foundation, 385–403. [pdf] https://www.bbvaopenmind.com/wp-content/uploads/2013/02/National-Cultures-Organizational-Cultures-and-the-Role-of-Management_Geert-Hofstede.pdf

Hopper, L.S., Weidemann, A. & Karin, J. (2018). The inherent movement variability underlying classical ballet technique and the expertise of a dancer. *Research in Dance Education*, 19(3), pp. 229–239. DOI:10.1080/14647893.2017.1420156

Humphreys, M. & Hyland, T. (2002). Theory, practice and performance in teaching: professionalism, intuition, and Jazz. *Educational Studies*, 28(1), pp. 5–15. DOI:10.1080/03055690120090343

Jarvis, P. (2012). Learning from everyday life. *Human and Social Studies Research and Practice*, 1(1), pp. 1–20.

Kabat-Zinn, J. (1994). *Wherever You Go, There You Are: Mindfulness Meditation in Everyday Life*. (Reprint and Retitled 2004). Hyperion.

Lakoff, G. & Johnson, M. (1999). *Philosophy in the Flesh: The Embodied Mind and Its Challenge to Western Thought*. Basic Books.

Lave, J. & Wenger, E. (1991). *Situated Learning: Legitimate Peripheral Participation*. Cambridge University Press.

Leigh, J. (2019). *Conversations on Embodiment Across Higher Education: Teaching, Practice and Research (Routledge Research in Higher Education)*. Routledge.

Lemos, E.S. (2011). The meaningful learning theory and its relationship with teaching and research on teaching. *Rev Aprendizagem Significativa*. 1(3), pp. 47–52. http://www.if.ufrgs.br/asr/artigos/Artigo_ID17/v1_n3_a2011.pdf

Lewin, A. & Volberda, H. (1999). Prolegoma on coevolution: a framework for research on strategy and new organization forms. *Organization Science*, 10(5), pp. 519–534. DOI:10.1287/orsc.10.5.519

Loncar, T. (2021). A decade of 'Power Posing': where do we stand? *The Psychologist*, 34(6), pp. 40–44. https://www.bps.org.uk/psychologist/decade-power-posing-where-do-we-stand

Marques, I. (2012). Dança na escola: Arte e ensino. Competência: Caderno pedagógico Notas sobre *o corpo e o ensino de dança*. 8(1), pp. 31–36.

McColl, J. (2016). Mindfulness research in higher education: student perspectives, educator perspectives and the research gap. In Garcia Medina, I. & Martin Llaguno,

M. (eds.), *Business, Economy and Society: Issues for Research in a Knowledge and Information Society*. Glasgow Caledonian University and University of Alicante Spain, pp. 18–24.

Mezirow, J. (2009). An overview on transformative learning. In Illeris, K. (ed.), *Contemporary Theories of Learning*. Routledge, pp. 90–105.

Moreira, M.A. (2012). After all, what is meaningful learning? *Rev Qurriculum*, 25, pp. 29–56. http://www.if.ufrgs.br/~moreira/alfinal.pdf

Newport, C. (2016). *Deep Work: Rules for Focused Success in a Distracted World*. Grand Central Publishing.

Polanyi, M. (1966). *The Tacit Dimension*. Peter Smith.

Porges, S.W. (2011). *The Polyvagal Theory: Neurophysiological Foundations of Emotions, Attachment, Communication, and Self-regulation*. WW Norton & Co.

Reese, D.D. (2015). Dashboard effects challenge flow-learning assumption in digital instructional games. In Tettegah, S. & Huang, W.D. (eds.), *Emotions, Technology, and Games*, pp. 231–287. Elsevier. DOI:10.1016/B978-0-12-801738-8.00011-7

Ribeiro, M. (2015). *Cognição e afetividade na experiência do movimento em dança: conhecimentos possíveis*. In Katz, H. & Greiner, C. (eds.), *Arte & Cognição: Corpomídia, política e educação*. Annablume Editora.

Rohrer, T. (2007). The body in space: dimensions of embodiment. In Ziemke, T., Zlatev, J. & Frank, R.M. (eds.), *Body, Language and Mind Vol 1: Embodiment*. Mouton de Gruyter, pp. 339–378.

Rosenberg, T. (2012). New beginnings and monstrous births: notes towards an appreciation of ideational drawing. In Garner, S. (ed.), *Writing on Drawing: Essays on Drawing Practice and Research*. Intellect Books, pp. 109–124.

Scott, C. (2018). *Elucidating Perceptions of Ageing Through Participatory Drawing: A Phenomenographic Approach*. PhD thesis, University of Brighton. https://research.brighton.ac.uk/en/studentTheses/elucidating-perceptions-of-ageing-through-participatory-drawing

Scott, C. (2020). Drawing. In Crawford, P., Brown, B. & Charise, A. (eds.), *Companion for Health Humanities*. Informa, pp. 302–310.

Scott, C. (2021). Drawing. *Arts for Health Series*. Emerald Publishing Limited.

Scott, C. (2024). Drawing edges: exploring the boundaries of drawing practice and research. In Devis-Rozental, C. & Clarke, S. (eds.), *Communities of Practice in Higher Education: Informal Spaces to Co-Create, Collaborate and Enrich Working Cultures*. Routledge.

Stolz, S.A. (ed.). (2022). *The Body, Embodiment, and Education: An Interdisciplinary Approach*. Routledge.

Tversky, B. & Suwa, M. (2009). Thinking with sketches. In Markman, A.B. & Wood, K.L. (eds.), *Tools for Innovation*. Oxford University Press, pp. 75–84.

Vaughan, K. (2005). Pieced together: Collage as an artist's method for interdisciplinary research. *International Journal of Qualitative Methods*, 4(1), pp. 1–21. DOI:10.1177/160940690500400103

Walsh, M. (2017). *Centring: Why Mindfulness Alone isn't Enough*. Unicorn Slayer Press.

Walsh, M. (2020). *Embodiment – Moving Beyond Mindfulness*. Unicorn Slayer Press. https://www.theembodimentbook.com/illustrations/

Walsh, M. (2021). *The Body in Coaching and Training: An Introduction to Embodied Facilitation*. Open University Press.

Wenger, E. (1998). *Communities of Practice. Learning Meaning and Identity*. Cambridge University Press.

West, O. (2007). *In Search of Words: Footnotes Visual Thinking Techniques*. OPB West.

Ziemke, T. (2003). What's that thing called embodiment? *Proceedings of the 25th Annual meeting of the Cognitive Science Society*, pp. 1305–1310.

Chapter 4

Expertise is ... never having to say you are sorry

Academic development and the artistry of improvisation

Jennie Mills, Jenni Carr, Natasha Taylor, and Catriona Cunningham

Introduction

In this chapter, we explore the inherent tension of academic development identity and practice and consider the relationship between improvisation and expertism. The authors are academic developers and as such we are experts in the field of higher education (HE) pedagogy and the shared endeavour of educational enhancement. Our role, knowledge, understanding, and institutional function situates us as experts at the centre of this social learning network. Some of us are actively charged with nurturing communities of practitioners, drawing them in and towards the centre. We are intermediaries recognising and validating the expertise of others via the Professional Standards Framework (PSF: AdvanceHE, 2023), academic qualifications, and awards. Despite acknowledgement of our expertise at many levels within the higher education sector, recognition at an institutional level can be precarious (Gordon, 2023).

Additionally, our own identity as experts can be fractured by the contexts in which we practise. Our work as gatekeepers belies our institutional habitus, we operate through everyday interactions in classrooms, not boardrooms, with VLEs more than PVCs (Virtual Learning Environments more than Pro-Vice Chancellors). To make our expertise palatable we adapt to our context (Kensington-Miller et al., 2015); we are professional readers of rooms, performing various adaptations of ourselves as experts shaped to meet the needs or demands of our audience.

Our audience members are experts in their own disciplinary fields, and are often overworked, overloaded, and overwhelmed. Coaxing them to invest time in deliberate pedagogic practice often requires us to improvise a more immediate, more palatable version of expertism. The professional understanding and practice of how to communicate our knowledge of pedagogy in situations which are uncertain, unstable, and unique (Schön, 1992, p. 49) is a significant aspect of our own artistry and expertise. We can find ourselves disavowing our own expertise to engage our audience and to enable them to connect meaningfully with teaching and learning. We intuit,

DOI: 10.4324/9781003437826-6

with exquisite accuracy, the first signs of resistance and our pedagogic muscle memory bobs a curtsy to disciplinary expertise and practitioner knowledge – and on we go.

Drawing on Bourdieu's concepts of cultural and social capital we will provide insights into the processes through which academic developers improvise their expertise and explore whether these acts of improvisation undermine our expertise. We will focus on Bourdieu's concept of *'illusio'* (1996, p. 215) and its relationship to different forms of knowledge and the ways in which these knowledges construct the role of 'expert' within different contexts. Having situated our identities and expertise within the contexts of cultural and social capital, we will draw on data generated through epistolary collaborative-autoethnography to offer four examples that illustrate how academic developers can negotiate the tensions between our expertise as academic developers and the need to improvise this expertise in different settings.

Finally, we will discuss how the insights offered might provide a potential way forward for the individual academic developer, as well as the broader academic development community. We are inviting our academic development colleagues to reflect and consider our examples in their own contexts.

Academic development and forms of capital

Before introducing examples from our data, we need to contextualise the theoretical framework for our analysis. Bourdieu (1986) outlines three forms of cultural capital – objectified, embodied, and institutionalised. Our focus in this chapter is on the embodied and institutionalised. Embodied social capital refers to the skills, attributes, and "long lasting dispositions of mind and body" (p. 243) of our professional identity as academic developers. It is this embodied nature of our expertise that underpins our proficiency to improvise in different settings. Academic development accumulates institutionalised social capital through the authority vested with it, via individual institutions and/or sector-wide bodies, to certificate competency in teaching and learning.

Academic developers' cultural capital, whether embodied or institutionalised, must be deployed within the setting of 'the Academy'. As such, the Academy represents the field where the cultural capital of its members is converted into social capital. Social capital coheres through a network of institutionalised relationships of mutual acquaintance and recognition. Each member of the network has the backing of collectively owned capital, which means this has a multiplier effect on the capital you own in your own right (Bourdieu, 1986). That multiplier effect is uneven – not everyone within the field has access to the same cache of capital. As with all systems of exchange involving capital, some are more advantaged than others. The precarity of academic development is indicative of its less than privileged access to social capital.

Within the knowledge economy of the Academy, it is helpful to relate access to social capital to knowledges and expertise. Bourdieu (1977) argues that this relationship can be understood through doxa, and in particular the boundaries between orthodoxies and heterodoxies. These boundaries are policed through accepted notions of what constitutes legitimate and valuable knowledges, and therefore expertise. Bourdieu states that a common *illusio*, an understanding of the rules of the 'game', enables this shared perception of the distinction between orthodox and heterodox positions. At the same time Bourdieu (1998) also argues that *illusio* enables dissent and change by all those that inhabit the field; in this context, the Academy:

> Every social field … tends to require those entering it to have the relationship to the field I call *illusio*. They may want to overturn the relations of force within the field, but for that very reason, they grant recognition to the stakes, they are not indifferent. Wanting to undertake a revolution in a field is to accord the essential of what the field tacitly demands, namely that it is important, that the game played is sufficiently important for one to want to undertake a revolution in it.
>
> (p. 78)

With this in mind, in the next section we will explore how we regard our expertise as more than simply a mechanism through which extrinsic, constantly mutating sector and institutional baselines and targets are met. As such we are not willing to sacrifice the cultural capital we possess to be 'allowed' to simply accumulate social capital. Although we are both invested in the game and understand the rules by which it is played, the deployment of our expertise is intrinsically motivated by what we see as the role of academic development within the serious business of teaching and learning; academic development is values driven. "It is high stakes. It is accredited. It is academic. It is reported. It is Important" (Carr et al., 2021, p. 63).

The extracts

In early 2020, we began exchanging handwritten letters about our lives and experiences in academic development. Over a period of 12 months, we exchanged 24 letters which were subsequently transcribed and analysed (the methodology and findings are discussed in Carr et al., 2021). In the sections that follow, we will apply the notion of *illusio* to four extracts from the letters. We explore the implications of this professional abjuration of our own 'expert power' and in doing so question whether this abjuration is merely an act of disavowal or whether, drawing on a different definition of abjuration, we cast a protective spell of improvisation. We examine whether surfacing our own narratives of resistance in this way can enable us to facilitate social change, reclaim our "agentic self" (McCune, 2022), and reconnect our authentic selves with our 'expertness'.

The rewards of compliance

This example depicts an improvisation of self as the letter-writer seeks to increase their social capital by buying in to the research game. Embracing the 'publish or perish' orthodoxy of academic advancement after a contractual change from professional services to academic, academic development hustles its way from the margins.

> Working on my promotion application turning into glory seeking publication whore so, frankly it's an attitude I'm embracing. It's a bizarre process trying to convince people to give you money and status. Not like a job application when you slip on your job seeking persona. Which brings me back to the familiar thought of what difference does it make? Shuffle that thought quickly into the jumbled kitchen drawer of intrusive thoughts ...

Research is recast as a transactional, desireless, and prosaic encounter, far removed from research as a sort of courtly love: noble, selfless, and transcendent. This candid statement of ambition *implies* honesty, openness, and reflexivity. This not the "lucidity of the excluded" (McNay, 1999) but an in-game hallucination – a spectre conjured by the *illusio*. Further, the *illusio* is sustained by this reflexive performance, as the "reflection game" is an orthodoxy within the field (Macfarlane & Gourlay, 2009). Bourdieu admits little possibility for an individual beyond the field to lay bare the social mechanisms by which the Academy operates:

> [P]ersons, at their most personal, are essentially the *personification* of exigencies actually or potentially inscribed in the structure of the field, or more precisely, in the position occupied within this field.
> (Bourdieu 1989a, p. 449 in Wacquant, 1992, p. 44)

Although the 'bizarre process' of promotion is discomforting, it conjures a self which is more authentic than the commonplace switcheroo of self in job applications. This exchange of 'self' for 'status' captures the essence of the academic 'game' – the accumulation of social capital with the promise of economic reward.

The emotional investment, and costs, are high. Success within the field depends upon intellectual labour, temporally and emotionally embodied within academic research and writing.

Journal rejection rates are consistently high (c. 60–65%, Bjork, 2019), but the Academy normalises the negative emotions of rejection as orthodoxy – everyday experiences which are 'just part of the job'. Rejection is something for individual academics to manage, and so literature on 'academic rejection' is overwhelmingly preoccupied with guidance on coping strategies (Allen et al., 2020). *Illusio* is not mandated or institutionalised, but perfidiously springs from individuals' aspirations and commitments, as they find themselves "entrapped by their own dispositions which make them value the stakes of the game above everything else" (Lupu & Empson 2015, p. 1332).

Community collusion, Bourdieu's concept of "*collusio*" (2000, p. 145), within the field, collective enchantment or social magic, ensures that each individual fully suffers for the game and fully benefits from the capital that the group shares. The trajectory of the contractually 'academic' academic developer exerts a social force on the field, spinning it closer to the Academy from which it is often set apart – as an identity, as a practice, and as a discipline. Publication as a subversive or subverting act, reflexive surfacing of the exchange inherent in 'publish or perish' in a flicker of insurrection itself upholds the *illusio* of the Academy.

So, whilst the letter writer offers a version of Macfarlane and Gourlay's penitent (reflective) self, the seemingly self-deprecating question 'what difference does it make?' throws down a gauntlet. This is a challenge which resists apology as professional persona (2009). The letter writer is an imposter from the margins – embodying a heterodoxic esteem for teaching, who not only stakes a claim to the social capital of research, but who interpellates their position in the field. The antidote to imposterism is assumed by the embodied *collusio* of 'publish or perish'.

Perhaps the possibility of resistance lies in this flash of unthought thought, the thoughts "which delimit the thinkable" (Bourdieu 1982a, p. 10 in Wacquant 1992, p. 40). The familiar 'intrusive thought'– 'what difference does it make?' – calls for us to scrutinise the position of the observer. As an academic developer, caught-up in the micros-mesos-macros and morals of impact and enhancement asking the question – what difference does our work make – not only challenges the orthodoxy but makes visible our position and power within the Academy.

Not failing

This example encapsulates how absence of power can lead to events and actions being experienced as failure even though the agent has not in fact failed. This illustrates tension at the boundary between orthodoxy and heterodoxy within the Academy, and the ways in which they create and resist narratives of failure. The expert academic developer may 'fail' to challenge individual beliefs rooted in academic orthodoxies, but an ability to choose the right battles might win the game.

The example comes from a story about teaching on the Postgraduate Certificate in Higher Education (PGCert). The academic developer (and teacher in this scenario) reflects on the experience of having a difficult colleague in the group. The difficult colleague makes sweeping generalisations about students. He patronises younger and less-experienced members of the group. Worst of all, he displays meanness and disrespect to students in his teaching observation. All of this leads to our letter writer confessing that he is a colleague she actively dislikes. She writes:

> Clearly, I kept my professional mask firmly in place to conceal my feelings. The point of this letter isn't to share my dislike but to unearth the truth about teaching, which is rarely voiced aloud. My response was a timely reminder that, yes, I am human, but also that there's very little I could say or do in this situation to make a difference. Yes, I fed back on his teaching observation, and we had a lengthy, if ultimately futile conversation about him becoming more inclusive in his practise with both students and with his colleagues. However, he made little of this in his final summited assignments and yet was still able to meet the learning outcomes of the module and pass.

There is a clear tension here. He has broken the rules. He does not fit the mould. He does not act or respond in line with the core values of the PSF. And yet he passes the course because he meets the learning outcomes.

Bourdieu's concepts of heterodoxy and orthodoxy are useful lenses through which to explore this tension (Bourdieu, 1984). Orthodoxy can be found in the formal structures of the course itself. The learning outcomes and the assessment processes are official mechanisms within which we operate as educators. There is a shared acceptance that curricula, assessments, and quality processes are robust and fit for purpose. This is institutionalised cultural capital and it legitimises much of the work we do as academic developers.

However, evident in the letter writer's frustration is a strong expression of heterodoxy. As a group of academic developers, we have our own cultural expectations, based on our norms and values. These expectations form our embodied cultural capital, based on extensive experience and expertise in our field. The letter writer is deeply upset because a key assumption has been undermined: as academic developers, we assume and expect our students (who are teachers) to share our core values. We need them to like students, to respect each other, to embrace reflexivity and to want to be better. Yet rarely will you see these things explicitly written into a learning outcome. So, she finds herself immersed in a tension between the institutionalised cultural capital and her embodied cultural capital.

As she grapples for a way to understand the dilemma, the power dynamics come to the fore. Bourdieu (1984) argued that heterodox knowledge is often dismissed or marginalised by those in power, who have the ability to define what is considered legitimate or orthodox knowledge; heterodox ideas and practices are often seen as deviant or illegitimate. The letter writer feels powerless and speaks of needing to improvise, making use of her 'professional mask' to hide her frustration. She feels that it is necessary to suppress her deeply held beliefs and values and give precedence to the institutionalised doxa. Although she herself possesses both embodied and institutionalised capital, she nevertheless feels that her share of social capital within the Academy is somehow inferior or imbalanced.

It does not seem to occur to her that the "obvious" solution moving forward is to change the learning outcomes of the course. She has the power to transform and shape the institutionalised capital, to ease that tension between the embodied and the institutional values. In so doing, she may be able to embezzle a greater share of social capital within the Academy. She has not underestimated the power of her status as expert, but rather estimated it perfectly through a masterful reading of the field. This quote makes visible the masterful flex which successfully deals in institutional capital whilst protecting self, sanity, and security to stay in the game. It points to a failure of the system (a feature not a bug) within which admirable personal values do not guarantee social capital.

Kind of in between?

The aim of this example is to see how the boundaries between heterodoxy and orthodoxy are slippery, constantly in motion.

> At the moment I'm having (intellectual) difficulties with "being kind". I think that "kindness" carries all sorts of loaded norms and is potentially a mechanism by which to silence critique, shut down debate and keep people in their (pre-destined) lane. I think most of all I'm exhausted by the "consensual hoorah!" ideas that no one is going to disagree with but which have become empty and meaningless. Like "being human" and "being kind" (Sometimes a good scolding is in order! :)

The letter writer exposes how the notion of 'kindness', so embedded in the compassionate and caring practices of academic development, was used, colonised even, by many across the sector as a term (a weasel word?) to embody and practice with our students and our colleagues, thereby becoming part of the dominant discourse of the Academy. Implicit in its widespread use was the idea that the university infrastructure is therefore not kind. The idea that the university dehumanises us and denies individual agency as we become cogs in the machine is an orthodox belief, but the notion that we are expert custodians of academic kindness initially presented a heterodox challenge.

The continuum between improvisation–expertise can be seen in this slippage between orthodoxy and heterodoxy which brings power and positions our expertise, acknowledged through the universalism of 'kindness', in the dominant discourse of pandemic times. Here, however, our letter writer is consciously attempting to disentangle herself from this discourse, calling out the taken-for-granted assumption of our profession's values-based approaches and our collaborative and caring ways of working. This emphasis came from senior leaders in universities, a top-down imposition of 'kindness' in a sector-wide culture that is often far from kind. This strange dissonance between the words we hear and then use ourselves is interesting to explore further in the context of *illusio*.

Implicit here is that the dominant discourse defines those who learn and teach in higher education and curtails our actions and even our development as we stay in our 'pre-destined lane'. There is also something dangerous about the imposition of values, as well as the tension between 'being kind' in our representation as change agents, representatives of a university's approach to learning and teaching and the system itself, which is far from kind and in which injustice is embedded in the very infrastructure of the university system itself. It was the heterodoxy of kindness that was being improvised in the pandemic space in an attempt to gain greater influence within the social capital of the academy. But in this instance the improvisation was potentially harmful.

From this perspective, there is something more insidious about the *illusio*; we, as academic developers, are indeed "complicit in the machinery" (Roxå & Mårtensson, 2017) of the academic system and yet we are somehow powerless to resist the temptation to stay in the game. This intentional submission to the *illusio* keeps us in place, performing our roles, acknowledging our expertise and yet unable to break free. As academic developers, we offered certainty, which in turn helped our universities to continue to function, masking perhaps the fear and sheer unknowability of where this pandemic would take higher education. In this sense academic developers were straddling a very fine line between the demands of the university machine and the more traditional academic development role (Bamber, 2020).

Perhaps academic developers can now be more honest about this tension with ourselves and with our communities. In the pandemic context we were seen to be leaders; colleagues looked to us to help them adapt their learning and teaching practices at a shocking pace. We need to acknowledge that our leadership within these unkind systems exists and explore how we can subvert, circumvent, and even combat these systems.

Do we, as academic developers, align with this toxic leadership by promulgating the very systems we purport to stand against (e.g., PGCert, Key Performance Indicators on Higher Education Academy Fellowship numbers etc.), in part from a desire for self-certainty amidst the ambiguity of our roles? In this way, being 'sorry not sorry' is a way of finding our own subversive take on it all, helping us to negotiate the improvisation–expertise continuum. There is hope and power in this acknowledgement. We are kind of in-between, but what opportunities lie in this liminal space?

Visions of the possible

This next example explores what evolved into one of the biggest improvisations of all – the response to the coronavirus pandemic – and highlights the ways in which this provided an opportunity to build the social capital of academic developers within the Academy. It highlights, however, that making the most of this opportunity may have led to academic developers compromising aspects of embodied cultural capital, the principles and values that many argue underpin academic development practice. Did this longed-for opportunity to own our expertise, to be loved, to not ever have to say we were sorry allow our ego to sabotage us?

The extract is taken from a letter written during the period when universities were preparing to bring students back onto socially distanced campuses:

> I've just seen a couple of posts from Uni A and Uni B re. COVID-19 campuses. Looks like Uni A have plastered every square metre with "keep your distance" stickers. The pics from Uni B are heart-stoppingly terrifying. Lots of yellow tape around individual front facing chairs – like an active learning murder scene. Do these people really not see the pedagogic horror show? I was going to say I feel so sorry for the students, but then thinking about my own undergrad experience – nah – they'll be fine. None of us did any active learning and we turned out okay.

This quote exemplifies the fluid relationship between orthodoxy and heterodoxy, and how the memory traces of old orthodoxies and the knowledges and expertise that maintained them can reassert themselves at times of crisis and rupture. It is through exploring these shifts across knowledge borders and threats to different forms of capital that we can examine the *illusio*.

At the beginning, the letter writer highlights the "active learning murder scene" that is represented by the images posted on Twitter. Active learning, a fundamental principle that underpins much current pedagogical expertise, has come to the classroom to die! Very quickly, however, a more pragmatic approach asserts itself. The sentence "None of us did any active learning and we turned out okay" might be viewed as a humorous style of writing, which was very common in the exchanges. But it also highlights a potential tension within the academic developer identity. Many of us, when learners, will not have experienced the approach to learning and teaching that we now promote. How did we become such advocates for current pedagogical approaches? Objectively, we could argue that our current enthusiasm is rooted in the evidence-based development of these approaches. Subjectively, however, we can ask whether there are other aspects that appeal. We rely on our institutional cultural capital (e.g., PSF and Advance HE–accredited programmes) to gain access to the social capital distributed within the Academy. Our expertise is validated by developments in pedagogical knowledge to which we have access and, perhaps more importantly, we have some influence over the strategies that embed these as 'good practice'. Once accepted as good practice, our roles are validated and there is a need for our brand of expertise.

But then came what we have referred to elsewhere as the Great Reckoning (Carr et al., 2021). Everyone's worlds were turned upside down, and pandemic teaching was the game that had to be played. We do not mean to suggest that there were not great efforts made to continue to bring good practice into learning spaces. The sharing of practice, advice, and resources during the pandemic reflected the strength and generosity of our academic development community.

In *Opening Lines: Approaches to the Scholarship of Teaching and Learning*, Hutchings (2000) argues that "every scholarly and professional field is defined in part by the questions it asks" (p. 4). Drawing on their taxonomy of SoTL questions, our main focus has been on 'what works' type questions. In many ways this is understandable. To not attempt to make some good emerge from such traumatic experiences would be perverse indeed! But now the immediate drama is over and we are speaking with our "louding voices" at conferences and in journal papers about the 'lessons learned', we should also recognise that we are buttressing our expertise, consolidating our access to what we believe to be our share of the social capital accrued through membership of the Academy. (In the book *The Girl with the Louding Voice* by Daré, 2020, "louding voice" is used by people that speak their opinions with a confidence that is legitimised by and through a "Western" education.)

We could argue that we also need to explore lines of enquiry into what Hutchings describes as the "Visions of the Possible". We need to pay attention to the quieter voices – the noises off – and consider if by drawing on the narratives that validated our expertise in normal times, and improvising them in that pandemic space, we betrayed the values that so many of us argue underpin our practice. Is now the time to put at risk some of our newly acquired social capital by questioning and researching how students might have learned best and under those extraordinary conditions?

Conclusion

Together, these examples tell us something important about the expertise of academic developers: we are at once cogs in the machine of the Academy, amplifying the dominant discourse and thereby promulgating the orthodoxy. However, we also have agency, and power to affect change. Academic developers have both opportunity and authority to exercise and deploy our embodied and institutional capital – informally through corridor conversations, in email exchanges, social networks, and workshops and through our formal taught programmes and recognition work to legitimise and challenge accepted ways of knowing, doing, and being in higher education.

We are invested in the Academy and constitute it as it constitutes us. Academic developers are not in the margins – lonely and irrelevant, but actively creating orthodoxies which, as this chapter demonstrates, can be both helpful and harmful to those within the field. The field is important to academic developers, and we cannot feign indifference or claim distance, rehearsing powerlessness, unwitting compliance, or outsider status.

Academic developers are empowered not only to manifest expertise but also to create expertise, willing it into being as we weave through institutional structures, shape-shifting, and improvising. Importantly, we listen. We hear the whisperings of the heterodox, and tune in to the sometimes silenced and unheard voices of our colleagues and students, amplifying their needs and perspectives amidst the noise. We speak the heterodox – loudly and frequently.

Key take-aways

As individual academic developers, we need:

- To give careful thought to the processes through which we engage in and with the Academy;
- To acknowledge our power, our position, and the ways in which we legitimise the systems of which we are a part;
- To find our own ways to draw on our shared/collective expertise to challenge, subvert or revolutionise the orthodoxies which run counter to our values – and to pick the right battles;
- To forgo bitter self-recrimination when we find ourselves having to improvise, and abandon belief that such improvisations diminish our expertise.

As a collective, a community of practice, academic developers can harness this open discussion about our agency and strength to be explicit about our institutional impact. Finally, we, the authors, extend our collective to all educators working within higher education. The honesty of these exchanges is not haphazard, and in sharing our discomfort we do not admit defeat. Rather, by harnessing critical apparatus and theoretical frameworks for thinking, we can share and shape discussion and reflection to show the way forward.

References

AdvanceHE. (2023). Professional Standards Framework. https://www.advance-he.ac.uk/teaching-and-learning/psf
Allen, K.-A., Donoghue, K., Pahlevansharif, S., Himerson, S.R., & Hattie, J.A.C. (2020). Addressing academic rejection: recommendations for reform. *Journal of University Teaching and Learning Practice*, 17 (5). DOI:10.53761/1.17.5.19
Bamber, V. (2020) *Our Days Are Numbered: Metrics, Managerialism, and Academic Development*. SEDA.
Bjork, B.-C. (2019). Acceptance rates of scholarly peer-reviewed journals: a literature survey. *El profesional de la información*, 28(4). DOI:10.3145/epi.2019.jul.07
Bourdieu, P. (1977). *Outline of a Theory of Practice*. Cambridge: Cambridge University Press. DOI:10.1017/CBO9780511812507
Bourdieu, P. (1984). *Distinction: a Social Critique of the Judgement of Taste*. London: Routledge.
Bourdieu, P. (1986). The forms of capital. In: Richardson, J., *Handbook of Theory and Research for the Sociology of Education*. Westport, CT: Greenwood, pp. 241–258.

Bourdieu, P. (1996). *The Rules of Art: Genesis and Structure of the Literary Field*. Trans. S. Emmanuel Oxford: Polity Press.
Bourdieu, P. (1998). *Practical Reason: On the Theory of Action*. Cambridge: Polity Press.
Bourdieu, P. (2000). *Pascalian Meditations*. London: Polity Press.
Carr, J., Cunningham, C., Mills, J., & Taylor, N. (2021). 'It's all fun and games until someone loses an 'I': identity and the imaginary in playful academic development. *Journal of Play in Adulthood*, 3(2), pp. 62–81. DOI:10.5920/jpa.849
Daré, A. (2020). *The Girl with the Louding Voice*. London: Sceptre Books.
Gordon, C. (2023). Taking aim at old hierarchies. *LSE Higher Education Blog*, May 4 2023, https://blogs.lse.ac.uk/highereducation/2023/05/04/taking-aim-at-old-hierarchies/
Hutchings, P. (2000). *Opening Lines: Approaches to the Scholarship of Teaching and Learning*. Palo Alto, CA: Carnegie Foundation for the Advancement of Teaching.
Kensington-Miller, B., Renc-Roe, J., & Morón-Garcia, S. (2015). The chameleon on a tartan rug: adaptations of three academic developers' professional identities. *International Journal for Academic Development*, 20(3), pp. 279–290. DOI:10.108 0/1360144X.2015.1047373
Lupu, I., & Empson, L. (2015). Illusio and overwork: playing the game in the accounting field. *Accounting, Auditing and Accountability Journal*, 28(8), pp. 1310– 1340. DOI:10.1108/AAAJ-02-2015-1984
Macfarlane, B. & Gourlay, L. (2009). The reflection game: enacting the penitent self. *Teaching in Higher Education*, 14 (4), pp. 455–459. DOI:10.1080/13562510903050244
McCune, V. (2022). Academic identities in contemporary higher education: sustaining identities that value teaching. *Teaching in Higher Education*, 26 (10), pp. 20–35. DOI:10.1080/13562517.2019.1632826
McNay, L. (1999). Gender, Habitus and the Field: Pierre Bourdieu and the Limits of Reflexivity. *Theory, Culture and Society*, 16 (1), pp. 95–117. DOI:10.1177/02632769901600
Roxâ, T. & Mårtensson, K. (2017). Agency and structure in academic development practices: are we liberating academic teachers or are we part of a machinery supressing them? *International Journal for Academic Development*, 22(2), pp. 95–105. DOI:10.1080/1360144X.2016.1218883
Schön, D.A. (1992). *The Reflective Practitioner: How Professionals Think in Action*. Abingdon: Routledge. DOI:10.4324/9781315237473
Wacquant, L. (1992). Toward a Social Praxeology. In P. Bourdieu and L. Wacquant. *Invitation to Reflexive Sociology*. Chicago: University of Chicago Press.

Chapter 5

The artistry of teaching as culturally self-aware, learning-centred, imaginative co-creation

Anna Santucci

Introduction

The first time I taught an undergraduate class I was a 25-year-old PhD student. Just a few years older than my learners, I remember wanting to dress for the part that morning; I ended up wearing a dark blue dress-suit, which I had specifically purchased over the summer for "when I would start teaching". That attire was so "not me" that I don't think I ever actually wore that dress again in my life. And yet that day I felt the need for that prop/costume to enter the stage for the first time as a higher education teacher.

I fondly remember that group of students, and how quickly getting to know their wonderfully unique selves convinced me that I really didn't need to be anything else than myself to help them learn. I was teaching Elementary Italian, first semester in their language curriculum; a typical teaching assignment for a second-year PhD in a language department at Brown. All of us language instructors would teach according to a curriculum and course structure determined by our coordinator faculty member, with whom we met every week. Under her guidance and advice, all daily lesson planning, classroom interactions, assessment feedback, and grading were our responsibility. This was a wonderful, practice-based experiential opportunity to learn and grow in our role as educators. It was one of the main appeals that drew me to this PhD program, together with Brown's Sheridan Center for Teaching & Learning – which would eventually open my eyes and heart to a professional pathway in the field of academic/educational development.

When I first walked into that classroom as a 25-year-old graduate student, I had no idea of what was to come in my trajectory. I didn't know I would discover a fervent vocation for academic/educational development (Santucci, 2022a), write my interdisciplinary Arts & Humanities PhD dissertation with a strong Scholarship of Teaching and Learning (SoTL) lens, and choose to dedicate my career to Teaching & Learning in Higher Education. All I knew was how anxious I was about not having taken my Theory and Methods of Foreign Language Teaching course yet; our regular PhD curriculum would have had me complete that in my first year, in preparation for commencing our teaching

DOI: 10.4324/9781003437826-7

duties in our second year. Yet as destiny would have it, that course was cancelled in my first year; so while I did take and enjoy it in my second year, when I first crossed my metaphorical threshold as a teacher I had not had any formal preparation whatsoever. Now, it goes without saying that I deeply believe in the importance of professional development and intentional learning about how to be effective teachers. Yet looking back to that first semester, and maybe especially considering what I do and know now, I can honestly say that I sincerely treasure the spontaneity and authenticity which that experience as a raw novice afforded me. Had I had more formal educational layers prescribing for me what being a teacher should mean, I don't think that dress suit would have come off as easily, or that I would have allowed my teaching persona to become holistically part of me as fast and with as much confidence in myself and in my students as I did.

Gravett and Winstone (2020) use the language of artistry, performance, and improvisation in relation to the importance of authenticity, meaningful connection, and relational engagement in teaching. As Eisner articulates, adaptive problem solving as expert teachers "requires sensibility, imagination, technique, and the ability to make judgements about the feel and significance of the particular. Teaching profits from – no, requires at its best – artistry" (2002, p. 382). This chapter explores how intentionally striving for cultural self-awareness helps us develop expertise in the artistry of teaching, specifically in relation to fostering critical and cyclical reflection on how our identity informs our ability to imaginatively co-create learning-centered practice. Our beliefs about learning and our values as educators guide our curiosity to learn in action; they determine the questions we ask, the types of resources we seek, and the strategies we choose to implement. Hence while we may occasionally share some portions of the journey along the roads we stride in our growth as teachers, the path is inevitably and beautifully different for each of us. There is no perfect formula, no magical step-by-step recipe to follow mechanically.

Discussing "Why College Faculty Need to Know the Research About Learning", Gary Smith (2015) employs an effective baking metaphor to describe how a teaching practitioner needs to know *why* innovations to their teaching are expected to work and not just *how* to implement them. In his metaphor, the artistry of the baker lies in their ability to not simply follow a recipe blindly, but rather consider all situational factors and constantly diagnose what to tweak or adjust. I would add that in asking ourselves as often as possible both "how" and "why", inclusive practitioners strive for awareness that as instructors we are ourselves part of those situational factors and cannot not factor into the picture what we bring to the table ourselves. In Smith's metaphor, the artistry of the baker remains largely demiurgically situated: if the teacher is the expert baker, where is the contributing agency of the learners? They surely cannot be just the baked goods, the raw ingredients to be shaped into form and substance. While as teachers we do indeed embody crucial responsibilities as the experienced designers, our role cannot be defined as puppeteers located outside of the learning experience. This is why the landscape of co-created performance practice is for me a better metaphor to both theorise and actualise the artistry of teaching. Teachers as actors, directors, theatrical ("seeing and being seen") and dramatic ("storytelling") facilitators, and most of all ensembles' co-improvisers are at the center of my work on critical embodiment and intercultural development for inclusive education.

To unpack this, I propose here three interrelated concepts; the following sections will discuss how the artistry of teaching is:

1. *Culturally Self-Aware* – Exploring who we are and how we experience difference;
2. *Learning-Centred* – Designing for liberation of human learning;
3. *Imaginative Co-Creation* – Envisioning possibilities, which transforms us forward.

Culturally self-aware

Our positionality inevitably informs our practice as scholarly teachers (Santucci & Vaccaro, in press). Hence if we truly want to foster professional development that improves our effectiveness and well-being, exercising self-awareness is a key component of the type of artistry this volume wants to articulate. As we are all along continued journeys in our teaching and learning "expertise" development, it is crucial to acknowledge how our multifaceted contexts, cultures, disciplines, habitus (Bourdieu, 1977), and epistemologies inevitably shape our ways of interpreting the world and making meaning in constant process.

In pursuing more just futures through our educational practice, I often use the language of 'we' – yet *we* must come to terms with the fact that 'we' is not an easily defined or definable variable. Since each of us is a unique combination of cultural traits that make us who we are, the best way I have found so far to wrap my head around the key issue of intersectionality in understanding systems is through intercultural development (Bennett, 2017; Acheson & Schneider-Bean, 2019). The Intercultural Development Inventory (IDI) defines 'culture' in these terms: "Each of us has a worldview that is related to participation in one or more culture groups. These groups are often defined by national and/or racial or ethnic boundaries, but they may also represent other affiliations, such as region, religion, gender, sexual orientation, ability, [socioeconomic status], etc." (IDI, 2023). Thinking about cultural 'belonging' helps us realise how each of the myriad traits that make us who we are feels, and effectively is, differently salient to our present experience depending on situational and contextual factors, such as location, moments in life, and so on. What does such a uniquely contextualised multiplicity of difference imply for our practice as educators? Beyond easy rhetoric around fostering a sense of belonging among diverse populations, what does Intentionally Equitable

Hospitality (Bali, 2021) look like, and how can we radically enact "Education in an Ethics of Hospitality" (Ruitenberg, 2011)?

Maha Bali (2021) is among several inspiring scholars who have embraced the language of hospitality to conceptualise inclusive educational spaces. In relation to the notion of "setting intentions for equity", she discusses "Intentionally Equitable Hospitality" as a mindset in which "the facilitators of a space view themselves as hosts, responsible for welcoming every participant, questioning for whom the space might be hospitable/welcoming and for whom it might not be". Ruitenberg (2011) urges us to recognise in educational spaces such a "call of hospitality" that poses a fundamental "ethical challenge": engaging with any student "in a way that lets [them] be in otherness, that does not seek to recognize or otherwise close the gap with this singular other" (p. 32). Ruitenberg (2011) distinguishes "hospitality" from "inclusion" – according to her, where inclusion presupposes a desire or intention to "fit the guest into the space of the host," hospitality "accepts that the arrival of the guest may change the space into which he or she is received" (p. 32). Ruitenberg thus pushes our boundaries in proposing that "in an ethic of hospitality, the question of whether the host feels comfortable in the presence of the guest is irrelevant" (p. 33).

Embracing discomfort and sitting with the trouble as we continue to courageously ask the hard questions rather than settling on easy answers is a key aspect of self-reflection and awareness development in the work of inclusive education towards more equitable and just futures. Schön (1983) encourages us to search "for an epistemology of practice implicit in the artistic, intuitive processes which some practitioners bring to situations of uncertainty, instability, uniqueness and value conflict" (p. 49). Indeed, experiential learning for intercultural transformation requires us to "dance with discomfort", tiptoeing back and forth right across the boundary of our comfort zone and into our learning zone but not as far as our panic zone (Harvey, n.d.). In seeking continued growth, our learning zones need to be what I call "safely brave enough" (Arao & Clemens, 2013) – for we can never be completely safe for truly transformative learning to occur: learners need to play, experiment, stumble, make mistakes, explore possibilities, and fail forward.

The models of equity-minded (Artze-Vega et al., 2022), critically inclusive practice I espouse require educators to authentically engage in self-reflection towards increased awareness of who they are. This is a common trait across approaches advocating for pedagogies grounded in critical principles of cultural relevance, anti-racism, decolonisation, and feminism (see rich resource collections such as Georgetown University's Center for New Designs in Learning and Scholarship's Inclusive Pedagogy Toolkit or Elon University's Center for the Advancement of Teaching and Learning's Teaching for Equity and Inclusion). For example, Dewsbury's Deep Teaching model (2020) suggests that increased teachers' self-awareness results in better ability to have empathy for the student experience, which in turn encourages us to utilise varied pedagogies, develop a trusting classroom climate, and effectively leverage our networks. Dewsbury, Murray-Johnson, and Santucci (2021) further unpack the steps that lead from self-awareness to empathy. Discussing how faculty development experiences aiming to foster inclusive teaching practices involve difficult dialogue and active listening processes, they highlight specific intercultural skills needed to "engage realities that potentially challenge long held understandings about one's own experience" (p. 59) and articulate the progressive development of these skills in four stages:

a) **Self-awareness**;
b) **(Cultural) humility**, described as the ability to recognise "one's cumulation of behaviors, habits, & experiences as only one specific set among human plurality" (*ibid*);
c) **Cognitive flexibility**, described as the ability to shift "frameworks of reference beyond the ones we have been socialised into" (*ibid*);
d) **Experiential and epistemological empathy**, described as "the (never completely obtainable) goal of entertaining experience, feelings, and thoughts like another" (*ibid*).

Diatta-Holgate and Hyder's (2023) current work in progress on a "unifying framework" for "applying equity-oriented pedagogies for inclusive teaching and learning" also highlights the crucial cyclical nature of these reflexive processes that nurture empowerment through self-reflection, fostering community and belonging and critical engagement with difference.

The ability to critically engage with difference, as articulated in Bennett's Developmental Model of Intercultural Sensitivity (2017) and the Intercultural Development Continuum (IDC, IDI; Hammer, 2023 – see Figure 5.1), has been helpfully further reframed as a pendulum model by Acheson and Schneider-Bean (2019 – see Figure 5.2): through the metaphor of a perpetually oscillating pendulum, their model allows us to identify in our lived experience both 'magnets' that pull us towards a hyper-focus on similarity or difference, and 'anchors' that help ground us towards what I call a fundamentally utopian state of adaptation (see Figure 5.3).

Learning-centred

As teachers, we often attempt to provide others who are less experienced than we are with scaffolded resources and support in a particular area; yet most importantly, we hold space that nurtures others' own growth. Learning is transformative growth, and no one can own, dictate, or direct someone else's transformation. I often observe with gratitude the facilitation practice of great colleagues whose work I admire, aka the artistry in their teaching. For example, Dr Mays Imad often starts her workshops on inclusive teaching by gracefully highlighting for participants that anything they need to know, they already do. The human-centredness of her remarks is a great example of what

Intercultural Development Continuum® (IDC)

Monocultural Mindset → Denial (Misses difference) → Polarization (Judges difference) → Minimization (De-emphasizes difference) → Acceptance (Deeply Comprehends difference) → Adaptation (Bridges Across difference) → **Intercultural Mindset**

© 2023 IDI, LLC

IDI Intercultural Development Inventory®

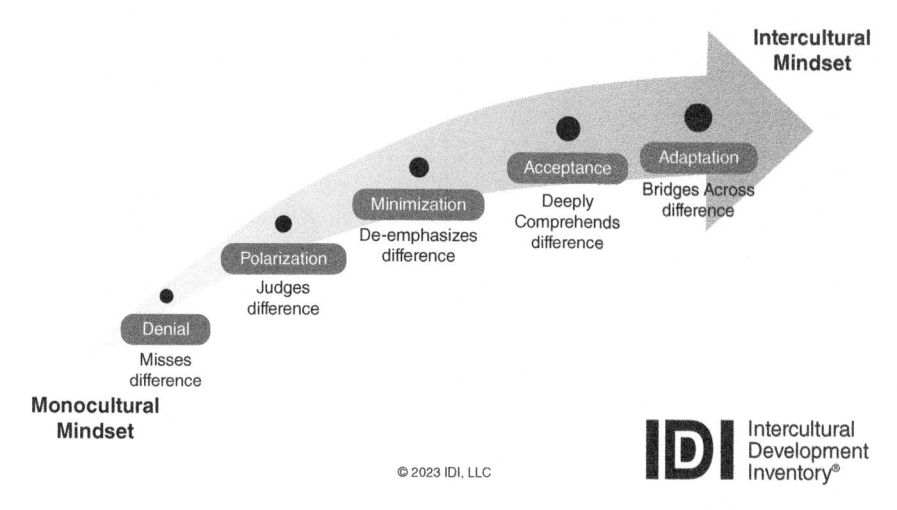

Figure 5.1 The Intercultural Development Continuum (IDC, IDI; Hammer 2023) in the Intercultural Development Inventory

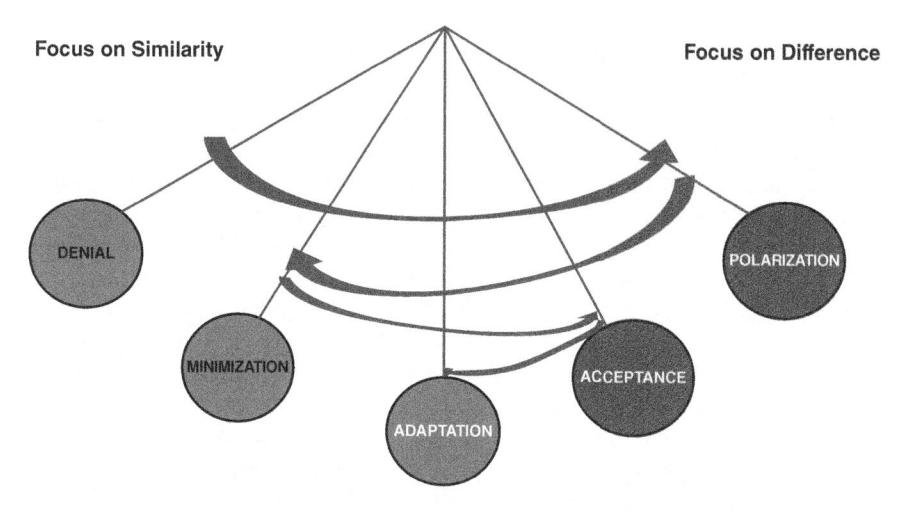

Focus on Similarity — DENIAL, MINIMIZATION, ADAPTATION, ACCEPTANCE, POLARIZATION — **Focus on Difference**

Figure 5.2 Representing the Intercultural Development Continuum as a Pendulum Model
Figure 2, p. 9 in: Acheson & Schneider-Bean, 2019

I have recently heard her theorise as "Pedagogies of (re)awakening". Discussing the "optimization of educational practice", Randy Bass has poignantly stated that "the end game should be the continuous pursuit of the existential project to help 'humans get better at being human' (Bass, 2018 p. 34)" – urging us to

80 Anna Santucci

Focus on Similarity

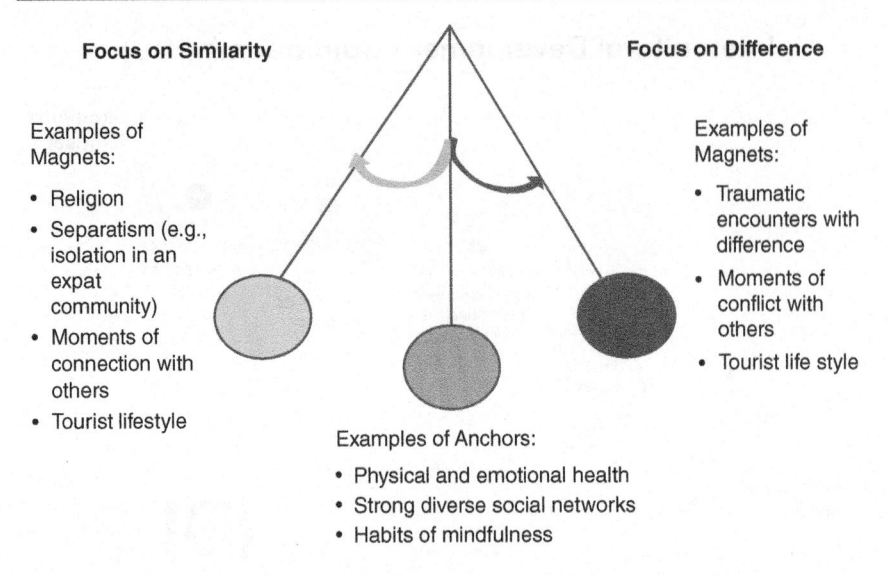

Examples of Magnets:

- Religion
- Separatism (e.g., isolation in an expat community)
- Moments of connection with others
- Tourist lifestyle

Focus on Difference

Examples of Magnets:

- Traumatic encounters with difference
- Moments of conflict with others
- Tourist life style

Examples of Anchors:

- Physical and emotional health
- Strong diverse social networks
- Habits of mindfulness

Figure 5.3 Magnets and Anchors on the Intercultural Development Pendulum Model
Figure 4, p. 13 in: Acheson & Schneider-Bean, 2019

"restlessly and authentically open up the questions of learning and higher education as if our human future depended on it" (Bass, 2020).

Pedagogies of (re)awakening help humans get better at being humans by centring learning facilitation and design based on our human grounding in love, hope, and beauty (Imad et al., 2022). Reawakening as teachers means valuing our intuitions and undoing dangerous cognition/emotion divides too often revered in academic settings. Reawakening, as teachers and humans, means stepping into a situation with our fullest possible self, acknowledging that all we can do is our best – and committing, to harken a quote famously attributed to Maya Angelou, to do better when we know better.

Education has the transformative potential to liberate, yet it is also historically a means of oppression. Much great work by decolonisation scholars reminds us how elite and dominant groups repeatedly dictate through schooling the ways to speak and even think to be deemed proper or acceptable, erasing the multiplicity of diverse ways of being and knowing. Educational spaces are therefore intrinsically shaped by complex intersectional layers of power, privilege, and culture. One of the noticeable consequences in our classrooms is that many learners are alas implicitly habituated to conceive of learning as passive, as their previous experiences may not have celebrated and leveraged the unique individuals that they are and are becoming. Embracing the incredible richness of our diversity, we know that no one instance of a teaching and learning interaction can ever be the same as another – simply because the people involved are never the same in their constant becoming.

Hence developing expertise in the artistry of teaching means realising that we do need to have a plan for well-designed courses and activities, but we also need all participants (including the teacher!) to allow themselves to be present and open to improvising together. An example of this is offered in Box 5.1, where Monica Ward describes the student-centred pedagogy of Challenge Based-Learning.

Box 5.1   Adapting, improvising and releasing of control – teaching in a Challenge Based Learning paradigm

Monica Ward

Challenge Based Learning (CBL) is an innovative approach to teaching and learning where learners get the opportunity to explore a challenge, investigate options, and develop a possible solution to the challenge (Leijon et al., 2022). It is a holistic approach and has many potential benefits for learners, but it requires several skills on the part of the CBL educators. There is sometimes, but not always, a technology aspect to CBL and challenges often relate to the UN Sustainable Development Goals (SDGs). In the CBL paradigm, there are many unknowns. The known unknowns include: What SDG will students choose as their focus? What technologies will they investigate as part of the solution? What solutions will be "sensible"? Will they find sensible solutions? There are also unknown unknowns which can add to the unpredictability of the CBL approach.

In this unpredictable environment, there are three key approaches that can be used: a) adaptivity, the ability to react when things do not go according to plan, b) improvisation when there is a need to change direction, and c) the ability to release control and embrace a student partnership approach. There are five key skills that are helpful to educators in this context: 1) modelling good practice when issues arise as it shows students not to panic, 2) good problem-solving skills help to overcome difficulties that arise, 3) resilience helps when problems seem particularly hard, 4) in this uncertain environment, it is helpful for students to see that the educator can also be vulnerable and that they too are on a learning journey, and 5) it is helpful if the educator has good educational technology skills.

We used a CBL approach with a cohort of computing-for-business students in their final year of an undergraduate honours degree programme. They looked at using innovative and disruptive technologies to address different SDGs. Topics included retrofitting commercial buildings in

Dublin, a solar panel farm in Kenya, and wearable tech for health in India. The feedback from the students at the end of the module was very positive. They liked the focus on real-world problems and that they could choose the topic themselves. As one student commented "*it encourages students to be 'active and engaged learners'*".

Delivering the CBL module was both challenging and exciting at the same time. It is important to 'walk the talk', demonstrating the ability to be flexible and deal with uncertainty, showing (real) curiosity and also not to be too afraid of not knowing something. While many aspects of the module deal with transversal skills, there are also key research skills incorporated into the module, including how to conduct literature searches and the use of white and grey literature. There are also key communication skills involved in the module, including explaining a technical topic to a non-technical audience.

In summary, educators need to be adaptive, comfortable with improvisation, and comfortable with releasing control. Smart, tailored professional development is required for educators to get them up to speed. CBL is scary and exciting at the same time.

As Derek Baylor perfectly summarised during one of our *Yes, And ... Higher Education* (YAHE Network) gatherings: "Don't educate me ... let me learn!" As we implement interventions based on high-impact practices regarding transparency, impostor syndrome, stereotype threat, hidden curriculum, and so on – can we ask ourselves: since my learners' past experiences accumulation influences their current interpretation of their learning context (Aguilar et al., 2014), where and how can I, however minimally, (re)set the stage towards a learning-centred mindset? The CUNY Innovative Pedagogy Team, in collaboration with UVA's Motivate Lab, wonderfully spelled out an easy-to-remember GPS for "learning mindset:" G for Growth Mindset (the belief that intelligence can be developed through hard work, the use of effective strategies, and help from others when needed); P for Purpose and Relevance (Belief that schoolwork is valuable because it is personally relevant); S for Sense of Belonging (Belief that one is connected to and respected by peers, cared for by teachers and mentors, and fits in with the culture) (CUNY Mindset Workshop, 2020). I find these three fundamental components significantly align with the key levers of intrinsic motivation as articulated in self-determination theory as well: sense of Competence (feeling effective through development); sense of Autonomy (having a voice, mattering as an individual); sense of Relatedness (feeling connected to others) (Ryan & Deci, 2017).

Teaching expertise conceived as learning-centred artistry thus cuts through dangerous rhetoric that perpetuates damagingly false dichotomies between the "science" and "art" of teaching and learning (McMurtrie, 2021). The artistry of teaching *includes* making expert decisions based on what we scientifically know about how learning works; or, better articulated from my perspective as an arts-based humanist: on what each of us chooses to consider, based on our values, beliefs, and epistemological frames of reference, what "we know" about how learning works.

Imaginative co-creation: what if??

Ruitenberg's framing of "Education in an Ethic of Hospitality" does get us in the right direction in terms of de-centring the self in the pursuit of critical self-awareness, as explored earlier. However, Ruitenberg's articulation of hospitality considers "the question of whether the host feels comfortable in the presence of the guest" as "irrelevant" (2011, p. 33). I believe this theorisation is insufficient on its own to create truly liberatory educational spaces that work towards reconciliation of historical injustice. If for the "guest" to matter, as it should always, the "host" needs to stop mattering, then we risk falling into too-prescriptive Diversity, Equity, and Inclusion policies and top-down approaches for institutional implementation. What if we, rather, radically embrace our shared responsibility of co-creating each other? Improv can help us conceive of such a space: "Building the world is both everyone's responsibility and no one's – in this paradox sits the democratic potential of improv to accept the invitation to co-create emergently" (Perone & Santucci, in preparation).

In our highly siloed, territorial, and competition-driven neoliberal institutions, how might we attempt to truly address the need to advocate for systemic change that enables reflection on purpose, belonging, and growth-oriented agency towards (more) equitable practices for *all* teachers and learners – and teachers *as* learners? Envisioning a different higher education through an improv-informed mindset affords us some ways to think and feel this through. Perone and Santucci (in preparation) theorise such "transformative potential of emergent co-creation" by offering an approach that "acknowledges, values, and builds on the practice of 'Yes, and...' […] in four interrelated ways: […] relational curiosity, love through vulnerability, completion, and the dialectic of being/becoming." Bearing in mind that our intersectional identities and capitalistically situated roles mean we cannot all afford to take risks or be vulnerable in the same ways (see for example recent debates on the complex issue of bias in Student Evaluations of Teaching; Artze-Vega et al., 2022, pp. 205–224), I ask us to reflect on what it might look like to act differently when we see an opportunity within our sphere of influence to be 'safely brave enough' and do so: What might it look like if in higher education we entertained more often the possibilities of co-creation and shared responsibility? What if we played more generously, and worried less about status? What if we were more often authentically receptive and open, truly *present*, having a plan of where we want to go but figuring out together how we'll get there? What if we were more often willing to be vulnerable? What if we validated more often how others' perspectives and ideas complete us, welcoming them as gifts to build together in our constant state of becoming? (Santucci, 2020). What if…?

While arts teachers have long made the case for the generative power of 'what if' in advocating for the importance of drama/theatre for/in education (Santucci, 2019), what I am hoping to highlight in this chapter is the transdisciplinary relevance of such 'what-ifs'. Mindful of the contours I tread in my professional identity, I strive to acknowledge a distinction between specific signature pedagogies (Shulman, 2005) of arts for justice-oriented change and my focus here on Teaching and Learning elements that have applicability across diverse disciplines. The approach I propose applies signature pedagogies of participatory performing arts practice for educational and professional development purposes; it encourages post-secondary educators to shift from fearing the scary 'what if' of losing control ('what if" tech doesn't work in the classroom? 'What if' students don't submit the assignment in time?) to embracing the nurturing 'what if?' of co-creative meaning making that has the power to unbridle unlimited potential. Such approach helps all of us exercise our muscles towards building artistry skills that are core to teaching expertise: it promotes self-discovery, heightens self-awareness, fosters empathy development, encourages presence, and increases the ability to hold ambiguity and process discomfort (Santucci, 2022b).

Randy Bass has defined "the essence of integrative higher education" as "the cultivation of distinctly human capacities: creativity, personal empowerment and agency, well-being, relationships, empathy, and the ability to reflect and act in conditions of complexity and uncertainty" (2018, p. 39). I believe that the ability to imaginatively co-create discussed in this section, to envision that-which-is-not-yet-here and act upon such vision in community, is a key qualifying trait of such distinctly human capacities. Critical educators who advocate for *Radical Hope* (Gannon, 2020a) share a sense of urgency driven by the utopian desire to perform into existence the world we want to see: we simply cannot "abide by the status quo because [we] know what could be, not just what should be" (Gannon, 2020b). Participatory performing arts practice for educational development affords us to envision possible futurities and play through imaginative experiencing that empowers us to act for change. If we can imagine a different future, we can start rehearsing it and are therefore one step closer to performing it into existence.

Augusto Boal's *Theatre of the Oppressed* techniques encourage us to "de-mechanize" not only our minds, but also our bodies: in order to rehearse towards revolutionary futures, we need to step out of habituated ways of being, predetermined roles that limit possibilities for change (Boal, 1979; 1992). "To de-mechanize the body is to awaken one's awareness of muscular potential, the relationship between self and other, […] how we physically carry ourselves in the world and our abilities to perceive ourselves as doers, agents of change" (Cahnmann-Taylor & Souto-Manning, 2010 pp. 40–1). Becoming agents of change means unlearning our habituated repertoires – for example, how we have been taught ourselves. Developing teaching expertise as artistry means exploring such expanded repertoires.

Conclusion

I consider practising and investigating the artistry of teaching to be at the heart of our professional identity as educators. As an Educational Developer and scholar of teaching and learning whose background combines intercultural studies and applied theatre, I am fascinated by the ritual of teaching and learning understood through a performance studies lens (Schechner, 2006; Turner, 1982) and curious about the ways in which the creative meaning-making skills of theatre arts help us develop our cognitive, affective, and bodily capacities as inclusive educators, our expanded repertoires of muscular potential as agents of change (Cahnmann-Taylor & Souto-Manning, 2010). To name a few core ones: they promote self-discovery and awareness, they foster empathy and authentic presence, and they enact ethics of care by increasing our ability to hold ambiguity and process discomfort (Santucci, 2020; 2022b). Teaching as dramatic artistry goes well beyond applications such as persuasive communication, charismatic oration, and command of space and audience (Santucci, 2023); while these are certainly relevant and useful, reflexively improvisational awareness of our teaching persona also encompasses deeper "ensemble" facilitation traits needed to build and hold brave spaces (Arao & Clemens, 2013) for learning where all participants can grow with courage and generosity, what I call "safely brave enough" Zones of Proximal Development (Vygotsky, 1978) in which to experiment, take risks, fail forward, and explore new possibilities – and thus experientially rehearse for revolutionary action (Boal, 1979; Freire, 1988). Infusing participatory performing arts in educational development work provides uniquely powerful tools to scaffold intercultural competence skills (Bennett, 2017; Deardorff, 2014) that allow educators to engage in transformative change: self-awareness, humility, cognitive flexibility, empathy (Dewsbury, Murray-Johnson & Santucci, 2021). The ability to articulate such skills plays a significant role in developing confidence in our teaching roles, and thus helps increase a sense of competence that is conducive towards sustaining motivation to continuously improve teaching. These skills are useful for our professional identity beyond the classroom, across our spheres of influence in the roles we occupy in the academy, as they increase our ability to find movement and breath in moments of tension and conflict, allowing us to feel more consciously grounded in our values when making decisions and stepping into action (Takayama, Santucci & Caldwell-O'Keefe, 2022).

Key take-aways

As we say in theatre labs, let's seal the practice! I conclude this chapter by offering three final 'take-aways' in the form of reflective questions summarising how, as I have attempted to discuss in the preceding sections, the artistry of teaching is:

- **Culturally Self-Aware**: Who am I? What are my 'magnets' and grounding 'anchors' in my relationship with difference? How does that inform how I conceive of learning? How might this foster mattering, belonging, and trust for me and others?
- **Learning-Centred**: How do my teaching practices reflect my beliefs about learning and my educational values? How can my choices intentionally design liberating opportunities to unbridle human learning?
- **Imaginative Co-creation**: What possibilities do I envision? What does it look like to embark on and facilitate "safely brave enough" learning zones for myself and others where we can be authentically present, experiment, discover, and grow together?

References

Acheson, K. & Schneider-Bean, S. (2019). Representing the intercultural development continuum as a pendulum: addressing the lived experiences of intercultural competence development and maintenance. *European Journal of Cross-Cultural Competence and Management*. https://hubicl.org/publications/3/1

Aguilar, L., Walton, G. & Wieman, C. (2014). Psychological insights for improved physics teaching. *Physics Today*, 67(5), pp. 43–49. DOI:10.1063/PT.3.2383

Arao, B. & Clemens, K. (2013). From safe spaces to brave spaces: a new way to frame dialogue around diversity and social justice. In: Landreman, L.M., ed. *The Art of Effective Facilitation: Reflections from Social Justice Educators*. Stylus Publishing, LLC, Sterling, Virginia, pp. 135–150.

Artze-Vega, I., Darby, F., Dewsbury, B. & Imad, M. (2022). *Norton Guide to Equity-Minded Teaching*. W.W. Norton, New York.

Bali, M. (2021). *Intentionally Equitable Hospitality & Liberating Structures*. https://blog.mahabali.me/pedagogy/intentionally-equitable-hospitality-liberating-structures/

Bass, R. (2018). The impact of technology on the future of human learning, *Change: The Magazine of Higher Learning*, 50(3–4), pp. 34–39. DOI:10.1080/00091383.2018.1507380

Bass, R. (2020). What's the problem now? *To Improve the Academy: A Journal of Educational Development*, 39(1). DOI:10.3998/tia.17063888.0039.102

Bennett, M. (2017). *Development Model of Intercultural Sensitivity*. https://www.idrinstitute.org/resources/a-developmental-approach-to-training-for-intercultural-sensitivity-2/ From: Bennett, M. (2017). Constructivist approach to intercultural communication. In: Kim, Y. (ed.) *International Encyclopedia of Intercultural Communication*. Wiley, Hoboken, N.J.

Boal A. (1979). *Theatre of the Oppressed*. Theatre Communications Group, New York.

Boal A. (1992). *Games for Actors and Non-Actors*. Routledge, London.

Bourdieu, P. (1977). *Outline of a Theory of Practice*. Cambridge University Press.

Cahnmann-Taylor, M. & Souto-Manning, M. (2010). *Teachers Act Up!: Creating Multicultural Learning Communities through Theatre.* Teachers College Press, New York.
CUNY Mindset Workshop. (2020 August). *UVA's Motivate Lab & CUNY Innovative Pedagogy Team.* https://www.cuny.edu/academics/faculty-affairs/cuny-innovative-teaching-academy/promoting-mindset-supportive-practices/
Deardorff, D.K. (2014). *The Sage Handbook of Intercultural Competence.* Langara College, Vancouver, B.C.
Dewsbury, B. (2020). Deep teaching in a college STEM classroom. *Cultural Studies of Science Education* 15, pp. 169–191. DOI:10.1007/s11422-018-9891-z
Dewsbury, D., Murray-Johnson, K. & Santucci, A. (2021). Acknowledgement and its role in the faculty development of inclusive teaching. *The Journal of Faculty Development* 35 (3), pp. 53–62.
Diatta-Holgate, H. & Hyder, M. (2023). *Workshop: Applying Equity-Oriented Pedagogies for Inclusive Teaching and Learning.* Kaneb Center for Teaching Excellence, University of Notre Dame.
Eisner, E.W. (2002). From episteme to phronesis to artistry in the study and improvement of teaching. *Teaching and Teacher Education* 18, pp. 375–385.
Elon University Centre for the Advancement of Teaching & Learning. *Teaching for Equity and Inclusion.* www.elon.edu/u/academics/catl/inclusiveteaching/
Freire, P. (1988)*Pedagogy of the Oppressed.* Continuum, New York.
Gannon, K. (Guest) (2020b, April 9). Radical hope: a teaching manifesto (No. 304) [Audio podcast episode]. In *Teaching in Higher Ed.* https://teachinginhighered.com/podcast/radical-hope-a-teaching-manifesto/
Gannon K.M. (2020a). *Radical Hope: A Teaching Manifesto.* West Virginia University Press, Morgantown.
Georgetown University Center for New Designs in Learning and Scholarship *Inclusive Pedagogy Toolkit.* https://cndls.georgetown.edu/inclusive-pedagogy-toolkit-landing/
Gravett, K. & Winstone, N.E. (2020). Making connections: authenticity and alienation within students' relationships in higher education. *Higher Education Research and Development,* 41(2), pp. 360–374.
Hammer, M. (2023). The intercultural development continuum. *Intercultural Development Inventory (IDI).* https://www.idiinventory.com/idc
Harvey, T. (n.d.) *Beyond the Comfort Zone: Activity Facilitation Guide.* True North Intrcultural. https://d31kydh6n6r5j5.cloudfront.net/uploads/sites/633/2021/03/Beyond_the_Comfort_Zone_Facilitation_Guide.pdf
Imad, M., Santucci, A., Caulkins, J. & Wuetherick, B. (2022). Love, hope, and beauty: nurturing a shared vision for justice-oriented change in higher education. *ISSOTL 2022 Conference.* (Kelowna, BC, Canada – November 2022).
Intercultural Development Inventory: IDI (2023). *Definition of Culture Within the IDI.* https://idiinventory.zendesk.com/hc/en-us/articles/360041563253-Definition-of-Culture-Within-the-IDI From: Hammer, M. (2019). The Intercultural Development Inventory® (IDIv5). IDI, LLC: Olney, MD.
Leijon, M., Gudmundsson, P., Staaf, P. & Christersson, C. (2022). Challenge based learning in higher education–A systematic literature review. *Innovations in Education and Teaching International,* 59(5), pp. 609–618. DOI:10.1080/14703297.2021.1892503
McMurtrie, B. (2021). The k: Despite decades of evidence, good teaching is still considered more art than science. *That's Hurting Faculty and Students Alike.* The Chronicle of Higher Education. https://www.chronicle.com/article/the-damaging-myth-of-the-natural-teacher
Perone, L. & Santucci, A. (Manuscript in preparation) Performing higher education: Improv is/as radical co-creating. In: Perone, L. (ed.), *Improvising Community,*

Learning, and Development in Higher Education: A Performance Approach. Palgrave Book Series: Studies In Play, Performance, Learning, and Development.

Ruitenberg C.W. (2011). The empty chair: education in an ethic of hospitality. In: Kunzman, R. (ed.) *Philosophy of Education 2011.* Philosophy of Education Society, Urbana, Illinois, pp. 28–36. DOI:10.47925/2011.028

Ryan, R.M. & Deci, E.L. (2017). *Self-Determination Theory: Basic Psychological Needs in Motivation, Development, and Wellness.* The Guilford Press, New York.

Santucci, A. (2019). *Performing Language and Culture: Teaching and Learning Italian through Critical Embodied Encounters.* [Doctoral dissertation, Brown University]. Brown Repository.

Santucci, A. (2020). Inclusive teachers & learners as artists... what's (dis) comfort got to do with it? *Deep Teaching Residency.* NSF-funded STEM Faculty Development Program, Washington DC, USA.

Santucci, A. (2022a). Belonging as an academic/educational developer: breathing for justice, together. *International Journal for Academic Development*, 27(4), pp. 308–309. DOI:10.1080/1360144X.2022.2140544

Santucci, A. (2022b). *Dancing with Discomfort: Towards Inclusive Pedagog(ies.)* IDEA (International Drama Education Association) 9th World Congress, DRAMA 4ALL (Reykjavík, Iceland – 4–8 July 2022).

Santucci, A. (2023). Setting the stage: our classrooms as rehearsals for action. In: Dewsbury, D. & Murray-Johnson, K. (eds.) *Education for Freedom MOOC.* Howard Hughes Medical Institute, Chevy Chase, MD.

Santucci, A. & Vaccaro, A. (In Press) An invitation into authentic dialogue about positionality in SoTL. *New Directions for Teaching and Learning.*

Schechner, R. (2006). *Performance Studies: An Introduction.* Routledge, London.

Schön, D. (1983). *The Reflective Practitioner: How professionals think in action.* Basic Books, New York.

Shulman, L.S. (2005). Signature pedagogies in the professions. *Daedalus*, 134(3), pp. 52–59.

Smith, G.A. (2015). Why college faculty need to know the research about learning. *Insight, A Journal of Scholarly Teaching*, 10, pp. 9–18.

Takayama, K.M., Santucci, A. & Caldwell-O'Keefe, R. (2022). *Embodied Stories: Human-Centered Sustainable Educational Dev.* ICED 2022 Conference, Sustainable Educational Development. (Aarhus, Denmark – May 31–June 3 2022).

Turner, V. (1982). *From Ritual to Theatre: The Human Seriousness of Play.* Performing Arts Journal Publications, New York.

Vygotsky, L. (1978). *Mind in Society.* Harvard University Press, Cambridge, MA.

YAHE: Yes, And... Higher Education Network East Side Institute https://eastsideinstitute.org/yes-and-higher-education-network/

Part II
Authenticity and professional identity

Chapter 6

Authenticity in delivering contextual pedagogy and materials in cybersecurity

Abdullahi Arabo

Introduction

As educators, getting your students involved and engaged, either online or face to face, through lectures and practicals, can be vital in bringing out the best in them. This is even more crucial due to the internationalisation of the cohorts within universities. From experience within the context of cybersecurity education, student engagement can be effective, and an educator can get the best out of students if we constantly show care and contextualise materials in a way that is authentic, inclusive, and enables their understanding. Using real-world examples/scenarios to contextualise complex topics, and even using examples that resonate with the cohort, improves not only engagement but also performance. This involves getting to know the student(s) and for the educator to be authentic to themselves as well as to the students, in conjunction with the materials and resources used during delivery. The essence of authenticity lies in loving your work, which in turn radiates and inspires authenticity in others. As a result, innovation blossoms, real-life scenarios unfold, and interactions between stakeholders and pedagogies converge to cultivate an inclusive and effective learning environment.

This chapter provides real examples, where the application of authenticity of curriculum design and learning materials has resulted in positive engagement from students. These tried and tested strategies demonstrate the value-added to inclusivity, engagement, and performance, while students get an inclusive experience that enables their best performance and sharing of knowledge. Specific examples are explored of how to engage students via:

1) Real-world examples and scenarios that demonstrate how the concepts they are learning are relevant to their own lives;
2) Hands-on activities that actively involve students in their learning, meaning they are more likely to be engaged and retain information;
3) Opportunities to collaborate with others: as they work together, they learn from each other and develop critical thinking skills;

4) The use of technology to create interactive learning experiences: technology can be a fantastic way to engage students and make learning more fun;
5) Timely feedback: by regularly providing constructive feedback that is specific, actionable, and supportive, students track their performance, identify areas for improvement, and stay motivated;
6) Reflecting and adapting to continuously evaluate the effectiveness of our teaching strategies: by seeking student feedback, understanding their needs, analysing assessment results, and reflecting on our teaching practices, we can achieve flexible approaches to adjust as needed to optimise student engagement and learning outcomes.

Through our experiences, our teaching teams have found that employing these strategies – individually or in combination – has consistently fostered an engaging and supportive learning environment. This approach has been instrumental in facilitating our students' success. Furthermore, these strategies empower educators to navigate situations characterised by uncertainty and instability, fostering a culture that values creativity and imagination to tackle the challenges inherent in real-world teaching scenarios. Our observations indicate that students have not only effectively learned but also thrived, fostering growth and creativity.

Teaching in cyber security

Teaching a complex subject to a diverse cohort within the field of cybersecurity, a field that is constantly evolving, requires encouragement from educators to students to be aware of the constant changes. This can increase students' awareness of the latest threats, potential solutions, and/or future threats to the landscape. This consequently improves students' desire to acquire more knowledge and explore their curiosity. The best way of doing this is to be authentic to yourself, and with the cohort, respect who they are and be able to provide a learning environment that is inclusive and respectful.

This pedagogical approach has proven successful in the context of teaching complex and practical cybersecurity modules, as evidenced by positive student engagement and feedback. Importantly, these principles are not limited to cybersecurity alone but can be applied across various disciplines. They enable educators to dynamically cater to students' needs, infusing creativity and imagination into the learning process while staying connected to real-world discipline-specific challenges. This approach facilitates direct interaction between students and teachers, promoting effective and enriching learning experiences.

Assessment strategies for individual modules can be effectively designed to provide real-time feedback that is inclusive and authentic. When we are authentic, and use authentic sources, assessment materials, and feedback strategies, not only will the teaching and delivery be easier, but this also allows the cohort to be seen as individuals and be inclusive and authentic (King, 2022). In our teaching, authentic assessment and feedback strategies that have started in a single module have gradually influenced the whole programme and programmatic assessment. Using real-life contextual (Duignan & McGraths, 2022) assessment and providing feedback before marks are released allows the cohort to digest the feedback (Arabo & Serpell, 2019). Additionally, students can serve as co-markers and staff as moderators (Arabo & Serpell, 2019). This provides a real-time engagement with assessments, marking, and feedback (Gravett, 2022). Our teaching team has observed an improvement in marks as the cohort progresses throughout their programme of study. To be fully effective at module and programme level, this approach can be embedded by asking students to provide reflective commentary on their submitted work within the submission.

The concept of authenticity and inclusivity

Inclusivity in teaching and learning within higher education (HE) is a way of empowering individuals and treating them as unique entities; this includes delivering curriculum, teaching, and assessments and providing an environment that respects all and brings out the best in individuals. Figure 6.1 provides some key issues to guide authenticity from both the perspectives of the educators and how the educator should relate to the student's cohort. Consequently, as an educator, understanding that we (both students and other educators) are all different and unique, with different abilities that may contrast to one another, that we are all from diverse backgrounds, ethnicities, nations, and tribes means that if we respect and appreciate, without distinguishing, one another, we bring out the best in each other.

Research has shown that inclusivity is about the ways in which pedagogy, curriculum, and assessments are presented and designed as well as delivered, which engages and encourages student learning (e.g., Duignan & McGrath, 2022; Arabo & Serpell, 2019). These processes should be meaningful and relevant, that is, contextualised within recent developments and understanding of the targeted cohort. These should also be accessible to all. Therefore, the core elements of inclusivity – considering and treating each student as a unique entity and seeing individuals and individuals' differences as a means of diversity – when addressed appropriately will enrich the outcomes and learning experiences of others.

Further to the preceding, Bransford et al. (2000) and my teaching team's experience resonate with how inclusivity in curriculum, design, delivery, and assessment can be achieved through aspects of ethnicity. Educators are only able to get the best out of students if they constantly show care and contextualise materials in a way that is authentic and enables their understanding. Through discussions, peer observations, and insights gathered from fellow educators, it becomes evident that an educator's authenticity in teaching

Be Authentic

Allow	Yourself to be vulnerable
Be	Open–Making connections via authenticity
Show	Care
Encourage	Participation
Use	Examples from your personal experience–not compromising secrecy
Use	Examples within the cohort
Get	To know them – the cohort
Reflect on	On experience from other cohorts

Figure 6.1 How to be an authentic educator

may be influenced by factors such as ethnicity and exposure to diverse cultures. In my experience, educators with broad international experiences tend to embrace constructive criticism from both peers and students. In contrast, other cultures perceive educators as authoritative figures beyond questioning, which can impact the perceived authenticity of teaching. In such cases, educators from these backgrounds may hesitate to acknowledge their mistakes or admit when they do not have an answer during sessions. A further impact of this type of culture is that this trains students to write down what they have been told, without questioning what has been said. Consequently, this can create an atmosphere that lacks authenticity from the students, and for a proper authentic setting and education system, authenticity needs to be both ways. Hence, we need to provide a curriculum that empowers all stakeholders and affirms the required future critical thinkers and leaders. King (2022) has suggested that "a teacher with expertise will have care". In this way, when we are authentic and make effective use of authentic sources and assessment materials, not only will the teaching and delivery be easier, but this also allows the cohort to be seen as individuals and have a teacher that motivates them.

Pierson (2022) argues and embodies the effects, implications, and needs of a champion or a role model that will be able to believe in an individual's ability and encourage them to explore and engage in the learning process and be the best they can. Duignan and McGrath (2022) have also explored the issue of authenticity in teaching, which they argue is based on a context of a given cohort and involves cultivating authentic spaces for effective teaching. Making connections via authenticity can also provide good relations with the cohorts both amongst the teaching team and cohort peers. One approach for bringing our authentic selves into the classroom is described by Mary Jacob in Box 6.1.

Box 6.1 Let's get real: authenticity for building community

Mary Jacob

Bringing our authentic selves into the classroom has value for community building and dialogic learning, but what is authenticity? Harriet Schwartz (2021) says authenticity is "bringing our humanity to work while also retaining role clarity". Patricia Cranton and Ellen Carusetta (2004, p. 7) say authenticity in teaching includes "being genuine, showing consistency between values and actions, relating to others in such a way as to encourage their authenticity, and living a critical life". In their study of student perceptions of teacher authenticity, Pedro De Bruyckere and Paul Kirschner (2016) identify "expertise, passion, unicity and distance" as key characteristics. Elaborating on unicity, they say teachers should "not feel restrained by the curriculum" but rather have freedom to adapt to student needs. This requires adaptive expertise in which teachers improvise in response to and with their students. Bransford et al. (2000, p. 45) similarly describes adaptive expertise as "helping people remain flexible and adaptive to new situations". De Bruyckere and Kirschner's fourth criterion, distance, requires appropriate distance between students and teacher, neither falsely familiar nor too distant for real communication.

When we show students our authentic selves in all our imperfection, we give permission for them to be authentic, too. As leader of the Postgraduate Certificate in Teaching in Higher Education at Aberystwyth University, I make an intentional effort to be authentic by sharing my passion for pedagogy, teaching experiences, and small things about everyday life. I am open about common frustrations we all face.

> To promote authenticity and inclusion, I say things such as:
>
> - I'll be honest with you.
> - We all have different prior knowledge and experience, so every one of you has something valuable to contribute.
> - There is no 'one right way to teach'. Find whatever fits your context.
> - No one is perfect, including the course team, so we don't expect perfection from you.
> - Tell us how we can help you.
>
> I communicate this right from the start through induction and needs analysis meetings. The message is reinforced in seminars, informal meet-ups, coaching sessions, and email. I foster informal sharing by starting meetings early to allow time to check in and share how we feel at the moment. This creates a communal space where we often discover common experiences.
>
> To know each other as full human beings rather than just in our roles as students and teacher, I invite participants to share pictures such as their pets on a Padlet. At informal meet-ups, we use adaptive expertise to follow topics relevant to the group, which may be about the course, their teaching, or life in general. Participants can offer support and share teaching experiences without anxiety or fear of failure. These optional activities help us bond and enact our authentic selves, creating a safe space for learning.
>
> As a result of intentional authenticity and community building online, we feel no communication barrier when we meet in person for the first time. Relational closeness allows us to form supportive bonds that can reduce anxiety and build an inclusive learning community where all can flourish and learn.

Inclusive curriculum design needs to be centred, and constantly evolve, around contextualised themes and domains, where the curriculum and expected learning outcomes provide room for educators to use and be inspired by real-world scenarios and the latest developments in the field. This includes the usage of inclusive language and examples that will cater for all learners to make them feel involved and provide a sense of belonging while at the same time cultivating potential and developing a conducive and inclusive learning environment. Inclusive curriculum designs need to provide an environment that can facilitate individual ownership of the curriculum and the ability and possibility of making it flexible so that students can demonstrate learning outcomes by adding their own stamp and context.

The ownership and flexibility of an inclusive curriculum enable students to feel empowered as well as being able to make informed decisions and choices on how to further explore and enhance their careers or time in HE. This means considering what to study within the curriculum and at what stage of their learning journey, when and how to get assessed, and ways to be fully involved in the curriculum, where appropriate. An inclusive curriculum design should be able to create a culture and environment in which educators and students can develop and extend their digital capabilities, help each other, and facilitate, as well as improve, the learning and teaching of each other in diverse contexts and environments that are supportive, tailored, and inclusive.

Authenticity comes a long way in making sure a curriculum design is inclusive; this should ensure that the curriculum, assessment tasks, and how the curriculum is developed and designed are relevant to students' subject areas, while at the same time making it relevant to the employment sectors through real-world problem-solving and to contexts of further study to provide a roadmap for progression opportunities. For example, including some elements of and links to industrial requirements, standards and demands is critical for the advancement of curriculums or programmes, as well as making use of real-life problems and case studies during assessments that are linked with industrial inputs and partners. The design of the curriculum and assessments needs to provide a culture that encourages contextualisation and creative programme design. An inclusive curriculum design needs to be informed by an awareness of student differences, needs, cultures, individuality, and understanding of peripheral difficulties, and provide better and decontextualised perceptions of structural, economic, individual, and societal barriers.

In this era of rapidly advancing technology, intense competition in academia, a fiercely competitive job market and the constant evolution of skill requirements and gaps, it is imperative to maintain an inclusive curriculum design. This means ensuring that the curriculum remains adaptable and open to ongoing reflection, allowing for continuous review and critique of its delivery, assessment methods, and contextualisation. To achieve this, incorporating real-world examples and scenarios that provide context, as well as soliciting feedback and feedforward from students, industry professionals, peers, and other key stakeholders is essential. As an illustration in the realm of cybersecurity, establishing partnerships with small and medium-sized enterprises offers the opportunity to immerse students in authentic, real-world cyber-attack scenarios. This hands-on approach allows selected students to engage in ethical hacking exercises, addressing live website and system vulnerabilities. Furthermore, integrating ongoing, large-scale cyber threats and attack incidents directly into the curriculum delivery enriches the learning experience. By doing so, we can ensure a sustained continuity, authenticity, and improvement of our policies, practices, and processes.

Contextual pedagogy and materials

Contextual pedagogy is all about the way the delivery of authentic and reliable materials is linked to reflecting the understanding of the target audience – in other words, the ability to ensure that each student can relate to the facts presented in a way that they individually feel connected with the materials. It is particularly important in the context of teaching complex issues with cybersecurity. Contextual pedagogy as a teaching approach underlines the importance of understanding the needs and experience of a given cohort as well as the context in which students learn. This means that as educators we need to be aware of the students' prior knowledge, experiences, and interests, and then use this information to design, deliver, and test learning experiences that are relevant and meaningful to them.

To achieve such an environment and the ability for each cohort member to appropriately be involved, we need to be flexible and able to adapt the learning materials to make them relevant to the cohort. For example, real-world authentic examples and the latest articles from authors that the students can relate to make such resources relevant to the students' learning goals. Our teaching team have been able to provide supporting materials within the session that are authored either as videos, articles, or invited talks from experts that mirror the diversity of the student cohort. Contextual materials can also include real-world examples, simulations, games, and other interactive activities that allow students to explore concepts in a hands-on way and use technology.

There is a growing body of research that supports the use of contextual pedagogy and materials to help facilitate authentic learning experiences. Studies have shown that students who learn in a contextually rich environment are more likely to be engaged, motivated, and successful in their learning (Arabo & Serpell, 2019; Bransford et al., 2000). By using contextual pedagogy and materials, educators can create learning experiences that are relevant, meaningful, and engaging for their students.

Strategies for delivering authentic contextual pedagogy and materials

To effectively create an authentic environment that fosters means and ways to deliver authentic contextual pedagogy and materials, we need to develop some strategies. This can be done based on experience and can be changed dynamically to fit the required scenario and cohort. One such tried and tested strategy involves incorporating real-world scenarios and case studies into the curriculum. Real-world scenarios can be obtained from industrial partners or the latest articles or news, for example from social media. By presenting students with authentic challenges and dilemmas faced by professionals in the field, educators can foster critical thinking and problem-solving skills (Srivatanakul & Annansingh, 2022). From the context of the practices of the teaching team, we have used real-world and the latest cyber-attack theories and case studies to contextualise teaching materials. We have applied this to assessment, where students are allowed to penetrate-test real companies, with legal agreements and scopes provided by such companies, hence acting within the law of ethical hacking. If an educator is not able to go that far, then students can be tasked with analysing and responding to simulated cyber-attacks, allowing them to apply theoretical knowledge to practical situations.

Another strategy is to establish partnerships with industry professionals and organisations. What we have done in some instances is to work with our collaborators, clients, and contacts to provide either a case study or an invited talk concerning a real attack. By collaborating with experts in the field, educators can bring real-world perspectives into the classroom and expose students to current trends and practices in cybersecurity (Ukwandu et al., 2022). Guest lectures, workshops, and internship opportunities can further enrich the learning experience and provide students with valuable insights and networking opportunities.

Furthermore, the use of authentic assessment methods is crucial in delivering contextual pedagogy and materials. Traditional exams and quizzes may not effectively capture the complex and dynamic nature of cybersecurity. Instead, educators can implement performance-based assessments, such as hands-on projects and simulations, where students are required to demonstrate their skills and knowledge in realistic scenarios (Arabo, 2023). These assessments provide students with authentic opportunities to apply their learning in practical contexts and receive feedback for improvement. By implementing these strategies, educators can deliver authentic contextual pedagogy and materials that bridge the gap between theory and practice, preparing students for the challenges and demands of the real-world cybersecurity landscape.

To contextualise the complete process, there is also a need to provide an authentic assessment that aligns with the principles of contextualised pedagogy and contextualised learning materials. Developing authentic assessments that align with contextual pedagogy and materials is crucial in promoting meaningful learning experiences in cybersecurity education. Therefore, to provide students with the means to test their learning, we need to provide authentic assessments to give them the opportunities to apply their knowledge and skills in real-world contexts, hence, mirroring the challenges they may face in professional settings. We have tried and tested several strategies including using real-world case studies of penetration-testing from our partner organisations and the use of online real-world case studies for penetration-testing from 'bug bounty' sites.

Effectively incorporating hands-on projects and/or supplemented use of simulations as assessment tasks can provide authentic and contextualised assessments that require students to tackle authentic cybersecurity scenarios, for example, running most or all of the required stages to test security and, where possible, fix the vulnerabilities found, thus identifying vulnerabilities within systems and networks at large. Hence, using these practical tasks students can demonstrate their understanding of key concepts and their ability to apply them in realistic and real-world situations, not only making them apply theory into practice but also readying them for the world of work.

Where students find it difficult to apply these skills in a real-life situation, we have provided the use of case studies as assessment tools. Students are provided with complex, real-world scenarios that require critical analysis, problem-solving, and decision-making skills (Halpern & Dunn, 2021). The use of a case study can be either in the form of a simulated environment that requires practical demonstration of skills or a theoretical scenario that enables the students to analyse and devise appropriate cybersecurity strategies, considering factors such as ethical considerations, legal requirements, and industry best practices.

To build students up for a more complex assessment, our teaching team have also adopted the strategy of using performance-based assessments, where students are required to regularly demonstrate live or simulated tasks to their tutors with some guidance. We have done this in two stages: a demonstration based on a simulated environment and students tasked with performing a live penetration test on a simulated system, and live real work systems from 'bug bounty' websites. This enables individuals to demonstrate their ability to respond to either a simulated or real cyber incident. In one case we provided a collaboration with one of the educator's contacts for real penetration-testing. These assessments provide students with hands-on experiences that closely resemble the tasks they may encounter in professional cybersecurity roles.

Benefits of authentic contextual pedagogy and materials

Figure 6.2 provides a summary of what we have tried and tested on the issue of contextualising and providing authentic materials based on the strategies discussed earlier. These efforts highlight the flexibility to dynamically choose from various teaching facets, fostering effective learning, creativity, and imagination among all stakeholders. From the case studies, experiments, and assessments that we have conducted for almost ten years now in various modules and levels we can summarise the key benefits of these strategies. By and large, providing an authentic and contextualised pedagogy and materials in cybersecurity education leads to a range of benefits that enhance the learning experience and prepare students for real-world challenges. These benefits stem from the alignment and creation of a balance between educational content and the actual contexts (materials, student cohorts, etc.) and practices of real-world expertise within the cybersecurity field. Some key benefits of incorporating authenticity into pedagogy and materials are numerous; we have focussed on four main benefits.

Contextualise Materials

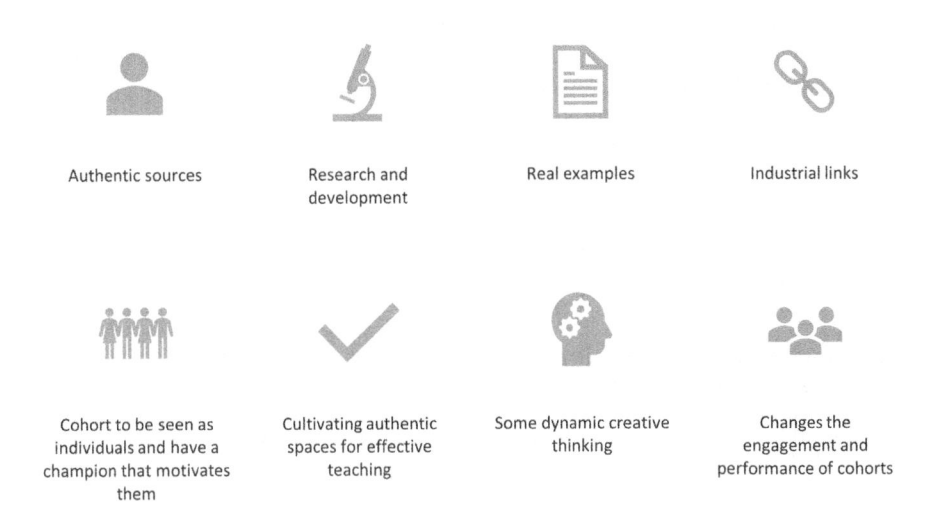

Authentic sources | Research and development | Real examples | Industrial links

Cohort to be seen as individuals and have a champion that motivates them | Cultivating authentic spaces for effective teaching | Some dynamic creative thinking | Changes the engagement and performance of cohorts

Figure 6.2 Tools and strategies of contextualising and providing authentic materials

Firstly, it promotes the development of practical skills and knowledge that are directly applicable and transferable to the real-world cybersecurity profession. By engaging with real-world scenarios, students gain hands-on experience in problem solving, critical thinking, and decision-making, which are essential skills in the field (Martínez-Argüelles et al., 2023).

Secondly, it nurtures student motivation, innovation, engagement, and maturity. We have seen students who have developed faster, demonstrating self-fulfillment and confidence in what they are doing, while also applying this in other modules or their day-to-day life commitments and issues. When students can see the relevance of their learning to the real world, they are more likely to be actively involved in their education; as a result, we have seen more lively engagement within and outside lectures. Authentic materials, such as case studies, simulations, and real-world examples, capture students' attention and create a sense of purpose and authenticity in their learning journey, especially if these materials and/or authors of such materials relate to students' background. These serve as role models for them to follow and inspire them; here the educator has the chance to push the boundaries and bring out aspects that the students are not aware of about themselves.

Thirdly, this encourages and fosters interdisciplinary and collaborative learning. Cybersecurity, like most other fields, is a multidisciplinary field in nature that intersects with areas such as psychology, law, sociology, and business. By incorporating authentic materials from such sources and with authors from diverse backgrounds and disciplines, students can develop a holistic understanding of cybersecurity, be able to picture themselves on what area(s) they can contribute and specialise in, and make sure that they are better equipped to address complex challenges in the field.

Lastly, as we have seen through the years, it enhances the transferability of knowledge and skills. The more the students are exposed to and engaged with authentic contextual pedagogy and materials, they gain experiences that closely resemble real-world situations. Consequently, this enables them to transfer their learning to new and unfamiliar contexts (in our case other modules, personal projects, and employment), making them adaptable and resilient professionals in the ever-evolving cybersecurity landscape (Khan et al., 2022).

Challenges and limitations of authentic contextual pedagogy and materials

Although authentic contextual pedagogy and materials offer significant benefits in cybersecurity education for students, educators, and the wider community, it is also a challenging concept to adapt by both educators and students. When our team first started to use this, most students found it strange, firstly because they were not used to it and secondly, because they believed that it was impossible to be able to find the latest developments that contextualise the preset curriculum and learning outcomes regularly. This confirms the traditional method of teaching, where everything is purely based on textbooks, and little is done to make it relevant to the dynamic nature of the 21st century. Having said that, it also comes with certain challenges and limitations that educators must understand and navigate. Familiarisation and contextualising these challenges are essential for effective implementation and maximising the benefits of authenticity. Here are some key challenges and limitations to consider based on the literature and the author's experience.

Within all disciplines, a key challenge is the availability and accessibility of authentic materials from a wider audience that reflects the nature of the cohort. Most materials are authored or secured in one direction, with a narrative that is not inclusive, hence why we are now facing the issue of decolonising the curriculum. Also, regarding cybersecurity as a discipline, incorporating real-world scenarios and resources into the curriculum can be either impossible, as most companies try to hide the fact that they have been attacked, or vulnerable, or time consuming and resource intensive as the discipline evolves in seconds. Educators may face difficulties in finding up-to-date and relevant materials, especially in a rapidly evolving field like cybersecurity, or might not have time to stay up to date with developments due to the nature of the job and lack of time (Mufarrohah & Munir, 2022).

Providing authentic assessments can be a complex and complicated issue for distinct reasons, such as it being more complex to design to get real-world examples and collaborators/partners and more complex to administer and evaluate compared to traditional assessments. Also, students might struggle to meet the challenge and requirement to perform excellently in that assessment. From our experience, we must balance this by providing a safety net for students who are not able to demonstrate the skills and ability for a real-world cybersecurity attack and vulnerability. They may require specialised tools or environments, making coordination challenging for educators (Barrientos Hernán et al., 2022). Additionally, assessing students' performance in authentic tasks can be subjective and requires clear rubrics and guidelines.

Finding one or more real authentic examples in an academic year is not that challenging, in comparison to maintaining the authenticity of materials and scenarios over time year on year within the evolving landscape. When the students get the state of authentic contextualisation in one session, they demand more for each session and keeping up with the demand per session or for all assessments can become impossible or highly demanding. As we know, technology, techniques, and threats in cybersecurity evolve rapidly and materials can quickly become outdated. Ensuring that the contextual pedagogy and materials remain relevant and aligned with industry practices requires continuous updates and collaboration with industry professionals (Karjalainen & Ojala, 2023).

Lastly, we can argue that there are limited resources, as well as other constraints within educational institutions which can pose limitations. These depend on the discipline and people at management levels, but they include factors such as budgetary constraints, limited access to technology and equipment, inadequate training for educators, and lack of facilities and support, which can impede the effective implementation of authentic contextual pedagogy and materials (Nguyen et al., 2022).

Conclusion

This chapter has explored and argued the importance of authenticity in delivering contextual pedagogy, materials, and assessment in cybersecurity education as a tool of artistry in educational development and delivery. The chapter has shown that this can be accomplished by incorporating real-world scenarios, some case studies for hands-on based projects, case studies from partners and collaborators, use of online tools or social media to enable educators to bridge the gap between theory and practice, and hence, enhancing the learning experience for students. The chapter has provided some benefits of the concept of authenticity as a tool for the artistry of teaching including the development of practical skills, increased motivation and engagement, interdisciplinary learning, and improved knowledge transferability. Some of the challenges have also been highlighted such as the availability of authentic materials, assessment complexity, maintaining authenticity over time, being vulnerable as an educator, and resource limitations. Nevertheless, considering the discussed challenges, if educators and the educational system can embrace authenticity, this holds immense potential in preparing students for the complexities and demands of the field, shaping students' cohorts into competent and adaptable professionals.

Key take-aways

- **Authenticity enhances the learning experience**: incorporating authentic contextual pedagogy and materials in cybersecurity education provides students with practical and real-world experiences. This promotes deeper understanding, critical thinking, and problem-solving skills, preparing students for the challenges they will face in the field.
- **Industry collaboration is crucial**: establishing partnerships with industry professionals and organisations is vital for delivering authentic contextual pedagogy and materials. Industry collaboration brings real-world perspectives, up-to-date practices, and networking opportunities to the cohorts, enriching the learning experience and bridging the gap between academia and industry.
- **There are challenges and limitations which require careful consideration**: while authenticity offers significant benefits, challenges such as resource constraints, assessment complexities, and maintaining relevance over time should be addressed. Educators need to plan and adapt their strategies, collaborate with industry partners, and allocate resources effectively to overcome these challenges and fully influence the benefits of authentic contextual pedagogy and materials.

References

Arabo, A. (2023). The use AI (ChatGPT) for offensive cyber security. *2nd International Conference on Computing Innovation and Applied Physics (CONF-CIAP 2023)*, Keynote Talk.

Arabo, A. & Serpell, M. (2019). Pedagogical approach to effective cybersecurity teaching. In: Pan, Z., Cheok, A., Müller, W., Zhang, M., El Rhalibi, A., Kifayat, K., (eds.) *Transactions on Edutainment XV. Lecture Notes in Computer Science*, 11345, pp. 129–140. Springer, Berlin, Heidelberg. DOI:10.1007/978-3-662-59351-6_11

Barrientos Hernán, E.J., López-Pastor, V.M., Lorente-Catalán, E. & Kirk, D. (2022). Challenges with using formative and authentic assessment in physical education teaching from experienced teachers' perspectives. *Curriculum Studies in Health, and Physical Education*, 14(2), 109–126. DOI:10.1080/25742981.2022.2060118

Bransford, J.D., Brown, A.L., Cocking, R.R. et al. (eds.) (2000). *How People Learn: Brain, Mind, Experience, and School*. Expanded Edition. The National Academies Press, Washington, DC. DOI:10.17226/9853

Cranton, P. & Carusetta, E. (2004). Perspectives on authenticity in teaching. *Adult Education Quarterly*, 55(1), pp. 5–22. DOI:10.1177/0741713604268894

De Bruyckere, P. & Kirschner, P.A. (2016). Authentic teachers: student criteria perceiving authenticity of teachers. *Cogent Education* 3(1), 1–15. DOI:10.1080/2331186X.2016.1247609

Duignan, C. & McGrath, D. (2022). Authenticity in teaching and learning: How far do we need to go? *All Ireland Journal of Higher Education*, 14(1).

Gravett, K. (2022). Feedback literacies as sociomaterial practice. *Critical Studies in Education*, 63(2), 261–274. DOI:10.1080/17508487.2020.1747099

Halpern, D.F. & Dunn, D.S. (2021). Critical thinking: a model of intelligence for solving real-world problems. *Journal of Intelligence*, 9(2), 22. DOI:10.3390/jintelligence9020022

Karjalainen, M. & Ojala, A.L. (2023). Authentic learning environments for in-service training in cybersecurity: a qualitative study. *International Journal of Continuing Engineering Education and Life Long Learning*, 33(1), 128–147. DOI:10.1504/IJCEELL.2023.127853

Khan, M.A., Merabet, A., Alkaabi, S. & Sayed, H.E. (2022). Game-based learning platform to enhance cybersecurity education. *Education and Information Technologies*, 27, 5153–5177. DOI:10.1007/s10639-021-10807-6

King, H (ed.) (2022). *Developing Expertise for Teaching in Higher Education*. Routledge/SEDA.

Martínez-Argüelles, M.J., Plana-Erta, D. & Fitó-Bertran, À. (2023). Impact of using authentic online learning environments on students' perceived employability. *Educational Technology Research & Development*, 71, 605–627. DOI:10.1007/s11423-022-10171-3

Mufarrohah, S. & Munir, A. (2022). Authentic materials of choice among English lecturers. *Linguistic, English Education and Art (LEEA) Journal*, 5(2), 162–174. DOI:10.31539/leea.v5i2.1280

Nguyen, C.D., Huynh, T.N. & Tran, N.H. (2022). Overcoming contextual constraints: implementing classroom pedagogical innovation through teacher leadership. *International Journal of Leadership in Education*, 1–19. DOI:10.1080/13603124.2021.2013543

Pierson, R. (2022). Every Kid Needs a Champion – TED Talk. https://www.ted.com/talks/rita_pierson_every_kid_needs_a_champion

Schwartz, H.L. (2021). Authentic teaching and connected learning in the age of COVID-19. *The Scholarly Teacher*. https://www.scholarlyteacher.com/post/authentic-teaching-and-connected-learning-in-the-age-of-covid-19

Srivatanakul, T. & Annansingh, F. (2022). Incorporating active learning activities into the design and development of an undergraduate software and web security course. *Journal of Computers in Education*, 9(1), 25–50. DOI:10.1007/s40692-021-00194-9

Ukwandu, E., Ben-Farah, M.A., Hindy, H., Bures, M., Atkinson, R., Tachtatzis, C., Andonovic, I. & Bellekens, X. (2022). Cyber-security challenges in the aviation industry: a review of current and future trends. *Information*, 13(3), 146. DOI:10.3390/info13030146

Chapter 7

Developing online communities of practice through relational pedagogy

James Layton

Introduction

In this chapter, I argue that using online discussion forums as a relational pedagogical approach can be as effective as the shared enactment, discovery, and collaborative imagining that occurs in the physical space of a drama studio, whereby processes of social exchange become a fundamental part of successful learning. Ultimately, this relational approach contributes towards the building of successful and sustainable online communities of practice which operate interchangeably with face-to-face interactions.

Using examples from a module delivered entirely online (2020–22) on a Scottish university BA (Hons) Performance programme, I explore how discussion forums on Virtual Learning Environment (VLE) Moodle and Learning Experience Platform (LXP) Aula were used to create shared dialogues among students and argue that communities of practice are developed, which Etienne Wenger (1998) suggests are composed of mutual engagement, joint enterprise, and shared enterprise.

The online context

According to Sam Brenton, the advent of the World Wide Web has "enabled networks of interest and communities of practice to flourish across physical distance with an immediacy and breadth that was impossible a generation ago" (2009, p. 85). Despite these advances in technology, teaching and learning has remained largely focused on face-to-face delivery. VLEs and Learning Management Systems (LMS) have been a part of education for many years although they are underutilised by both staff and students, often being considered an adjunct rather than integral teaching and learning components. More recently, LXPs such as Aula have focused on making virtual learning more social. Ko and Rossen note from their research that "over one hundred institutions in more than a dozen different countries reported in 2014 that while nearly all institutions have a learning management system in place, the greatest use faculty make of their LMS is just to push out content" (2017, p. 138).

DOI: 10.4324/9781003437826-10

This is a familiar picture across UK higher education institutions (HEIs) with the notable exception of the Open University (OU) who have always foregrounded flexibility in reaching a wide range of students in innovative ways. Their model of supported open learning rather than blended, distance, or online learning suggests a flexible but entirely remote learning experience. Open learning can be defined as giving students maximum flexibility in terms of pace, time, place, and methods of interaction. Conversely, blended learning suggests a combination of asynchronous and synchronous methods, such as the combining of face-to-face teaching with VLEs, whilst distance or online learning suggests an entirely remote learning experience.

The increased use of Massive Open Online Courses (MOOCs) has broadened access to online education, building on the already established work of the OU, who have been market leaders in open learning since the 1960s (Open University, 2021a). The term 'MOOC' first appeared in 2008, at the University of Manitoba, and by 2012 there had been significant growth in the USA and UK, such that HEIs were aware of both potential disruption to the traditional models as well as the opportunities for developing their own MOOCs (Advance HE, 2021). In fact, the growth of MOOCs was so great that by 2015, a Future Learn MOOC in English language learning had over 440,000 participants (Future Learn, 2015).

The model of supported open learning is described on the OU website as comprising four areas: flexible, all-inclusive, supportive, and social (Open University, 2021b). One of the OU's strategies for delivering the social aspect of learning is the use of course forums: online spaces where students can participate in discussions, exchange of ideas, debates, and more. Even though this is not a new idea, I suggest it is an innovative approach to engaging students in discussion. The simplicity of a forum offers the potential for rich communities of practice to develop; this opportunity was made available by the enforced transition to remote teaching and learning in early 2020. The remote nature of students' experience in this context might suggest that it would be difficult for social engagement to take place, and this is a problem I wanted to explore. The nature of learning in drama, theatre, and performance often supports interaction and social exchanges, particularly in practical work. In some instances of practically 'doing' drama such as site-specific contexts, this bodily co-present interaction between individuals is extended to sensory engagement with environment where smell, touch, and taste are as important as sight and sound (Layton, 2020). The highly social nature of practical learning amongst students in this discipline also carries over into more theory-focused modules. As such, peer-to-peer interaction is an important means of ensuring learning occurs. A problem, then, might be presented when these opportunities for face-to-face social interactions are unavailable. In this case study, I explore how forums on the VLE Moodle were used to develop social interactions between students. In doing so, I suggest that communities of practice are formed that are fostered through mutual engagement, joint enterprise, and a shared repertoire.

Creativity and relational pedagogy

In discussing creativity in schools, Ken Robinson notes that "good drama teachers are experts in [...] facilitating the complex processes of collaborative inquiry and personal questioning upon which deep learning so often rests" (Aronica & Robinson 2015, p. 113). This notion extends into teaching drama, theatre, and performance in HE, where shared practice and collaboration are of utmost importance. In theatre workshop and rehearsal processes, the concept of ensemble is, according to John Britton, when people "work together for an extended period, rather than a single project" (2013, p. 5). Robert Cohen concurs with this although he adds that "ensemble is a long-term relationship: a day-in, day-out collaboration in shared living, thinking and creating" (Cohen 2011, pp. 16–7, cited in Britton, 2013, p. 5). In contemporary art practice, Nicholas Bourriaud suggests that artists' work that is relational "bring[s] into play modes of social exchange [... demonstrating] processes of communication in their concrete dimensions as tools that can be used to bring together individuals and human groups" (1998, p. 165). These artists offer "spaces where we can elaborate alternative forms of sociability, critical models and moments of constructed conviviality" (Bourriaud 1998, p. 166).

In a similar way, "drama is a relational pedagogy that opens possibilities for dialogue and shared imagining among students, teachers and community. Drama involves creating alternative presents and futures through processes of shared enactment, discovery and collaborative imagining" (Prentki & Stinson 2016, p. 5). Whilst commonly accepted in practical explorations of the subject, these possibilities are less apparent in theoretical exploration of drama which, in many instances, has moved online. Despite the obvious differences between face-to-face and online teaching and learning, the possibilities for relational pedagogy to be utilised are just as tangible. Relational pedagogy is not just important in the teaching of drama. The principles of shared experience and imagining together are applicable to a range of disciplines, particularly those that utilise collaborative learning. That is, to say, all subjects. A particular challenge for learning collaboratively online in the creative arts arises when the object of creativity is physical, such as a ceramic piece, as outlined by Jennifer Savage in Box 7.1.

Aitken et al. suggest that "[r]elational pedagogy in the Arts occurs when teachers work alongside [learners] to explore where learning *may* go rather than teachers determining where it *will* go" (2007, p. 16). In a manifesto of relational pedagogy, Biesta et al. propose that "[h]uman relations exist in and through shared practices", that "[a]uthority and knowledge are not something one has, but relations, which require others to enact" (2010, p. 7). Echoing this, Biesta notes that "learners learn from their participation in a social situation" (2010, p. 18) and that it is only through teacher/learner interaction that education is "done". Karen Bell (2022) discusses improving student satisfaction through relational pedagogy and notes that approachability, empathy, and

Box 7.1 Exploring tacit skills remotely

Jennifer Savage

Having the right environment in which to teach and learn is vital to successfully gaining knowledge and understanding. Learning a practical skills-based subject without an appropriate physical teaching space can have a real impact on the subject and student experience.

When COVID-19 hit, this was felt by all subjects; face-to-face teaching stopped and online delivery began. For practical subjects such as ceramics, making the jump to online delivery felt like an impossible task, with sessions delivering haptic knowledge such as throwing or even as simple as wedging clay ready for use now being taught theoretically online.

The importance of the environment in which we, as creatives, design and create is highlighted by Kamalipour and Peimani (2022, p. 4): studio settings are where students are engaged "shifting between analytic, synthetic and evaluative modes of thinking in different sets of activities (drawing, conversing and model making)." This describes a place where the drawing and discussing of ideas happens simultaneously with the modelmaking and the value placed on it, an experience that was impossible to recreate during the pandemic. The chance encounters between students within the studio and with technical staff and tutors, as well as the opportunity to respond to feedback, were removed.

When the University's ceramics studio space was restricted during lockdowns, the replacement video conferencing environment wasn't able to replicate the usual learning experience. To work through ideas in the three dimensions physically, such as in discussions about the altering of objects, students had construction paper around a mug to explore shapes or used acetate and objects such as beads threaded to create 3D transparent forms to emulate glass. However, there is only so far that alternative methods can replace the physical experience of learning. It was evident when we returned to the workshops that, although theory had been learnt and students had used this to advance the ambitions of their designs, the experience-based learning with the material had been missed.

Niiranen (2021, p. 85) notes that "an interesting characteristic of technology education, [is] the high degree of tacit knowledge inherent to it. Tacit knowledge and skills, i.e. understanding how various materials behave and knowing how to manipulate them, can be gained only through concrete experience." To combat the gaps in this knowledge, extra practical support was needed, helping to make the connections between the students' design experience and the making experience.

> When looking at students' abilities within practical work, it is beyond a simple "what they know" or "how they apply it". It becomes more physical – how they hold their bodies in relation to the work, the angle they hold their hand and how tense their movements are. In this sense, the art behind teaching these skills starts as conversation and feedback to understand what is trying to be achieved and ultimately how they are going to move to get their desired result: "learning by iteration from feedback and failure; and by noticing and troubleshooting in dialogue with ideas, materials and people" Niiranen (2021, p. 84).

staff/student interactions are strong indicators of student satisfaction; caring, sensitive, and proactively engaged staff and students support a culture of belongingness. On a similar theme, Murphy and Brown (2012) argue for relational pedagogy as a means of improving student experience in an HE landscape of student as consumer, whilst also presenting an alternative model of pedagogy based on psychoanalysis and critical theory. Mark Ingham argues for students having "more agency in their own learning and becom[ing] agents in all of the learning spaces and places they inhabit while at university" (2020, p. 49).

Communities of practice (CoPs)

For Etienne Wenger (1998), there are three dimensions of communities of practice: mutual engagement, a joint enterprise, and a shared repertoire. I use these to explore how students fostered online CoPs.

Mutual engagement

Wenger suggests that membership of a CoP is "a matter of engagement. That is what defines the 'community'" (1998, p. 73). Geographical proximity can assist with engagement although it is not always the case that being in the same room equals interactions, meaningful or otherwise. Although Wenger's study is based on workplace settings, it is also relevant to educational contexts. Individual participant contributions allow unique positions and identities to emerge, which are "both integrated and further defined in the course of engagement in practice. These identities become interlocked and articulated with one another through mutual engagement, but they do not fuse" (Wenger 1998, p. 76). Thus, individual and diverse voices are not lost in the development of online CoPs. Rather, they continue to operate within "a very tight node of interpersonal relationships" (Wenger 1998, p. 76). These mutual relationships are "neither a haven of togetherness nor an island of intimacy insulated from political and social relations" (1998, p. 77); where people come together, CoPs have all the usual challenges and triumphs.

Joint enterprise

Key to constructing an online CoP is that participants are part of a collaborative process which sustains the group. Wenger suggests that CoP are a "[...] result of a collective process of negotiation that reflects the full complexity of mutual engagement [...] defined by the participants in the very process of pursuing it. It is their negotiated response to their situation and thus belongs to them in a profound sense [...] it creates among participants relations of mutual accountability that become an integral part of the practice" (1998, p. 77–8).

Although each student arrives at a module with varying differences in academic and life experience and personal situations, the focus on the process of negotiation remains the same. It does not, however, mean that contributions are uniform. It is important that sharing and responding to ideas is emphasised by the educator and it is this sense of mutual support that helps build a CoP. In this process, the participants have a sense of ownership of the community they are building as well as an awareness of their mutual accountability. Wenger compares the enterprise of a CoP to rhythm in music: it is a "resource of coordination, of sense-making, of mutual engagement [.... If rhythm is] extracted from the playing, it becomes fixed, sterile, and meaningless, but in the playing, it makes music interpretable, participative, and shareable" (1998, p. 82).

Shared repertoire

Patterns of behaviour, routines of working, and shared language become important aspects of CoP. Similarly, Victor Turner's (1969) discussion of *communitas* suggests that individuals come together and share a bond because of certain experiences. *Communitas* can also contribute to the growth of a CoP because, like *communitas*, it emerges from "an essential and generic human bond, without which there could be *no* society" (Turner 1969, p. 97). Both *communitas* and CoP are ambiguous. Ambiguity, Wenger suggests, does not mean an "absence or lack of meaning. Rather, it is a condition of negotiability and thus a condition for the very possibility of meaning" (1998, p. 83). It is difficult to identify when shared repertoires become fixed and part of a community, perhaps because they are dynamic and reflect the constantly evolving nature of real people in real situations.

Context

In this section I outline the content of a Scottish Credit and Qualifications Framework (SCQF) Level 9 module (SCQF 2023), delivered annually between 2020 and 2022 as part of a BA (Hons) Performance programme. Contemporary Arts in Context (CaiC) explores the critical reception of theatre and live art performance from postmodern and postdramatic perspectives. Historically this module was delivered face to face, although lockdown and subsequent restrictions due to COVID-19 meant that delivery became an entirely online teaching and learning experience. Due to the online delivery, the use of a forum as an asynchronous activity became central to my pedagogic approach. Setting students specific tasks, such as responding to a reading or video to be completed at their own pace, became a key feature of the teaching and learning process as well as being a useful indicator of engagement. In 2020, the usual format of lecture followed by seminar was utilised much as it would have been in a face-to-face setting, albeit using a video conferencing platform (Zoom). Learning activities included live lectures, in which students could interact verbally and through the chat feature; recorded lecture material; taking part in breakout room discussions; and participation in practical creative activities. From 2021, all lectures were pre-recorded, and more time was given to discussion in the Zoom seminars.

Whilst using forums has always been a part of my blended learning approach, the predominance of face-to-face delivery has usually resulted in minimal or zero engagement with remote VLE activities. In my experience, the face-to-face learning environment becomes the dominant mode of learning interactions. The physical co-presence of others in a classroom, where the educator is the primary focus, can become privileged above other modes of learning which are more autonomous and independent and foster a greater degree of critical thinking.

The four key features of open learning identified by the OU – being flexible, inclusive, supportive, and social – are the distinct aspects of online delivery. Whilst the lecture plus seminar format was used as the primary means of teaching, these four features of open learning made the overall module experience very different. Despite the synchronous delivery of online lectures and seminars, students were able to access recordings of the sessions asynchronously which, for many, was a necessity, given the ongoing disruption to people's lives during the pandemic. For students with parenting and caring responsibilities, balancing their own studies with delivering home schooling presented challenges that would sometimes limit their capacity to attend live sessions. Asynchronous access to recorded material (and later pre-recorded as standard) was therefore a welcome feature, something that was not previously possible in an on-campus format. This flexibility increases the inclusivity of online delivery, as it allows students who may be constrained by caring responsibilities or financial limitations to access the learning materials.

This flexible and inclusive approach supports the various needs and circumstances of students, but what really makes the online delivery platform successful is the social possibilities. It may be counterintuitive to suggest that remote learning has many social possibilities in contrast with face-to-face settings. However, with the increased utilisation of VLE features, using forums as both learning and social spaces creates opportunities for CoPs to emerge. Using activities such as contributing to discussion forums, watching and interacting with video material, and posting extracts from draft essays for peer review leads to some blurring of lines between social and learning contexts. There is a degree of social interaction necessary for student-to-student discourse to take place, particularly when providing peer feedback. It is this increased utilisation of VLE forums as both learning and social spaces that created opportunities for CoPs to emerge.

Method

This study was carried out between 2020 and 2022. In this context of online delivery due to government restrictions and later through pedagogic choice, there was an opportunity to explore how a social learning approach might generate CoPs. Given that, initially, no on-campus activity was taking place, the online sessions were the only opportunities for students to interact with each other. To assess the ways in which students interacted on the module, I took an observational approach which was qualitative rather than quantitative. Whilst it was notable that there was an increased student use of the VLE compared with previous years, no data were available to support this. I therefore undertook qualitative observations of the interactions between students on the discussion forums. Rather than noting the actual number of interactions, I focused on the nature of them; for example, the depth and breadth of exchanges between students, observing how they were connecting ideas, offering feedback and mutual support, and developing a shared understanding of the ideas and concepts explored during the module.

Results

It was clear from my observations of the discussion forums that student engagement had increased substantially compared with normal VLE activity during face-to-face delivery and that this engagement showed a level of reciprocity between the students. My qualitative assessment of the content in discussion forums is organised into the following thematic areas: depth and breadth of contributions; reciprocity and shared understanding; improved student engagement; and development of critical dialogues.

Depth and breadth of contributions

From the sample of posts examined periodically during the module, they were more detailed than brief comments; posts were around 300 words or more. In general, the posts also addressed a wide range of ideas and concepts, often supported by reference to relevant literature. There was also evidence of connections being made (i.e., how the posts related to each other). The content of posts, in many instances, indicated that references were being made to previous posts. This did not always mean that students agreed with each other; rather, they counteracted opinions (often with evidence) which had an effect of offering provocations for further discussion.

Evidence of reciprocity and shared understanding

The content of the interactions outlined here suggested that students were operating in a supportive and collegiate manner. Whilst there was a difference of opinion evident in some interactions, the tone of the written comments indicated that students were mutually supportive. Through the process of peer support, a sense of the group working towards a shared understanding of the module content was apparent, if only through a qualitative appraisal of the language used in the posts.

Improved student engagement

As stated earlier, previous iterations of CaiC delivered in face-to-face settings saw limited student engagement with VLE activities. Other than downloading essential reading and lecture slides, interaction was scant. From the outset of online delivery in 2020, which became the default pandemic mode, it was clear that students were engaging with posting comments and participating in forum discussions. Many of the forum posts were substantial and presented ideas and opinions in some detail. An indicator of improved student engagement was evident from the high volume of posts as well as how students responded to these posts in sustained forum conversations. Whilst some students were more prolific than others in posting comments, this evidence suggests that most students benefitted from either reading or writing forum posts as well as engaging in discussions of the posts over Zoom in class time. Even if students were less active in contributing to a forum, the posts proved useful as students were able to review module material as they prepared for assessment. This was something flagged up in module evaluation responses as well as during informal feedback sessions held at various points.

Regular writing practice and the development of critical dialogues

Informal student feedback and module evaluation data indicated that participation in forums offers opportunities for regular writing practice, where important lessons are learned about appropriate style and register and the ways in which language can be used to persuade, argue, and convince a position. This same student feedback suggested that insights were often also learned from peers who may have been more developed and confident in articulating their thoughts. Having access to an overview of students' writing at an early stage in the module also provided valuable opportunities for diagnostic assessment and identifying potential support needs. There were, as might be expected, students who did not engage with contributing to the forum writing activities and therefore potentially slipped under the radar in terms of needing support. The opportunity was, nevertheless, present, and even without contributing directly to forum posts, all students could read their peers' work and benefit from essential critical dialogues. Exploring complex ideas and key debates in contemporary performance such as ethical issues around participation is one such example of these dialogues. These critical dialogues open many possibilities for debates to emerge, in which opposing positions are stated and argued. Within these debates, it is the necessary interaction that is essential in forming a CoP. Pre-pandemic, students often commented that both social and critical dialogues occurred during breaks or on journeys to and from university. With these opportunities less available, online spaces offer an alternative path to successful teaching and learning. Online spaces nurture CoP, offering some interesting and useful opportunities.

Discussion: how the relational aspects of drama are transposed to the online forum space

My observations of the students' interactions revealed that there was a clear reciprocity as a kind of mutual support or respect for everyone's contribution to the learning process. This reciprocity was demonstrated by the students' responses to posts which, importantly, happened both asynchronously and during the live sessions where discussions took place as part of usual class activity. The CoP, I suggest, began to emerge in these kinds of exchanges. Tacit mechanisms of mutual support surfaced, such as verbal exchanges between students that expressed appreciation for each other's contributions and enabled students to feel a sense of togetherness whilst simultaneously isolated; in other words, the learning interactions became social.

Mutual engagement

Pre-pandemic, the physical classroom environment created opportunities for useful peer-to-peer communication such as discussions, although this was often limited to small clusters of students. The online environment, conversely, brings about more inclusive interactions when using forums. Because the space is online and not limited to friendship clusters, students' written contributions and responses to the forums are further expanded during verbal discussions. The forums, then, enable engagement in a CoP that is diverse. It is this diversity of participants and their contributions that is important.

These discussions are not only useful at the time but can be beneficial as students review the module content when preparing for assessments. Whether delivered face-to-face or online, some students will take longer than others to form a clear picture and understanding of the assessment. Looking back over the posts can provide a throughline or narrative arc for the module which helps students in structuring their thinking and how they can meet the learning outcomes. Whilst there is currently no hard evidence that this is wholly true, informal student feedback has suggested that reviewing forum posts has been beneficial. It is, therefore, less important when the mutual engagement occurs, but rather, if it happens, a community will continue to grow.

Joint enterprise

Participation in online forums may come in various forms and although there were degrees of difference in the detail and quality of the posts, it is significant that the process remained a joint enterprise. Without the interaction between students, there is little opportunity for a CoP to develop; a process in which everyone plays a part in building successfully. Based on my observations of students' interactions in the forums, I suggest that the participants are more than willing to invest in this community in ways that support, nurture, and show kindness to others within it.

Shared repertoire

In using online discussion forums, the constantly evolving nature of developing a shared repertoire is its strength. As students contribute more to a discussion forum, followed up in live online conversations, the possibilities expand for recognising the shared processes, language, and tools being used to shape a CoP. From my observations of the students' interactions on the discussion forums and in live synchronous sessions, it was apparent that there was a sense of new relationships emerging and, in doing, new skills in collaboration were forged. One such skill developed from these collaborations was a more confident way of expressing ideas and opinions. Like any community there is a shared language; not as explicitly as common linguistic traits or style of expression but, more so, there is a mutually agreed way of being, of doing things, and of continuing to build the community of practice. Like Turner's (1969) notion of *communitas* which, he observed, usually becomes part of structure and law, nascent CoP pave a way for more formalised and permanent ways of working with others.

Conclusions

Etienne Wenger describes CoPs as "a process by which we can experience the world and engagement with it as meaningful" (1998, p. 51) although we must also "be alive in a world in which we can act and interact". My experience of utilising the discussion forums in delivering CaiC online has highlighted the crucial role such interactions play in developing a CoP that is meaningful and focused on supporting students in accessing a social interface for learning. The bigger picture might suggest that we should use the CoP developed online as a means of cultivating the face-to-face communities that already exist. In developing and nurturing these CoP, we could continue to examine how the online world and its tools, such as VLE forums, are made meaningful as a way of preparing students for inhabiting the real on-campus world. Many students have been profoundly affected by disrupted learning and the HE landscape has changed irrevocably. Therefore, being part of a community is more important than ever. Using online communities of practices as a means of healing damaged experiences of face-to-face settings is an opportunity not to be overlooked.

Based on these initial findings and conjecture around the ways in which online communities of practice can be developed alongside on-campus settings, I note two key learning points:

1. **Online learning is not simply an adjunct to or substitute for face-to-face delivery**. The co-existence of online and on campus worlds is mutually beneficial. Both worlds should be afforded the same importance so that they work together effectively. Online learning offers flexibility but also requires a good deal of individual motivation. For the student who may flounder in online learning contexts (whether synchronous or asynchronous), regular on-campus experience can be used as a means of continuing to motivate such learners. In a post-COVID context, many HEIs opt for a hybrid approach, in which face-to-face teaching and learning is still considered superior and more 'meaningful' than online experience. In the context of my subject area, this is often reserved for practical, studio-based teaching although there is a place for modules delivered online to also incorporate aspects of on-campus provision. Regardless of whether a module is considered 'practical' or 'theoretical', the important point is that on-campus work supports online work and vice versa.

   Being remote does not need mean being isolated. In the first lockdown of 2020, many people appeared to seamlessly continue their social lives by moving to online platforms, replacing face-to-face events with Zoom and FaceTime calls as a means of staying in touch. Whilst this was, of course, no substitute for face-to-face interactions, this demonstrated that it is possible to make an online world an extension of a 'normal' world. Again, significance here is placed on the connections between these two realities; if there is link between what is experienced face-to-face and what happens online, a digital experience does not need to feel detached. Therefore, if students can make connections (however small) between the screen and the physical classroom, this can have a positive effect on both experiences. As a hybrid model of both on-campus and online teaching and learning continues to become the preferred method of many institutions, there are opportunities to further explore how these online and face-to-face CoP can support and complement each other.

Key take-aways

- Successful social learning and collaboration are not limited to physical co-presence.
- Nurturing online communities of practice positively enhances relational learning experiences.
- Online collaborative enquiry and dialogue encourages deep learning.

References

Advance HE (2021). Knowledge Hub: Massive open online course (MOOC). https://www.advance-he.ac.uk/knowledge-hub/massive-open-online-course-mooc

Aitken, V., Fraser, D. & Price, G. (2007). Negotiating the spaces: relational pedagogy and power in drama teaching. *International Journal of Education & the Arts*, 8 (14), 1–18.

Aronica, L. & Robinson, K. (2015). *Creative Schools*. London: Penguin Books.

Bell, K. (2022). Increasing undergraduate student satisfaction in Higher Education: the importance of relational pedagogy. *Journal of Further and Higher Education*, 46 (4), 490–503. DOI:10.1080/0309877X.2021.1985980

Biesta, G. (2010). 'Mind the Gap!' communication and the educational relation. In: Bingham, C. & Sidorkin, A. (eds.) (2004). *No Education Without Relation*. New York: Peter Lang, pp. 11–22.

Biesta, G., Bingham, C., Hutchison, J.N., McDaniel, B.L., Margonis, F., Mayo, C., Pijanowski, C.M., Romano, R.M., Sidorkin, A.M., Stengel, B.S. & Thayer-Bacon, B.J. (2010). Manifesto of relational pedagogy: Meeting to learning, learning to meet. A joint contribution by all authors. In: Bingham, C & Sidorkin, A.M. (eds.) *No Education Without Relation*, Peter Lang Publishing.

Bourriaud, N. (1998). Relational aesthetics'. In: Bishop, C. (ed.) (2006) *Participation*. London: Whitechapel Art Gallery, pp. 160–171.

Brenton, S. (2009). E-learning – an introduction. In Fry, H., Ketteridge, S. and Marshall, S. (eds.) *A Handbook for Teaching and Learning in Higher Education: Enhancing Academic Practice*. Abingdon: Routledge, pp. 85–98.

Britton, J. (2013). *Encountering Ensemble*. London: Bloomsbury.

Future Learn (2015). *Future Learn delivers the largest MOOC ever*. https://www.futurelearn.com/info/press-releases/futurelearn-delivers-the-largest-mooc-ever-as-nearly-400000-learners-convene-for-english-language-learning

Ingham, M. (2020). Assembling agency – learning in liminal spaces. In: Campbell, L. (ed.) *Leap into Action: Critical Performative Pedagogies in Art & Design Education*. New York: Peter Lang, pp. 43–56.

Kamalipour, H. & Peimani, N. (2022). *The Future of Design Studio Education: Student Experience and Perception of Blended Learning and Teaching during the Global Pandemic*. https://orca.cardiff.ac.uk/id/eprint/147740/1/education-12-00140.pdf

Ko, S. & Rossen, S. (2017). *Teaching Online: A Practical Guide*. London: Routledge.

Layton, J. (2020). From space to (embodied) place: a manifesto for sensory learning in site-specific practices. In: Campbell, L. (ed.) *Leap into Action: Critical Performative Pedagogies in Art & Design Education*. New York: Peter Lang, pp. 165–167.

Murphy, M. & Brown, T. (2012). Learning as relational: intersubjectivity and pedagogy in higher education. *International Journal of Lifelong Education*, 31(5), 643–654. DOI:10.1080/02601370.2012.700648

Niiranen, S. (2021). Supporting development of students technical understanding in craft and technology education visa the learning through doing approach. *International Journal of Technology and Design Education*, 31, 81–93. DOI:10.1007/s10798-019-09546-0

Open University (2021a). *About the OU.* http://www.open.ac.uk/about/main/

Open University (2021b). *Teaching and research.* http://www.open.ac.uk/about/main/teaching-and-research

Prentki, T. & Stinson, M. (2016). Relational pedagogy and the drama curriculum. *Research in Drama Education: The Journal of Applied Theatre and Performance*, 21 (3), 1–12. DOI:10.1080/13569783.2015.1127153

SCQF (2023). *SCQF Level Descriptors Tool.* https://scqf.org.uk/about-the-framework/scqf-level-descriptors-tool/

Turner, V. (1969). *The Ritual Process: Structure and Anti-Structure.* Ithaca, NY: Cornell University Press.

Wenger, E. (1998). *Communities of Practice: Learning, Meaning, and Identity.* Cambridge: Cambridge University Press.

Chapter 8

The MIPA model of professional identities of dance teachers

Negotiating professional identities in and across higher education

Michelle Groves

Introduction

As I sit at my desk in preparation for writing this chapter, I take a fleeting moment to consider some of the other tasks which I have engaged with earlier in the day: approving committee minutes, recording a promotional video for student recruitment, advising a staff member on dealing with a conflict issue, identifying key performance indicators for the next five years, and replying to an email from an enthusiastic student seeking advice regarding their next steps in becoming a dance teacher. As I reflect on these activities, I am not so much struck by the diversity of tasks but rather on how my professional role as a Director of Education is constructed around a multiplicity of identities which I seem to instinctively navigate.

I have always been fascinated by the mechanisms through which individuals understand themselves, how others create their perceptions of others, and how personal and collective opinions of self and others are mediated. Only in more recent years have I begun to recognise how little I and others take purposeful 'time out' to consider our multiple identities, and the impact these identities have on our sense of professional selves. Theorising professional identity formation in higher education (HE) is not new (Benhabib, 1992; Henkel, 2000; Alsup, 2006; Fanghanel, 2012; Davey, 2013). For me, what has often been missing from various discourses on professional identity formation is practical guidance through which individuals can meaningfully interrogate their understanding and emerging possibilities of their professional identities. This 'gap' from theory into practice led me to devising the MIPA (Materialist/Idealist positioning and Passive/Active agency) Model of Professional Identities of Dance Teachers, the function of which is to act as a tool for professionals working in HE to reflect on their multiple identities.

My intention for this chapter is to take you, the reader, on a reflective journey of your own in thinking about professional identities and the implications of such thinking on the practices of being a professional in higher education. From outlining the principles which underpin the MIPA Model, I will present examples of how the model has been used in dance teacher education, before concluding

DOI: 10.4324/9781003437826-11

with some suggestions on how the model can be applied in supporting professionals in higher education becoming more reflective and reflexive of their past, present, and future professional selves. In framing teaching as artistry, I believe it is crucial for the 'artists' to interrogate their identities in tandem with their practices. The intention of the MIPA model is to facilitate such interrogation.

Framing the MIPA Model of Professional Identities of Dance Teachers

The MIPA Model of Professional Identities of Dance Teachers is a tool which can be used to nurture personal and professional development of dance teachers working in HE. The model aids identification of "self" within, across, and outside the subject field of dance and the disciplinary fields of dance education and teaching. In progressing through the various stages of the MIPA model, dance teachers are guided through revealing how their perceptions of their personal and professional selves impact their decision-making, which can subsequently empower or restrict identity development, professional practices, and career opportunities.

Rather than prioritising an end product, the MIPA model is constructed around process, the focus of which is engagement of the reflexive self in equal measure with engagement of the reflective self. While the work of Donald Schön (1987) and others (Gibbs, 1988; Johns, 2013; Sellars, 2017; Bolton & Delderfield, 2018) have been influential in developing the idea of dance teachers as reflective practitioners, being more reflexively attuned, that is, starting with an understanding of oneself, is sometimes lost in transference from theory into practice. Teachers, regardless of subject, are generally well versed in being reflective of their practices. What is often more challenging is being reflexive of who they are as 'self', how their personal or core selves inevitably seep into the professional selves. What can also be hidden away is a deeper understanding of how the professional selves of dance teachers reveal an intricate and often complex state of disequilibrium as they experience and navigate several different professional identities. In addressing the apparent imbalance between reflective and reflexive processes, the MIPA model sets out to embrace in equal measure the concept of reflective and reflexive engagement.

The unspoken worlds of dance teachers

Dance teaching is a profession which, to an outsider, is a bit of a mystery. That said, the same can be said of other professions, so the cloak of intrigue is not unique to dance teachers. As a result, dance teachers can sometimes be seen as enigmas, holding positions of innate knowledge and power informed and shaped by historical legacies of dance as an art form. While many dance teachers are comfortable talking about the 'what' and the 'how' of their practices, they are less forthcoming in talking about how they perceive and demonstrate their professional selves. Dance teachers struggle to bring their inner voices to the surface, which begs the questions: "If you can't say it, do you really know it, and how can I know it if you can't say it?". With dance teachers preoccupied in the 'doing' of teaching, they rarely take time out to think about the factors which shape their professional identities, let alone how their professional selves might be perceived by others. The circumstances outlined here may also resonate with educators outside of dance fields as they too grapple with how to authentically articulate their professional beings (the who).

Professional identity types in the MIPA model

The MIPA model presents four professional identity types.

The horizontal axis of Figure 8.1 relates to the degree of agency which dance teachers perceive to have in relation to professional opportunities across time (different points in their careers), space (the contexts where they teach), and practices (the extent to which dance teachers have autonomy in how and what they teach). The vertical axis relates to how dance teachers perceive their positioning in terms of normative expectations, for example articulating and adopting practices which align to more traditional expectations of how dance should be taught (and, by proxy, how dance teachers should teach), or stances which are shaped by innovation, pushing boundaries, and challenging 'tradition'. The labelling of the two professional identity types on the vertical axis are drawn from the writings of the dance critic Jack Anderson (1983). Anderson categorised audiences who watch dance works into two groups: Materialists who expect dance works to retain traditional characteristics of 'original' productions, and Idealists who perceive and value dance works through the lens of innovation and novelty. For those not familiar with discussions in and around dance aesthetics and criticism, the labels of Materialist

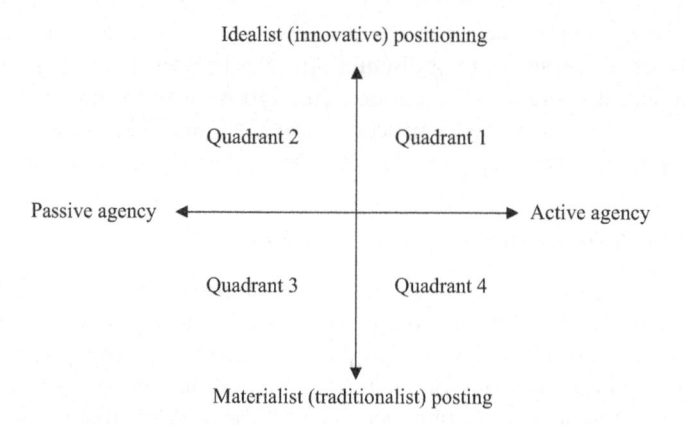

Figure 8.1 Co-ordinate plane for passive/active agency and materialist/idealist positioning

and Idealist may not be immediately understood. The rationale for the labels is that as the MIPA model emerged from needs emanating from the fields of dance and dance teaching, the terms Materialist and Idealist would hopefully be in the lexicon of dance teachers. Regardless, the proposition that some individuals are drawn to traditional-based values, beliefs, and attitudes while others are more open to challenging normative expectations is a dualism readily recognised across other professional domains.

Professional identity types are revealed through a process of guided self-reflection with the 'Speaker' (dance teacher) engaging in a conversation with the 'Listener' (a peer or more experienced other). The conversation is steered by the Listener through a series of prompt questions, akin to a semi-structured interview. Depending on the mutually agreed aim, the conversation may cover components of all four professional identity types or focus specifically on one or two aspects. For example, the Speaker and Listener may decide that the focus of the conversation should be on perceptions and experiences of passive and active agency as a means towards progressing or blocking career progression.

While 'process' is a key element of working through the MIPA model, the 'product' of the process is determined through an iterative cycle of conversational engagement (Figure 8.2).

The preferred terminology for this conversational engagement is discursive dialogue. The point of differentiation is that conversations between two people can often progress without moments of contemplative stillness. A discursive dialogue, on the other hand, has an ebb and flow carried by moments of longer, uninterrupted narratives while also punctuated by moments of pause, and vice versa.

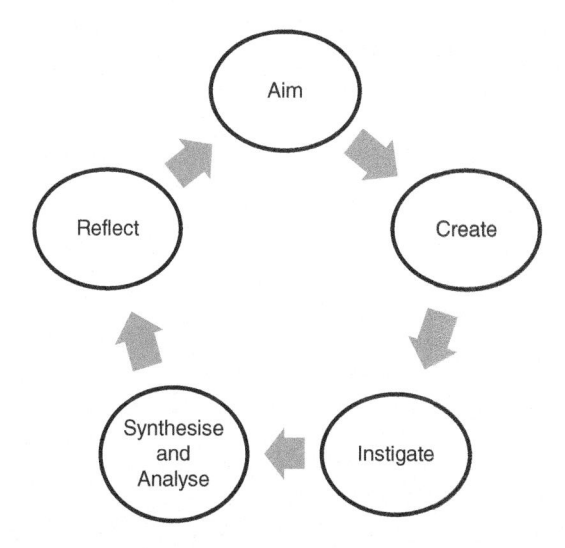

Figure 8.2 The iterative cycle of the MIPA model

Stage 1 (Aim) is for the Speaker and Listener to establish the aim of the discursive dialogue through mutually agreeing a focus. The initial coming together of Speaker and Listener normally takes the form of a brief meeting. There will be a multiplicity of reasons for initiating the coming together. It may be that the Speaker has become aware of a feeling which suggests they are experiencing some sort of blocker in making sense of a particular experience or perception. For example, a dance teacher (the Speaker) may come to their manager (the Listener) expressing frustration about not feeling able to move their teaching outside the confines of a rigidly set syllabus. The dance teacher's frustration may be triggered by feelings that their preferred positioning as an active agent has been destabilised, and that their innovative (Idealist) alternative approaches to delivering the set syllabus is being seen as unacceptable. Such destabilisation may be driven by the dance teacher's perceptions of their active and idealist positionings being curtailed because of the way in which their approaches are perceived by others as running contrary to normative expectations.

Another example for instigating Stage 1 might be that an early career dance teacher has expressed to their manager difficulty in understanding and establishing their identity as a dance teacher. While being competent in the 'what' and 'how' of their teaching, the early career dance teacher is experiencing a state of disequilibrium by not being able to express to themselves, let alone others, who they are as a dance teacher. Whatever the circumstances leading to agreeing the focus of the discursive dialogue at Stage 1, it is important that there is mutual agreement of the parameters of the dialogue.

Having established the aim of the discursive dialogue, the process moves on to Stage 2 (Create), where the Listener takes time out to create and shape the format of the discursive dialogue. The Listener devises a series of prompt questions which will engage the Speaker in reflexive thinking and dialogue in and around the agreed focus. The Listener will determine how the discursive dialogue is to be captured, for example by audio recording or through *aide memoire* notes, and share this decision with the Speaker ahead of Stage 3 commencing. Stage 3 (Instigate) is where the Speaker and Listener come together for the discursive dialogue part of the process. There is no set timeframe for the discursive dialogue. What is key, however, is that sufficient time is earmarked so neither party feels rushed, and for the dialogue to take its course unimpeded by time constraints.

The stage which will most likely take the most time is Stage 4 (Synthesise and Analyse). This is where the Listener will synthesise themes and emerging messages from notes or recordings taken from Stage 3. These themes and emerging messages are then plotted onto a MIPA model template which organises information into characteristics associated with each of the four potential professional identity types: Passive Idealist, Passive Materialist, Active Idealist, or Active Materialist. For example, the emerging messages from a Speaker who expresses frustration at feeling constrained by the normative expectations of the dance school where they work, while at the same time believing that their ideas and innovations which challenge the normative expectations of practice would benefit their students, could be interpreted by the Listener as exhibiting perceptions of passive agency with idealist tendencies. On the basis of these two messages alone, the Speaker would be characterised as a Passive Idealist professional identity type. The final stage of the iterative cycle is the Reflect stage. Here, the Listener and Speaker meet to reflect on the interpretation of the professional identity type which the Speaker has alluded to. It is at this stage that the discursive dialogue can take on a different shape as the Speaker and Listener interrogate together converging or diverging points of interpretation. At the Reflect stage, the Speaker and Listener might also explore how some of the perceptions and interpretations of the Speaker might support or hinder ongoing professional development and career aspirations.

Engagement with the MIPA model process may end at Stage 5, or it may instigate another cycle of discursive dialogue sometime in the future, starting fresh at Stage 1. The four professional identity types are not fixed; they are simply products of a process at a given point in time. For the Speaker who the Listener interpreted as a Passive Idealist, engaging with a future round of the MIPA model process may see the Speaker expressing characteristics of an Active Idealist as a result of a changing circumstances. Identifying as a particular professional identity type is not an end point; instead, it is a point of departure in understanding one's professional self at a given point in time.

Articulating the inner voice and decision-making through modes of reflexive thought

In working with dance teachers, I have found myself fascinated by the ease with which they articulate the 'what' and 'how' of their practices yet spend little time questioning why they make the decisions they do. The act of teaching is constructed, in part, around asking oneself a continuous loop of inner voice questions before enacting the outcomes of decisions made. In observing a dance class, a dance teacher's inner voice may question if the pace of the class is too slow, too quick, or just about right for what is to be accomplished. The inner voice may question if feedback needs to be given to the whole class or just to the student who is struggling with a dance routine. Beyond the reflective questions and decisions made about practice variables, dance teachers may also find their inner voices setting the stage for a state of reflexive unease as they attempt to externalise their values, beliefs, and attitudes. These inner contemplations shape perceptions of who they are as dance teachers, the decisions they may or may not make regarding their professional careers, or how authentically they operate in professional spaces shaped by normative expectations.

Dance teachers are sometimes oblivious to the factors which shape their decision-making, yet making certain decisions over others can significantly impact one's standing as a dance teacher. Often decisions are made intuitively, predicated by inner voice conversations. To better understand one's professional identity, and to be able to articulate to others who they are as professionals, dance teachers may benefit from identifying and unpicking the reasons for making certain decisions above and beyond alternative solutions and, in doing so, appreciate how those decisions may shape their professional identity types.

To augment identification of a professional identity type, the MIPA model process aims also to excavate nuggets of information in relation to how a Speaker understands, and is able to articulate to the Listener, the premises upon which they make decisions. By any reckoning, such introspective analysis is cognitively challenging, and particularly so for dance teachers exhibiting Passive Materialist tendencies. It is also challenging for a Listener to scan the discursive dialogue for examples of factors related to decision- making. The Listener can prompt the Speaker by asking questions such as "why do you think you made that decision?" as a means of identifying the foundations of decision-making outcomes. As a means of clustering expressions of reflexive thinking related to decision-making processes, the MIPA model process draws upon Margaret Archer's modes of reflexivity (2003, pp. 153–298) which identifies communicative, autonomous, meta-reflexive, and fractured ways of "thinking about thinking".

Dance teachers who operate a mode of Communicative Reflexivity in their decision-making will look towards professional peers for validation of their choices as a check against normative professional expectations, with early career dance teachers tending to have the Communicative Reflexivity mode as their default position. Dance teachers who engage in Autonomous Reflexivity patterns of decision-making do not look for external validation of their decisions but make choices akin to a 'lone wolf', while Meta Reflexivity is the *modus operandi* of dance teachers at ease in contemplating the impact of their decision-making through critical self-analysis and external consequences. Generally, dance teachers who demonstrate Meta Reflexivity modes in decision-making are more experienced practitioners who are able to draw on a wealth of professional experience, while dance teachers who have Autonomous Reflexivity as their default mode can be at any stage of the careers. The fourth mode of reflexivity, Fractured Reflexivity, is where dance teachers experience a sense of destabilisation as they try to work through the disorientation of inner voices with perceived external realities. Rather than supporting agency and action, a dance teacher whose decision-making is blanketed in a fractured mode of reflexivity may find themselves struggling to understand or make decisions without considerable inner turmoil.

During Stage 4 of the iterative process cycle, as well as identifying and interpreting professional identity characteristics expressed by the Speaker, the Listener will also note examples which indicate how the Speaker understands and expresses the drivers of their decision-making processes. If it is taken that professional identity types are fluid as opposed to fixed, and that dance teachers are able to shift their understanding and actions towards a professional identity type more congruent with their professional values, beliefs, and attitudes, then understanding the enablers and blockers of decision-making processes which can shape identity formation will potentially allow dance teachers to move towards reconstructing their professional identities towards a more harmonious sense of professional self.

Pen portraits as a product of personality types and decision-making style

At the Reflect stage, the Listener may share with the Speaker their pen portrait which the Listener has created through emerging themes and messages of the MIPA model process. The pen portrait can be shared ahead of the Reflect stage meeting as a starting point for the Reflect stage discussion. A pen portrait example of a fictional speaker, Isabelle, is presented here as an illustration of how a Listener's interpretive product can be delivered to a Speaker. This pen portrait shows Isabelle, a dance teacher of more than ten years' experience, occupying an Active Materialist professional identity type, with a Meta Reflexivity approach to decision making.

> Isabelle consistently refers to teaching as being intrinsic to her sense of personal self. For Isabelle, personal values and beliefs are fundamental to her dance teaching practices, as is the needs for constant reflection on the 'what', 'how', and 'why'. Isabelle values being able to work with other dance teachers, which leads towards a deeper contemplation of who she is as a dance teacher and the impact of her professional and career choices. With strongly expressed personal and professional values and beliefs, Isabelle is active in shaping her career, committed to the concept of lifelong learning, and proactive in supporting aspirations of early career dance teachers. Isabelle believes that the traditions and expected practices of a dance *genre*'s heritage are fundamental to her approach to teaching, suggesting a dominant Materialist positioning, though this is tempered with Isabelle recognising that her teaching needs to address the needs of individual students.

A pen portrait is not intended to be a 'blow by blow' account of the interpretations of a Listener. Rather, a pen portrait can act as a starting point for the Reflect stage discussion. Imagining how such a discussion may play out between 'Isabelle' and the Listener, it may be that Isabelle does not immediately recognise herself from the pen portrait's description. This mismatch of recognition provides an impetus for the Listener to once again guide the Speaker towards externally articulating perceptions, thoughts, and reckonings which are captured within the Speaker's inner voice. In Box 8.1, Julia Reeve provides another example of a reflection on professional identity where the author creates an analogy between their discipline of fashion design with their identity as a teacher.

> **Box 8.1 Fashioning a teaching identity**
>
> *Julia Reeve*
>
> > Being a teacher is a creative profession.
> >
> > (Robinson, 2011, p. 267)
>
> The roots of my professional identity lay within my original subject discipline of fashion. Having spent years working within the fashion industry, and subsequently as a fashion lecturer, my practice is now emphatically cross-disciplinary. However, my fashion background continues to inform my identity as a teacher.
>
> Fashion has both informed and challenged my personal philosophy as an educator. For example, problematic issues within the fashion industry, such as worker's rights, led me to not only develop a module on ethical practice in fashion, but ultimately to also focus on social justice more broadly.
>
> Ironically, it was leaving my design discipline that allowed my creativity as an educator to flourish. Getting away from my subject allowed me to explore further networks of like-minded colleagues and extend my visual, tactile learning and teaching approaches across multiple subjects and settings.
>
> "Having ideas through the process of making" (Gauntlett, 2011, p. 4) is central to my personal authenticity, and has come to be an essential part of my professional identity too. So, reflecting on the artistry of teaching in my own context via an infographic (Figure 8.3), where I could use imagery to convey the essence of the tactile fashion world, seemed wholly appropriate.
>
> Using fashion design as a metaphor for the art of teaching, I view the honing of pedagogic artistry as a craft, through a constructionist lens (Papert & Harel, 1990). I see parallels between fashion design processes and the development of my teaching practice. For me, fashion reaches far deeper than mere subject knowledge: it goes to the heart of who I am as a multisensory, cross-disciplinary pracademic.
>
> You may like to consider the following questions in response to 'fashioning a teaching identity':
>
> - Has this piece sparked any reflections on the relationship between your pedagogic identity and your discipline(s)?
> - Can you create a visual map, collage, infographic to illustrate this relationship?

The MIPA model of professional identities of dance teachers   129

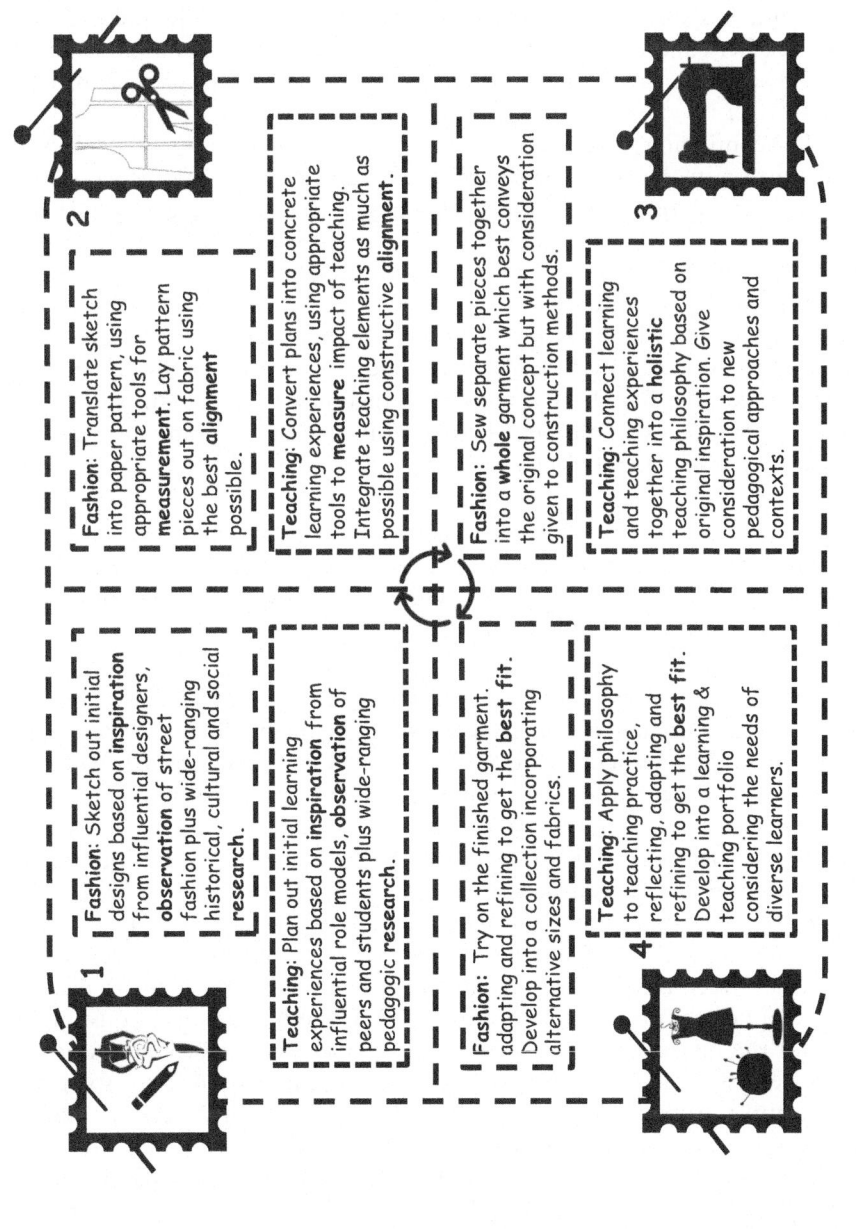

1
Fashion: Sketch out initial designs based on **inspiration** from influential designers, **observation** of street fashion plus wide-ranging historical, cultural and social **research**.

Teaching: Plan out initial learning experiences based on **inspiration** from influential role models, **observation** of peers and students plus wide-ranging pedagogic **research**.

2
Fashion: Translate sketch into paper pattern, using appropriate tools for **measurement**. Lay pattern pieces out on fabric using the best **alignment** possible.

Teaching: Convert plans into concrete learning experiences, using appropriate tools to **measure** impact of teaching. Integrate teaching elements as much as possible using constructive **alignment**.

3
Fashion: Sew separate pieces together into a **whole** garment which best conveys the original concept but with consideration given to construction methods.

Teaching: Connect learning and teaching experiences together into a **holistic** teaching philosophy based on original inspiration. Give consideration to new pedagogical approaches and contexts.

4
Fashion: Try on the finished garment, adapting and refining to get the **best fit**. Develop into a collection incorporating alternative sizes and fabrics.

Teaching: Apply philosophy to teaching practice, reflecting, adapting and refining to get the **best fit**. Develop into a learning & teaching portfolio considering the needs of diverse learners.

Figure 8.3 Fashioning my teaching identity

It's good to talk, isn't it?

Having outlined the processes involved in the MIPA model, two questions arise: "So what, and who cares?" In practice-based disciplines such as dance, much time is spent on the 'doing' and much less time on the 'saying'. As a dance teacher educator, I believe that the saying is as important as the doing if dance teachers are to achieve a 360-degree understanding of their professional selves.

While continuing to actively seek out opportunities for instigating purposeful discussions with peers as well as trainee dance teachers, I experience a deep sense of satisfaction when I hear responses such as, "Talking about 'it' reassures me that I'm on the right path" (affirmation), or "That's interesting, I haven't thought about 'it' in that way" (unfolding), or "I haven't really thought about 'it' at all!" (revelation). What the MIPA model provides me with is a framework within which purposeful discussions have a goal rather than being confined to a 'nice chat'. Indeed, some dance teachers experience a sense of gratitude that they have been able to bring their inner voices to the surface, as expressed by one dance teacher when asked if they had anything further they wanted to say after the Reflect stage:

> Just thank you. It was really nice to talk to someone about all of this because it has been on my mind. It's been really useful to talk through how I see myself as a dance teacher, so it's been great. I'd love to discuss things further with you when you have the time.

But, as with any process which interrogates and reveals one's inner voice, not all dance teachers are comfortable with engaging in discursive dialogue, which is a key component of the MIPA model. Some dance teachers will lack confidence in articulating their thoughts and perceptions, seeing themselves as 'doers' not speakers. Other dance teachers may be fearful of being judged, not only by their peers but also by those who look up to them as professional role models. Some dance teachers will feel unsettled by the potential ramifications of revealing too much of themselves to others, alongside being fearful of personally connecting with their most inner-held values, beliefs, and attitudes. Added to these reasons for not being 'ready' to engage in discursive dialogues, the processes involved in the MIPA model are time-consuming both for the Listener as well as the Speaker. Many dance teachers work on a freelance basis, where time is money and therefore time needs to be spent on what is most profitable. The challenge here, then, is to find ways of embedding and framing engagement with the MIPA model as a tool towards promoting ongoing professional reflection, development, and investment in career progression.

Applications of the MIPA model

To situate the MIPA model as a meaningful tool towards a better understanding of professional identities and decision-making practices, a number of practical applications are presented. While this chapter has focused the application of the MIPA model to dance teacher education, the model can be readily applied across other higher education disciplines.

A framework for mentoring early career professionals and tutors

Through my experience of working with early career professionals and tutors in higher education, I have witnessed tendencies for these colleagues to focus their thoughts on the 'what' and 'how' of what they do – reflection in and on practice – with little time or motivation given to thinking about the factors which shape and influence their professional identities – the 'why' of what they do. A crucial, yet often under-played role of a mentor is to encourage early career professionals and tutors to look beyond what they do and to actively question what they bring of themselves to their practices. Being reflective, and reflexive, are skills which require practice. A task for mentors is to identify and facilitate opportunities for both reflection on practice and reflexion of self. However opportunities might be constructed, the MIPA model provides a tool for mentors and mentees in supporting and initiating discursive dialogues, leading to a better understanding and appreciation of professional identity formation and development.

A tool to support observation and verbal feedback on practice

Formal observation and feedback on practice, particularly for early career tutors in higher education, is more times than not led by more experienced tutors well practiced in how to conduct 'peer' observations. Equally valid, and often less daunting for the individual being observed, is when the observations and feedback are led by others who do not hold positions of power. A potential barrier to the success of this peer-on-peer approach is the absence of a framework which can guide the verbal feedback of the observing peer. To connect the observation of the 'what' and the 'how' with the 'who', aspects of the MIPA model can be adapted and used as a template for delivering focussed feedback.

A framework for meaningful annual appraisals

The very mention of annual appraisals often instigates groans of discontentment from professionals and tutors in higher education as yet another example of a quality assurance tick-box exercise which has little perceived relevance for appraisees. Appraisal reports are often stored in desk drawers, only to be revisited a year later just ahead of the next appraisal meeting. An appraisal process which moves its focus away from what has been achieved over the year towards deeper consideration of why something has been achieved, in other words, recognition of how the appraiser has initiated action and change, may make annual appraisals more meaningful and insightful for both the appraisee and the appraiser. In addition, rather than annual appraisals being scheduled as an annual 'one-off', it may also be beneficial to embed a normative expectation of the appraisal process being continuous throughout an agreed timeframe. The five-stage iterative process cycle which underpins the MIPA model provides a potential foundation for implementing a continuous appraisal system. Each of the five stages can be scheduled at relevant points in the year, culminating in the Stage 5 Reflect coming together as a means of closing the cycle. In adopting continuous appraisal processes, engagement with the skills associated with being a reflective and reflexive professional in higher education are not reduced to an arbitrary end-point in time but are practiced and followed through the course of one's professional and career trajectory.

Identifying and mapping professional development needs

Being an agile professional in higher education has never been more crucial given the current uncertainty of higher education landscapes. Like annual appraisals, mapping out one's professional development is often conducted through a porthole of dealing with the now as opposed to projecting forwards to future horizons. Understanding and appreciating one's core personal characteristics, and how these characteristics can influence one's perceptions and presentation of the professional self, are important factors in pinpointing possibilities and identifying the barriers which may block the formation of professional identities. While the MIPA model is constructed around didactic interactions between a Listener and Speaker, many of the building blocks of the MIPA model can be extrapolated and reworked by individuals wishing to work solo towards greater personal agency and innovative enterprise. Likewise, line managers can draw on the MIPA model as a framework for identifying with staff any professional development opportunities which will enhance and extend an individual's professional identity formation beyond the here and now.

Conclusion

Being a dance teacher educator, I have always felt a moral and professional responsibility for the colleagues I am tasked with nurturing and supporting. I see my role as facilitating pathways for ongoing professional development and instilling an understanding of how professional identities are shaped and influenced. To understand other professionals, one needs to better understand one's own professional identities. I believe greater effort needs to be made across professional fields for individuals to connect the 'what' and the 'how' with the 'why' as a means towards self-actualisation. There is no getting away from the fact that implementing the MIPA model, even in a reduced form, is time consuming. Unless there is a prevailing institutional ethos that spending time in engaging in discursive dialogue outside of the "doing" is time well spent, it is unlikely that the MIPA model (or any other vehicle for reflexive practice) would be adopted as a tool for promoting professional development and identity appreciation. Always the optimist, I continue to believe that if professionals in higher education, who are tasked with mentoring and supporting colleagues, champion 'it's good to talk' hard enough and often enough, their efforts will be rewarded by ring-fenced time being allocated for understanding 'self as a professional'.

Key take-aways

- Professional identities are not fixed, but are deconstructed and reconstructed across time, space, and practices.
- Understanding one's professional identity is as equally important to understanding what one does as a professional.
- The MIPA Model Professional Identities of Dance Teachers provides a tool to guide reflexive engagement through democratic interactions.

References

Alsup, J. (2006). *Teacher Identity Discourses Negotiating Personal and Professional Spaces*. New Jersey: Lawrence *Erlbaum* Associates, DOI:10.4324/9781410617286

Anderson, J. (1983). Idealists, materialists and the thirty-two fouettés. In: Copeland, R. & Cohen, M. (eds.) *What is Dance? Readings in Theory and Criticism*. Oxford: Oxford University Press, pp. 410–419.

Archer, M. S. (2003). *Structure, Agency and the Internal Conversation*. Cambridge: Cambridge University Press. DOI:10.1017/CBO9781139087315

Benhabib, S. (1992). *Situating the self: Gender, Community and Postmodernism in Contemporary Ethics*. New York: Routledge. DOI:10.4324/9781003059516

Bolton, G. & Delderfield, R. (2018). *Reflective Practice Writing and Professional Development. 5th edition*. London: Sage Publications Ltd.

Davey, R. (2013). *The Professional Identity of Teacher Educators. Career on the Cusp?* Abingdon, Oxon: Routledge. DOI:10.4324/9780203584934

Fanghanel, J. (2012). *Being an Academic: The Realities of Practice in a Changing World*. Abingdon, Oxon: Routledge. DOI:10.4324/9780203818237

Gauntlett, D. (2011). *Making is Connecting: The Social Meaning of Creativity, from DIY and Knitting to YouTube and Web 2.0*. Cambridge: Polity Press.

Gibbs, G. (1988). *Learning by Doing: A Guide to Teaching and Learning Methods*. Oxford: Further Education Unit Oxford.

Henkel, M. (2000). *Academic Identities and Policy Change in Higher Education.* London: Jessica Kingsley Publishers.
Johns, C. (2013). *Becoming a Reflective Practitioner.* Oxford: Wiley-Blackwell.
Papert S. & Harel, I. (1990). Situating constructionism. In: Harel (ed.), *Constructionist Learning.* Cambridge, MA: MIT Media Laboratory.
Robinson, K. (2011). *Out of our Minds: Learning to be Creative.* Chichester: Capstone Publishing Ltd.. DOI:10.1002/9780857086549
Schön, D. (1987). *Educating the Reflective Practitioner: Toward a New Design for Teaching and Learning in the Professions.* San Francisco: Jossey-Bass.
Sellars, M. (2017). *Reflective Practice for Teachers.* London: Sage Publications Ltd..

Chapter 9

From disciplinary expertise to academic artistry

The shifting professional identity, expertise, and artistry of the programme leader

Jenny Lawrence

Programme leadership and leaders

Programme leaders are responsible for the academic, educational, and administrative coherence of the programmes in their keep (Lawrence & Ellis, 2018). The programme is the focus of the prospective student's attention when selecting a course of study in higher education (HE) and the nexus of the student experience. Data outlining student satisfaction, outcomes, and graduate destination are commonly organised by programme of study. Given the importance these play in global rankings and sector standing, those responsible for the programme of study are increasingly recognised as crucial to institutional success (Lawrence, Moron-Garcia & Senior, 2022a) and are "coming out of the shadows" (Caddell et al., 2022) as institutions invest in developing programme leadership. The role is demanding and time consuming: they must work across the entire institution to inspire academic peers' and professional service colleagues' commitment to the programme, understand and work to institutionally specific practices, engage with PSRB (Professional, Statutory or Regulatory Body) or validating body requirements, keep abreast of national policy, and operate within the wider context of HE (Lawrence, Moron-Garcia & Senior, 2022): a sector ever changing at an ever-increasing pace. They must be increasingly "agile, responsive and resilient" (Lawrence, 2021). It is in this agility that the intangible artistry of programme leadership lies.

The personal attributes and high degree of academic professionalism needed to lead a programme of study far exceed disciplinary expertise, represent considerable stretch for academic staff that come to the role as an expert in their disciplinary field, and have troublesome implications to the programme leader's academic identity.

Programme leader identity in HE

There is a "lack of parity between research-focused and education-focused careers" (Hulme, 2022, p. 108) which impacts programme leaders (Caddell et al., 2022) and extends across the worldwide HE (Lawrence, Moron-Garcia

DOI: 10.4324/9781003437826-12

& Senior, 2022). Following Hulme's (2022) lead, I borrow from Tajfel and Turner's (1979) social theory to understand how a context can be created where a positive academic identity might be constructed for and with programme leaders.

Academic identity is informed by how we understand ourselves within our academic context: by who is 'in'– those with attributes valued in HE, commonly winners of research grants and producers of high-impact research outputs – and who is 'out' – those who possess attributes undervalued in HE – often education-focussed capabilities (Hulme, 2022), such as educational, academic, and administrative leadership. Programme leaders have been, in the academy's "prestige economy" (Blackmore & Kandiko, 2011), out-siders (Caddell et al., 2022) that might experience a "lack of belonging" (Hulme, 2022, p. 108), which could arrest self-efficacy and hinder the leadership of those who possess the more valued research credentials.

However, the role is coming to be understood as central to a contemporary academic career as it is increasingly recognised as crucial to student, institution, and the individual programme leader success, appreciated across the sector (Lawrence, Moron-Garcia & Senior, 2022a, p. 7) and all kinds of provision (Lawrence & Hall, 2019). The role can be a source of professional and personal satisfaction, reward, and, as I argue here, a locus for a positive academic identity.

Method

In research funded by Advance HE two programme leader networks at a UK medium-sized (14,000 students), research-focussed university were evaluated using Appreciative Inquiry (Cooperrider & Srivastva, 1987). The first is a cross-university, central-formal network led by a central academic development unit; the second a local-informal network led by programme leaders in an academic department. The inquiry invited approximately 160 programme leaders to complete an online survey (30 responded); a workshop for each cohort of programme leaders (attended by 5 and 6 participants) and a second workshop that brought both cohorts together (attended by 8). Participants and researchers came to a shared understanding of a model for competence-based programme leadership (Lawrence & Scott, 2022), domains of reward and responsibility inherent to the role (Lawrence, Morrell & Scott, 2023), and the importance of socially mediated academic development for programme leaders (Scott & Lawrence, 2022). Here I read the model for competence-based programme leading through the lens of expertise and artistry and consider how the value this artistry holds in the learning community is integral to the development of a positive academic identity and how it might be nurtured by looking to developmental practices from across the globe.

Programme leader expertise

Programme leaders deploy a complex array of expertise: expertise in educational leadership by setting direction and influencing change in teaching, learning, and assessment; in academic leadership, linking research, teaching, and scholarship; and administrative leadership in attending to the programme's logistical requirements (Parkin 2017; 2022). All whilst marshalling academic and systemic complexity, and perhaps even dissonance amongst colleagues servicing their programme/s into coherence, programme leaders participating in this study thought their ability to "garner support" (programme leader) from colleagues made them a good programme leader. They are seldom prepared for the role (Lawrence & Ellis, 2018), and many institutions lack a role descriptor or guide for practice (Senior, 2018), though this is changing (Lawrence, Moron-Garcia & Senior, 2022a). The role encompasses encounters with the unknown every day. Programme leadership then aligns to expertise as King defines it as it has "learning, adaptability and flexibility at its heart" (King, 2022a, p. 4). It is commonly developed through experience rather than professional development (Ellis & Nimmo, 2018): as one participant pointed out, they are a good programme leader because they are "an old hand".

Programme leader artistry

Effective programme leadership exceeds being able to expertly deploy the well-rehearsed models of leadership described, yet what it takes is hard to define. Effective programme leadership is rooted in deep understanding of the institution in which it is practised yet "anchored" in the discipline (Lawrence, Moron-Garcia & Senior, 2022). It can be defined by its complex, multidimensional nature (Forsyth & Powell, 2022), encompassing attending to the professional, academic, and pastoral needs of staff, students, and stakeholders whilst balancing the regulatory requirements of host and validating institutions. This calls for highly skilled relational engagement with interested parties across an institution and beyond (Moore, 2022; Parkin, 2022). It is inherently challenging (Parkin 2022), yet is deeply meaningful for those committed to their students and their discipline (Lawrence, Morrell & Scott, 2023). As HE evolves at an increasing pace, and the student and staff experience becomes evermore administratively burdensome, the programme leader must be dynamic. When responding to the free text survey question "what makes you a good programme leader", programme leaders recognised strength in their ability to "adapt to changes in situations quickly … see outside the box" being "calm and organised" and "fearless" whilst "being the bigger picture/strategic thinker" and "hard working": almost a third (9) of the 30 programme leaders who answered this question cited this attribute. This dynamism is underpinned by a deep commitment to their students, programme team, and discipline

138 Jenny Lawrence

Table 9.1 Domains of reward and responsibility of programme leading to programme leaders (Lawrence, Morrell & Scott, 2023)

Domain of reward and responsibility	Description of the domain
Investment in the Programme	The pleasure and intrinsic reward of teaching of their discipline
Commitment to Students	The investment in their students' success; in sustaining their discipline and teaching the next generation of scholars
Individual interest	The reward found in exercising academic agency and creativity, of professional stretch in stepping up to the challenge of educational leadership and potential for career progression
Responsibility to Community	Dedication and devotion to their programme team, department, institution, discipline

identified in domains of reward and responsibility of programme leading (see Table 9.1).

Programme leaders cited their ability to make judgement calls in resisting initiatives for the good of their students, community, and programme as integral to what makes them a good programme leader. If expert programme leadership is the intelligent and creative act of deploying academic, educational, and administrative leadership in unpredictable and perhaps challenging circumstances, the academic artistry of programme leadership is realising these professional responsibilities ethically, authentically, and with compassion. This sense of being an "expert educator as ethical decision maker" (Morantes-Africano, 2022) resonates with programme leaders. One respondent considered themselves a good programme leader because they were "approachable, honest, to have integrity, to be organised".

The balance between professional and personal characteristics was a recurring motif; as one programme leader describes, there is "a need for enhancing motivation and fun, a good sense of humour, flexible, adaptable = what makes us human! Additionally, I am organised, rigorous, show attention to details, respect deadlines = what makes me a robot and seems to be appreciated more in terms of career progression etc.".

Academic development for programme leaders must take into account a comprehensive understanding not only of programme leader expertise – what they must know and do in their disciplinary and institutional ever-changing context, but also how they might develop the artistry of programme leadership – the intangible, meaningful, and inherently human elements of the role that allow the ethical and compassionate navigation of adversity at pace – and bring personal and professional satisfaction.

Developing programme leader artistry and identity: competence-based programme leading

Competence-based programme leadership (Lawrence & Scott, 2022; Lawrence, Morrell & Scott, 2023) offers a means of understanding how we might nurture the artistry of programme leadership whilst at the same time build a positive academic identity for the programme leader.

To be competent is to have the necessary experience, knowledge, and self-awareness to attend to a task effectively (Huxley-Binns, Lawrence & Scott, 2023). It is a process where these three dimensions exist in instantaneous dialogue, giving someone command to act in any eventuality. Competence-based education facilitates the ontological turn (Barnett, 2012) from knowing about a discipline, for example philosophy, to being able to apply and integrate that philosophical knowledge in a specific and perhaps unexpected context. It enables the essentially intelligent, creative, and innately human process of *being* a philosopher (Lawrence, 2020; Huxley-Binns, Lawrence & Scott, 2023). In co-creating a model for programme leading we used competence-based education as a foundation. The model can be used to facilitate the ontological turn from knowing about programme leading, the processes and practices necessary to undertake the role, to being a programme leader which we can understand to be exercising programme leader academic artistry: working creatively, with agility, adapting practices and processes to realise their responsibilities ethically and with compassion, and true to the discipline (see Table 9.2). Activities and resources which support the model for competence-based programme leadership were also compiled. These are framed in the understanding of programme-leading expertise and academic artistry.

Experience of programme leading

This dimension can be understood as the experience of working for or service to the learning community and is made possible by drawing on and sharing individual practice with fellow programme leaders through central-formal and local-informal networks of colleagues with comparable responsibilities (Scott & Lawrence, 2022). Here the programme leader's experience is taken as a seat of valued expertise: no one knows the complexity of the role and the canny solutions as well as another programme leader. It is here the "intangible characteristics" of programme leader academic artistry emerge and might be identified. These are the characteristics the programme leader draws on to deal with complexity and improvise in the navigation of fixed institutional structures to get the best result for their programme, students, and community. It is in this improvisation that programme leaders found satisfaction and, when sharing their experience with peers (when troubleshooting) or senior leaders

Table 9.2 Competence-based programme leading (based on Lawrence & Scott, 2022)

Experience of programme leading	Knowledge for programme leading	Self-awareness of the meaning of programme leading
Drawing on, sharing, and growing the effective practice of programme leading	Developing understanding and knowing where to find information, advice, and guidance on: • HE (global trends, national drivers) • Institution (the programme leader role, policy, and practice) • Discipline/Practice (sector wide) • Students (prospective, current, alumni)	Recognising the importance of the role to learning community and programme leader success, including • Responsibility to students, colleagues, programme, and institution • Standing in the department, institution, discipline, and sector • Motivation & reward: pride in the programme; professional development; career advancement; student success

(when being consulted on new initiatives), enjoyed positive identity formation. As one participant reflected, it is affirming to have a "place at the table".

This dimension acknowledges a programme leader will evolve as their experience widens and should be confident in the particularity of their specific, situated (either by discipline, organisational structure, or personal characteristics), and therefore authentic practice of programme leadership. Here the expertise of programme leading can be understood as "a process of experiencing and experimenting, rather than being better than others" (King, 2022a. p. 3). As one programme leader pointed out "… there are different ways to be 'good'. Different individuals have different natural strengths that they can bring to bear".

Knowledge for programme leading

The second dimension is the knowledge necessary for programme leading: knowledge of higher education, the institution, discipline, and learning community (students, stakeholders, and partners). This means knowing where to find the most recent information, advice, and guidance; policy documents; and accessing and deciphering data dashboards or, as one programme leader put it, having to hand an "explanation of the basic and most commonly encountered regulations and procedures".

Localised programme-specific repositories programme leads developed for their teams themselves or a centrally curated and systematically updated index of information and guidance relevant to the programme leader (hosted on the Virtual Learning Environment) were used effectively.

These first two dimensions speak of the generic characteristics of expertise outlined by King, where "high performance based on knowledge and skills [is] developed through study and experience and ways of thinking and practising" (King, 2022b, p. 19) and associated activities enable the development of responsive, creative, and therefore expert programme leadership. However, "experience alone is insufficient in developing expertise" (King, 2022c, p. 165).

Self-awareness of the meaning of programme leading

The third and potentially most important dimension is self-awareness of the meaning of programme leading to the programme leader and wider learning community. It speaks of the programme leader's responsibility to and standing in the learning community and includes explicit "appreciation of the *value* of programme leading" (Lawrence, Morrell & Scott, 2023), which programme leaders understood to be having some personal pride in the programme; the opportunity for professional development in the exercising of academic agency in the running of their programme/s; recognising programme leadership is academic career advancement; and holding onto the satisfaction of facilitating student success.

Self-awareness of the meaning of programme leading is sympathetic to the third generic characteristic of expertise: intentional learning and development (King, 2022b, p. 19), as programme leaders might recognise where to invest their developmental energies as they "question consciously all aspects of their practice in the quest for continual improvement" (Turner & Spowart, 2022, p. 130). It also resonates with the role of reflection in emerging expertise, identity building (Morantes-Africano, 2022), and recognising the learning community's influence on social standing in HE (Hulme, 2022), as programme leaders come to understand the high degree of expertise necessary to discharge their duties and find their own respected and esteemed "in-crowd" of programme leader peers benefiting from the role and being rewarded for their practice. As such, it is this third dimension where institutions, academic developers, and programme leaders might seed the positive academic identity "the programme leader" and where the shift from programme leader expertise to academic artistry might be made.

The appreciation of the value of programme leading is possible through active and purposeful reflection amongst peers, coupled with an enlightened institutional infrastructure. It is interesting to note that members of a local-informal network of disciplinary programme leaders recognised the importance of their role to their immediate learning community and found great satisfaction in securing student success. These programme leaders were more likely to call on each other to solve acute operational or student issues (Lawrence, Morrell & Scott, 2023). Those engaged with the central-formal network of programme leader peers, where activities aligned to Descriptor 3 of the Professional Standards Framework (PSF: Advance HE, 2023) and senior leaders attended to draw on the experience of programme leaders in reshaping systems and processes, saw the role as integral to their academic success. This success was manifest in career progression (promotion) or the award of Fellowship Higher Education Academy (HEA), with programme leadership used to make the case for both. Those rewarded and recognised for their programme leadership were the most confident in, and proud of, their standing in the learning community.

The institutional context the programme leader works within is integral to positive identity formation. In an institution where the role of the programme leader is recognised and rewarded, programme leaders might come to understand their education-focussed academic success as of comparable esteem to their research-focussed peers. Suitably graded job roles and opportunities for career progression based on the effective leadership of a programme of study signify institutional investment in and appreciation of programme leaders (Senior, Moron-Garcia & Lawrence, 2022).

Implications for the development of programme leaders' academic artistry and identity

The competence-based model for programme leadership offers a model for academic developers and HE leaders wishing to devise a comprehensive portfolio of socially mediated developmental activity that might nurture an individualised, situated, and therefore authentic academic artistry of programme leading and, in so doing, build for and with programme leaders a positive academic identity. The focus on experience and self-awareness allows specific, intangible, and authentic characteristics or artistry to emerge, be recognised by the individual, and, in the right context, celebrated or further developed, enabling the shift from discipline-based to an altogether more complex and nuanced academic identity based on fulfilling one of the most important roles in contemporary HE.

Practical, evidence-based ideas for developing programme leader artistry and identity

The following ideas draw on an evidence-based Manifesto for Sustainable Programme Leadership (Senior, Moron-Garcia & Lawrence, 2022) and the research presented here. They outline how we might facilitate the ontological turn from knowing about programme leading, that is, the processes and practices necessary to undertake the role, to being a programme leader, which we can understand as exercising expertise in programme leadership, working with agility to realise their responsibilities, and leading to academic artistry: adapting practices and processes ethically and with compassion for the good of the student, programme, and learning community.

Programme leader academic artistry might be nurtured through building the programme leader's deep, personal understanding of the high degree of academic artistry necessary to fulfil the role and the personal and professional rewards it might bring, rewards that are of comparable academic esteem as those available to research-focussed colleagues.

Facilitate connection and collaboration among programme leaders: the Manifesto for Sustainable Programme Leadership evidences the importance of "connection and collaboration" to programme leader development. Developmental activities are best built with and for community (O'Dwyer & Sanderson 2022; Scott & Lawrence, 2022) with a mind to a common purpose (Malone & Yorkstone, 2022) and co-designed with programme leaders (Petrova, 2022).

An effective community of programme leaders must sit within the discipline and draw upon the disciplinary identity and conventions, but at the same time placed within the wider university and higher education community (Ellis & Nimmo, 2018). This can be achieved through an integrated community of complementary formal and informal networks of peers (Scott & Lawrence, 2022), where programme leaders might reflect on their specific practice and learn from each other's experience.

Those that attend the central-formal programme leader network find the portfolio of activity useful to professional practice; one response to evaluation said it had "significantly improved my working life"; another recognised their increased efficiency is "good for my students". Most of the 60 (of 170) who regularly attend academic development events lead programmes that have enjoyed National Student Survey (NSS) uplift for "teaching on my course" from 2019 to 2022. Evidence of the sustained impact of support can be seen in NSS data pre and post these interventions (which began in April 2018). Note that in the given time scale satisfaction for teaching dropped across the sector by 5.56%, I cite the cross-disciplinary sector benchmark (BM) for comparison (Table 9.3).

Table 9.3 Impact of socially mediated academic development for programme leaders on programme NSS returns for "teaching on my course"

	2017 (BM = 85.5%)	2020 (BM = 84.33%)	2021 (BM = 79.82%)	2022 (BM = 79.94%)	Uplift
English	87.5%	94%	81%	92%	4.5%
Economics	79.5%	79%	89%	91%	11.5%

Instil deep understanding of the meaning of programme leading to the individual programme leader: "Expertise must consider critical reflection as a core skill" (Morantes-Africano, 2022, p. 40), opportunities must be presented for programme leaders to engage in "deliberate" (King, 2022b) and purposeful "critical evaluation of [our] ideas and experiences" (p. 40). Reflective practice can be nurtured within existing activities. The central-formal network aligned all activity to Descriptor 3 of the PSF (in 2018), raising the profile of Fellowship of the HEA. At the same time opportunities to reflect on individual practice were embedded in the schedule of network meetings. This saw an overall increase of 40% in applications for Senior Fellowship of the HEA (SFHEA): 27 of the 31 SFHEA awards made in 2019/20 were to programme leaders (this coincided with Fellowship being written into promotion criteria).

Reshape the prestige economy: recognise and reward programme leaders: As a whole university approach is necessary to developing teaching expertise (Gannaway, 2022) so too it is to that of programme leaders. This calls for a shift in organisational culture (Senior, Moron-Garcia & Lawrence, 2022): reshaping institutional structures (Forsyth & Powell, 2022) drawing on the programme leader's expertise and experience to create systems that are more humane (Lawrence, in review); defining (Maddock et al., 2022b), perhaps rethinking (Hamilton & Donaldson, 2022) the programme leader role to better reflect the high degree of expertise necessary to undertake it. Integral to this shift in organisational culture is the recognition of programme leaders' expertise and academic artistry. This recognition should be comparable to that afforded research-focussed peers, such as career progression or, for example, funding to lead enhancement projects (Maddock, Carruthers & van Haeringen, 2022a).

By raising the profile and standing of programme leaders an institution begins to reconfigure the prestige economy. The attributes that define belonging to HE's 'in-crowd' expand to include education-focussed academic practice, realised through the academic artistry of programme leading. The central-formal network at the host institution was often used by senior leaders to consult with programme leaders on change initiatives and recruit programme leaders to associated working groups. Here programme leaders used their expertise to make the systems and processes they must navigate more 'humane' (Lawrence, in review). Programme leaders gained experience and esteem useful to career progression and were promoted to: Associate Dean for Teaching and Learning; School Director of Teaching and Learning; Senior Lecturer; Reader and Head of Department.

Conclusion

Competence-based programme leading captures a means for understanding and developing the 'intangible characteristics' of the academic artistry inherent to effective programme leading, that is, the professional agility necessary to integrate disciplinary knowledge with institutional education strategy to design a distinct programme of study, navigate fractured university systems at pace, and steer dispersed and distracted programme teams to coherent commitment to the programme ethically, with compassion and authenticity. At the same time the model and suggested ideas open up opportunities for programme leaders to build a positive, personal, and therefore authentic professional identity 'the programme leader', which will afford greater confidence in leading within HE's prestige economy.

Key take-aways

1. Expertise in programme leadership is the effective discharge of the duties of the programme leader in a specific disciplinary and institutional yet ever-changing context.
2. The academic artistry of programme leadership is unique to the individual programme leader. It is the ethical and compassionate navigation of the role's responsibilities to the benefit or good of the programme, students, and learning community. This brings personal and professional reward to individual programme leaders.
3. Artistry can't necessarily be taught but it can be learned through connection, collaboration, and deepening programme leaders' understanding of the role's personal, professional, and social meaning.

Acknowledgement

Original research funded by Advance HE (GPG, no. 1296), and conducted with Professor Graham Scott at the University of Hull, who kindly gave his permission for primary data to be used here.

References

Advance HE (2023). Professional Standards Framework (PSF 2023). https://www.advance-he.ac.uk/teaching-and-learning/psf

Barnett, R. (2012). Learning for an unknown future. *Higher Education Research & Development*, 31(1), pp. 65–77. DOI:10.1080/07294360.2012.642841

Blackmore, P. & Kandiko, C.B. (2011). Motivation in academic life: a prestige economy. *Research in Post Compulsory Education*, 16(4), pp. 399–411. DOI:10.1080/13596748.2011.626971

Caddell, M., Ellis, S. Haddow, C. & Wilder-Davis, K. (2022). A national approach: foregrounding programme leadership in Scotland. In Lawrence, J., Morón-García, S. & Senior, R. (eds.), *Supporting Course and Programme Leaders: Practical Wisdom for Leaders, Educational Developers and Programme Leaders*. UK: Routledge.

Cooperrider, D. & Srivastva, S. (1987). Appreciative inquiry in organizational life. In Woodman, R.W. & Pasmore, W.A. (eds.), *Research in Organizational Change and Development*, Vol. 1, pp. 129–169. JAI Press.

Ellis, S. & Nimmo, A. (2018). Opening eyes and changing mind-sets: professional development for programme leaders. In Lawrence, J. & Ellis, S. (eds.), *Supporting Programme Leaders and Programme Leadership* (pp. 35–39). London: Staff and Educational Development Association, SEDA Special 39.

Forsyth, R. & Powell, S. (2022). Understanding and defining programme leadership in a large institution. In Lawrence, J., Morón-García, S. & Senior, R. (eds.) *Supporting Course and Programme Leaders: Practical Wisdom for Leaders, Educational Developers and Programme Leaders.* UK: Routledge.

Gannaway, D. (2022). A whole university approach to building expertise in higher education teaching. In King, H.(ed.) *Developing Expertise for Teaching in Higher Education: Practical Ideas for Professional Learning and Development.* London: Routledge.

Hamilton, J. & Donaldson, D. (2022). In pursuit of excellence: A collaborative and interdisciplinary framework for reconceptualising programme leaders. In Lawrence, J., Moron-Garcia, S. & Senior, R. (eds.) *Supporting Course and Programme Leaders in HE: Practical Wisdom for Leaders, Educational Developers and Programme Leaders.* UK: Routledge.

Hulme, J. A. (2022). Supporting and developing teaching-focussed individuals to professorial level: Career progression across boundaries. In Nutt, D. & Mackintosh, E. (eds.) *Studies in the Third Space: The Impact of the Integrated Practitioner in Higher Education.* UK: Routledge.

Huxley-Binns, R., Lawrence, J. & Scott, G. (2023). Competence-based HE: future proofing curricula. In Blessinger, P. & Sengupta, E. (eds.), *Integrative Curricula – A Multi-Dimensional Approach to Pedagogy.* UK: Emerald Publishing.

King, H. (2022a). *Developing Expertise for Teaching in Higher Education: Practical Ideas for Professional Learning and Development.* London: Routledge.

King, H. (2022b). Introduction: developing expertise in higher education. In King, H. (ed.) *Developing Expertise for Teaching in Higher Education: Practical Ideas for Professional Learning and Development.* London: Routledge.

King, H. (2022c). Professional learning for higher education teaching: an expertise perspective. In King, H. (ed.) *Developing Expertise for Teaching in Higher Education: Practical Ideas for Professional Learning and Development.* London: Routledge.

Lawrence, J. (2020). Assessing competencies could equip graduates for an uncertain post-covid future. *WonkHE blog,* https://wonkhe.com/blogs/assessing-competences-could-equip-graduates-for-an-uncertain-post-covid-future/

Lawrence, J. (2021). *Thriving on the Winds of Change: Repositioning Programme Leadership as a Career Thriller.* QAA Scotland Enhancement Theme: Resilient Learning Communities. https://www.enhancementthemes.ac.uk/docs/ethemes/resilient-learning-communities/thriving-on-the-winds-of-change.pdf?sfvrsn=57abd681_6

Lawrence, J. (in review). SoTL, Social Justice and Radical Compassion: academic development for transgression. *International Journal for Academic Development.*

Lawrence, J. & Ellis, S. (2018). *Supporting Programme Leaders and Programme Leadership.* London: Staff and Educational Development Association.

Lawrence, J. & Hall, G. (2019). Understanding the provision and perceived value of the academic and professional development practices of HE teachers in College Higher Education. *Journal of Post-Compulsory Education,* 23(4).

Lawrence, J. Moron-Garcia, S. & Senior, R. (2022). *Supporting Course and Programme Leaders in HE: Practical Wisdom for Leaders, Educational Developers and Programme Leaders.* UK: Routledge.

Lawrence, J., Moron-Garcia, S. & Senior, R. (2022a). Supporting Course and Programme Leaders in HE: positioning programme leadership as central to HE success. In Lawrence, J., Moron Garcia, S. & Senior, R. (eds.) *Supporting Course and Programme Leaders: Practical Wisdom for Leaders, Educational Developers and Programme Leaders.* UK: Routledge.

Lawrence, J. Morrell, L. & Scott, G. (2023). Building a competence-based model for the academic development of programme leaders. *International Journal of Academic Development.* DOI:10.1080/1360144X.2023.2166942

Lawrence, J. & Scott, G. (2022). *Competence-based Programme Directing.* London: Advance HE.

Maddock, L., Carruthers, S., & van Haeringen, K. (2022a). Developing programme leadership in an Australian University: An institutional approach to professional learning and development. In Lawrence, J., Moron-Garcia, S. and Senior, R. (eds.) *Supporting Course and Programme Leaders in HE: Practical Wisdom for Leaders, Educational Developers and Programme Leaders.* UK: Routledge.

Maddock, L., Curruthers, S., van Haeringen, K., Massa, H, & Love, C. (2022b). Developing a role statement for programme leadership. In Lawrence, J., Moron-Garcia, S. and Senior, R. (eds.) *Supporting Course and Programme Leaders in HE: Practical Wisdom for Leaders, Educational Developers and Programme Leaders.* UK: Routledge.

Malone E. & Yorkstone, S. (2022). Facilitating educational leadership: Building and sharing an understanding amongst the programme team. In Lawrence, J., Moron-Garcia, S. & Senior, R. (eds.) *Supporting Course and Programme Leaders in HE: Practical Wisdom for Leaders, Educational Developers and Programme Leaders.* UK: Routledge.

Morantes-Africano, L. (2022). Critical reflection as a tool to develop expertise in teaching in higher education. In King, H. (ed.) *Developing Expertise for Teaching in Higher Education: Practical Ideas for Professional Learning and Development.* London: Routledge, pp. 29–43.

Moore, S. (2022). Empowering programme leaders: Developing relational academic leadership. In Lawrence, J., Moron-Garcia, S. & Senior, R. (eds.) *Supporting Course and Programme Leaders in HE: Practical Wisdom for Leaders, Educational Developers and Programme Leaders.* UK: Routledge.

O'Dwyer, M. & Sanderson, R. (2022). It can be a lonely job sometimes: The use of collaborative space and social network theory in support of programme leaders. In Lawrence, J., Moron-Garcia, S. & Senior, R. (eds.) *Supporting Course and Programme Leaders in HE: Practical Wisdom for Leaders, Educational Developers and Programme Leaders.* UK: Routledge.

Parkin, D. (2017). *Leading Learning and Teaching in Higher Education. The Key Guide to Designing and Delivering Courses.* UK: Routledge

Parkin, D. (2022). Programme leaders as educational and academic leaders: A question of influence – relationships, behaviour and commitment. in Lawrence, J., Moron-Garcia, S. & Senior, R. (eds.) *Supporting Course and Programme Leaders in HE: Practical Wisdom for Leaders, Educational Developers and Programme Leaders.* UK: Routledge.

Petrova, P. (2022). A Collaborative and comprehensive approach to designing a cross-institutional development programme for programme leaders. In Lawrence, J., Moron-Garcia, S. & Senior, R. (eds.) *Supporting Course and Programme Leaders in HE: Practical Wisdom for Leaders, Educational Developers and Programme Leaders.* UK: Routledge.

Scott, G. & Lawrence, J. (2022). Harnessing the potential of formal networks and informal communities to support the holistic development of programme leaders in Lawrence, J., Moron Garcia, S. & Senior, R. (eds.) *Supporting Course and Programme Leaders: Practical Wisdom for Leaders, Educational Developers and Programme Leaders.* UK: Routledge.

Senior, R. (2018). The shape of programme leadership in the contemporary university. In Lawrence, J. & Ellis, S. (eds.) *Supporting Programme Leaders and Programme Leadership.* London: Staff & Educational Development Association.

Senior, R. Moron-Garcia S. & Lawrence, J. (2022). Celebrating Programme Leadership: A Manifesto for Sustainable Programme Leadership. In Lawrence, J., Moron Garcia, S. & Senior, R. (eds.) *Supporting Course and Programme Leaders: Practical Wisdom for Leaders, Educational Developers and Programme Leaders.* UK: Routledge.

Tajfel, H. & Turner, J. (1979). An integrative theory of inter group conflict. In Austin, W. & Worchil, S. (eds.) *The Social Psychology of Intergroup Relations* pp. 33–47. Monterey Books/Cole Publishing Company.

Turner, R. & Spowart, L. (2022). Reflective practice as a threshold concept in the development of pedagogical content knowledge. In King, H. (ed.), *Developing Expertise for Teaching in Higher Education.* London: SEDA Series, Routledge. DOI: 10.4324/9781003198772-12

Chapter 10

The many identities of a learning technologist (and how to make the most of them)

Evan Dickerson

What is a learning technologist?

The Association for Learning Technology (ALT), the professional association for those working in this space, defines learning technology as "the broad range of communication, information and related technologies that can be used to support learning, teaching and assessment" (ALT, 2010). The year 2023 marks the ALT's 30th anniversary which, of itself, indicates the maturity of the field, particularly in higher education.

There have been many attempts to define the work of those employed as learning technologists, such as Oliver (2002) and Vasant (2014). However Scott (2019) states that they are "people who are actively involved in understanding, managing, researching, supporting or enabling learning with the use of Learning Technology." ALT (2010) and Scott (2019) also point out that "you don't necessarily need to be called 'Learning Technologist' to be one".

That this remark holds true is easily reflected in an informally gathered survey of the job titles used in adverts for learning technology roles across the higher education sector, as observed in online adverts posted on the https://www.jobs.ac.uk/ website between 2019 and 2023 (Jobs.ac.uk, 2023). Job titles that regularly reoccurred included:

Academic IT Specialist/Technologist
Assistant Educational/Learning Technologist
Digital Education Developer/Support Analyst
Digital Learning Design/Developer/Manager/Technologist
Director of Online Learning
Educational Adviser/Developer (Technology Enhanced Learning)/Technologist/
    Technology Support Analyst
eLearning Adviser/Support Assistant/Support Officer/Technologist
Head of Digital Learning/Digital Teaching and Learning/eLearning/
    Learning Technology
Higher Education Adviser (Digital)
Instructional Designer/Learning Designer

DOI: 10.4324/9781003437826-13

Learning Enhancement and Technology Adviser
Learning Innovation Specialist
Learning Technologist (Accessibility/Artificial Intelligence/Lecture Recording/ Multimedia/Online Exams/Simulation)
Learning Technology Adviser/Assistant/Consultant/Officer/Services Manager
Lecturer (Blended Learning/Digital/Online Learning)
Senior Educational Technologist (Learning Designer/Digital Capabilities)
Senior Learning Technologist/Officer/Consultant
Service Desk Senior Adviser (Learning Technologies)
Technology Enhanced Learning Adviser/Senior Adviser/Officer/Materials Developer/Project Manager/Specialist
Researcher (Learning Technologies/Online Learning)

This list reveals a few different factors about the nature of learning technology roles. There are indeed a wide range of job titles associated with this area of professional services, and this is evident within both higher and further education. Also evident is the fact that roles exist at various levels of seniority. Furthermore, although a general learning technologist role is still reasonably common, it is probable that, particularly within larger universities, roles are appointed on a specialist and more focussed basis, either to support a specific remit (online or blended learning, for example), a specific technology (lecture recording, for example), or a specific aspect of the educational cycle (online exams, for example).

If one were to ask academic or senior management colleagues within a university what it is that a learning technologist contributes towards the support of teaching and the student experience, the responses might be narrowly focussed ones along the lines of: "they keep the VLE running", "they have helped integrate the VLE with other institutional systems such as student records", "they manage systems", "they help with induction and enrolment" or "they provide staff development so the academics can use technology platforms more effectively". Each of these responses I have anecdotally encountered in conversations with colleagues. Larger institutions are likely to appoint postholders in the listed roles to fulfil these functions; smaller institutions might well have one or more staff covering more than one aspect of a learning technologist's function. However, learning technologists are likely to have a much wider skill set and experience than at first may be apparent. Although some learning technologists have worked solely in the field, many – and particularly those with more experience – have wider skill sets and experience of working in higher education that can be drawn upon.

Were I to situate the learning technologist within a framework of organisational roles, I would suggest that they can exemplify the cross-boundary third space professional as defined by Whitchurch (2013, frontispiece), given that the nature of a learning technologist's work and remit can "be a safe haven for experimentation and creativity, and also a risky space in which there is likely to be contestation and uncertainty" in supporting teaching and assessment activities through the use of technology. It is this chapter's contestation that a failure to utilise the full range of skills and experience that a learning technologist or team of professionals in this field might possess is short-changing the educational experience for management, administrators, academics, and students within any university or college. Every learning technologist brings to their role a unique combination of personal and professional experiences, skill sets, and knowledge.

Lenses on 'identity' and 'becoming'

To help me understand more about my role and reflect upon my own lived experience as someone working in the higher education sector today, I have found two lenses particularly helpful:

Auto-ethnography. This reflexive lens articulates my unique journey to my present position, elaborating on some of the details and teasing out latent skillsets and hidden experience that are often worth acknowledging and making use of in a professional context. What can this tell me about myself and the role I now occupy?

The 'squiggly career'. During the COVID-19 pandemic, whilst I was in a highly pressured role as a head of service at a large research-intensive university, I read Tupper and Ellis (2020). Having gradually climbed the career ladder, I found myself re-evaluating what I thought was important in a role and made the decision not to pursue a 'status' position thereafter, but rather to work somewhere where I felt I would have relevant interests and agency and be able to offer more through taking the opportunities, often unwritten on a job description, that an apparently lower profile role might present me with. I also strongly felt that a role which necessitated contact with end users and hands-on work with learning technologies would once again give my role some much needed authenticity in the field.

A career journey to and within learning technology

During the early years of my career as a part time lecturer I was fortunate enough to be mentored by a learning technologist and have my teaching practice nudged towards the field of blended delivery. After she left to take up a post at another university and I was appointed as her successor to cover the learning technology role on a part-time basis alongside my teaching contract, I then seriously considered learning technology as a career path, which I have now followed in a variety of roles and forms for over 23 years.

During my learning technology career, I have been tasked with a wide range of activities that fall within the remit of the role at varying levels of seniority. These can fall into particular groups; however, it is important to realise that there are aspects of identity traits that are often relied upon and connect the various groups in subtle ways. These include evidence-based curated examples of practice and personal experience of having been an online student and teacher. Credibility and collaboration are the golden threads that run throughout a learning technologist's work and are likely key to sustaining a career at any level of operation.

In discussing the following various aspects, I will reference activities undertaken within my current role at Guildhall School of Music & Drama. From discussions with learning technology peers working in the performing arts conservatoire sector, it is apparent that we often work in small teams or, like myself, as the only post-holder within an institution. Sometimes we are based within a teaching and learning department, but not every conservatoire has such a department with educational developers and others in post. I am based within Guildhall's Library and Learning Resources team, as this is within the Student Experience Directorate. I see that my role and function is to complement the skill sets of my immediate team of colleagues and wider colleagues. Thus, I work closely with staff at all levels across the institution including the Head of Library and Learning Resources, Dean of Student Affairs, Associate Dean of Teaching and Learning, plus other Senior Management Team members including the Registrar and the wider team, Course Directors, Academics, Administrators, and IT staff including the Head of Business Systems, who is the budget holder for learning technology within the School. My multiplicity of roles requires:

- **Technological expertise**: this includes the piloting, rollout, and ongoing support of various technologies including virtual learning environments (e.g., Moodle, Blackboard, and Canvas), ePortfolio platforms (e.g., Mahara, MyProgress, or PebblePad), lecture capture systems (e.g., Planet eStream, Echo360, or Panopto), audience response systems (e.g., Mentimeter), or services to assess the authenticity of student submissions (e.g., Turnitin). Often, these technologies and others such as cloud storage require integration with each other or external systems, such as the institutional student records system, to effectively operate as a joined-up ecosystem.
- **Pedagogic expertise**: hands-on experience teaching in face-to-face, wholly online, blended or hyflex settings. Knowing how the use of specific technologies can be used effectively to facilitate teaching, learning, and assessments is key to the work of any learning technologist. Usually this practical knowledge of practical application is backed up by knowledge of the theories of specific pedagogical approaches and the ability to reference key thinkers and texts that provide an underpinning to the collaborative solution to be created. In smaller institutions, a learning technologist can be required to input pedagogic expertise by acting as a de-facto materials developer, educational developer, or academic developer (or a combination of all three roles, which would normally be undertaken by specialists

in larger universities). Ideally, the training function a learning technologist fulfils delivers both technological expertise and pedagogic knowledge.
- **Problem solving and investigative abilities**: a lot of a learning technologist's time is spent problem solving on behalf of the staff/students that are at the institution. Be it understanding a ticket requesting immediate support regarding a problem or understanding the needs of a larger project so that alternative solutions can be offered with their various pros and cons, enablers, and blockers, a learning technologist needs to investigate and offer viable, scalable solutions that not only are technically possible, but also are pedagogically applicable to the envisaged scenario of use. Inevitably, emerging agendas and topics in digital learning, that is, the growing use of Artificial Intelligence by students and the impact upon assessment and feedback practices, demand significant amounts of my own research time and form much of my own continuing professional development so that I can influence institutional thinking around the issues and technologies concerned within formal settings such as the Digital Strategy Group and the Programme Leaders Group.
- **Strategic thinking and awareness**: I am the service owner for the virtual learning environment and the e-portfolio system. I have had significant input to School's Teaching and Learning Enhancement Strategy with regard to digital learning; I am responsible for maintaining strategic oversight and actioning the relevant priorities within the strategy and reporting on progress against those priorities, all the time maintaining support at a grass-roots level for all staff and students. One major output to date has focussed on baseline standards for digital learning provision, which all modules should adhere to. These are designed to ensure that every student is provided with an equitable, accessible, and pedagogically robust supported learning, assessment, and feedback experience. I have contributed papers to Academic Board (e.g., regarding assessment and feedback practices or the Office for Students Enquiry into Blended Learning). I routinely contribute reports to re-validation boards regarding the use of digital learning and the future plans for use that programmes have. Learning technologists at larger institutions will be the service owners for a bigger suite of technologies. Heads of service need to have an overview of the learning technology requirements for the whole institution, ensure adequate resourcing for licence and support staff, ensure that staff development delivery meets institutional requirements, and so forth.
- **People skills and networking**: these are ever-present tools in a successful learning technologist's professional arsenal. Whether it be a careful response to a technophobe colleague or student, or judiciously used to foster student and staff engagement with technologies, a learning technologist's presentation and human interaction skills are almost always in evidence. Tact and diplomacy are essential elements, particularly when implementing service changes or projects that require effective cross-organisational working.

- **Delivering added value for the institution through subsidiary interests, skills, and knowledge**: whilst these can often enrich what we bring to the table as practicing professionals, sometimes there is the difficulty of getting these aspects of our identities recognised and accepted by colleagues. Over the years I have been a materials developer for specific projects and an instructional designer for specific programmes or modules. However, both these areas of activity are not within my specialist knowledge, although I know and can apply the frameworks used by colleagues who specialise in these areas of expertise. Through my personal professional network, I have contacts that I can informally consult in these areas should I need to.

I also make significant contributions to the professional development activities at the School that are outside of my official job description, but they serve to illustrate the added value that I bring to my role. I fulfil the remit of an educational developer as best I can when needed and am working on staff development concerning learning design as there is a small but growing level of interest in this. I mentor applicants through the School's accredited Advance HE Fellowship scheme at both Fellow and Senior Fellow level. Externally, I raise the School's profile and represent the conservatoire sector by being on the steering groups of the national Heads of eLearning Forum and the Association for Learning Technology M25 London Learning Technology network. My wider sector involvement is reflected through frequent conference or online presentations annually on digital learning, or by being a reviewer for Advance HE's CATE scheme in 2022 and 2023. I am a peer reviewer on digital learning for publications including the *Journal of Learning Development in Higher Education*.

Alongside my work, I have studied piano and singing in the past, although I do not perform publically. I am an acknowledged UK authority on the life and work of the Romanian composer and violinist George Enescu. I write programme notes on his music and wider repertoire for the London Philharmonic Orchestra, venues including Wigmore Hall, and various music festivals. I have been interviewed on Romanian radio and written feature articles and recording reviews for leading publications including *Fanfare* (USA) and *Gramophone*. Whilst this might not have a direct bearing on my learning technology work, it is useful in my current role to help gain agency and form working relationships with a large proportion of colleagues, as I can authentically demonstrate an interest in their discipline and have an understanding of the pedagogic approaches they employ.

The learning technologist's role and workflow within the academic lifecycle conceptualised in artistic terms

Having established that collaboration is a key thread in the professional working success of a learning technologist in an academic environment, it is important to note that this is also central to all creative disciplines. No performer, unless an artist performing a solo or reciting a monologue, ever practices their art in isolation; in fact, even then it should be said that their collaboration is with the composer or writer whose work is being performed. When establishing a learning technology presence or introducing a new system or service within an institution, the learning technologist collaborates with the early adopter academics and others who are willing to work with him/her to make the project a success. Thus, any specific project or innovation that involves learning technology might be similar to a violin and piano duo recital, let's say. The academic plays the leading violin part to an audience of students, whilst the learning technologist takes the role of piano accompanist; always present, but often with discretion, only coming to the fore when particular input or assistance is needed to keep the composition, teaching, or assessment activity moving forward as planned.

It is possible to take the performance analogy further still. As pointed out earlier, a learning technologist may fulfil several functions within a smaller organisation, whereas a larger organisation may have a team of specialist learning technologists and allied professionals at its disposal. Whatever the academic context, the learning technologist will bring an individual mix of pedagogical, technical, and other skills to the table. Thus, it is possible to see how and why a learning technologist needs to understand every side of the rationale for use regarding any technology they support: what the academic wants to achieve pedagogically, why and how the students will benefit as a result of using the particular technological solution. The learning technologist's role is to understand the functional capabilities of the platform, work through the scenarios of use with the collaborating colleagues, advise of the pros and cons of each potential scenario of use, and, once a decision has been made regarding the preferred method and rationale of use to best fit the pedagogic requirements, to then facilitate the implementation so those benefits are realised as intended. One could visualise the learning technologist as an ensemble player within a group for each project, having mastery of his/her own role and part. Mastering the part may be conceived as akin to learning a musical score or a play text, so that one is fully prepared for every stage of an activity that needs to be performed, be this the annual rollover of Moodle sites or providing training to a group or academics, for example. As the rollout of technologies become more widespread, collaborations with different departments and stakeholders grow, so the learning technologist often becomes a key participant in parallel projects, keeping several streams of work in play simultaneously. Take the analogy to its logical conclusion in a large university, and a head of service learning technologist is akin to the conductor of an orchestra, who alone possesses knowledge of every department's or instrument's requirements, how these fit alongside other requirements, and how they work together as a whole across a multi-term academic year, which may be thought of as a symphony in three movements.

Spotlight on the Postgraduate Certificate in Performance Teaching at Guildhall School of Music & Drama

The Postgraduate Certificate in Performance Teaching is an example of collaborative working that benefits both the staff and student experiences and illustrates how a learning technologist can support creative pedagogic delivery. The Postgraduate Certificate is the only wholly online award-bearing programme that is currently offered at the Guildhall School of Music & Drama.

As a learning technologist, my approach to supporting the programme team reflects that which I try to offer all teaching teams. I provide the programme team hands-on support throughout the academic year. At peak usage times, such as the start of the year, during key assignment submission periods, and the setup period for a new academic year, this contact can mean almost daily contact with members of the teaching team. Upon joining Guildhall, I quickly established my prior experience in delivering and supporting similar programmes at other universities. From this, an open and discursive relationship between myself and my colleagues developed that was responsive to their needs and proactive in suggesting improvements or tweaks to the models online and the tools used. Together the course team and I maintain a strong, student-first approach. As benefits a programme specifically of this nature and discipline focus, student creativity in their presentations and other collaborative activities is encouraged. Learning content and the other supportive materials provided are both created by the course team and curated from other sources as needed, often with the help of the library team. To help bring about a culture of reflection regarding the use of technology to support the educational experience, I attend the programme's annual away day to hear their experiences, discuss and prioritise potential improvements, and discuss any changes to teaching practice and innovations for the coming year.

Evidence of the impact that the close working relationship between the programme team and myself has had to date is reflected in the detailed use of Moodle for the programme. There have been impacts upon the professional practice of colleagues, as evidenced by this feedback from one lecturer:

> What I really value about working with you is that you are a techie and an online pedagogy expert (maybe pedagogy expert in general). Because of this I feel that you understand where I am coming from regarding a vision for the students' high quality learning experience. The shared language of pedagogy/andragogy makes it possible for us to work really well together. You gently coaxing and extending my knowledge of the technology and me not feeling like my aims for the student's learning experience are being thwarted by the affordances of the tech but rather that you will support me in exploring what is possible. This feels creative, collaborative and also like really personalised support. Especially in the performing arts, that

recognition of creativity in the process is really inspiring. … Furthermore, I enjoy creating and am motivated by it so that I think a lot of how you approach your role has influenced my enthusiasm for using technology to enhance teaching. In terms of your skillset, you communicate collaboratively so I don't need to worry if a question is too silly (I really value that). You share valuable and fascinating resources at pertinent times. You offer feedback really well. I get a sense that there is some sort of similarity in our work ethic too, and I really value your patient, speedy yet thoughtful communications. Working with you makes my practice better but also makes the process enjoyable!

At a programme level, the External Examiner has observed that:

[The use of] Moodle is even better [than before]; love the overall navigability and structure; easy connections [are/can be made] between micro/macro programme levels; Moodle use on a level with best established distance learning programmes in terms of quality.

Further evidence of the successful model of VLE usage employed by the Postgraduate Certificate Programme is found in the fact the course team are currently exploring the possibilities for expanding the use of Moodle to encompass both the onboarding of new students over the summer prior to the formal course start date and the creation of an online community of practice to allow the sharing of ideas and opportunities for collaboration post-graduation. From the 2023–24 academic year, the Postgraduate Research Programme at Guildhall School of Music & Drama adopted a similar multi-site approach that was developed and created as a staff–student collaborative initiative.

Tips to make the most of a learning technologist in your setting

By way of a conclusion, I will draw together several of the threads that run through this chapter to present tips that I have experienced working in practice to suggest how the skill sets of a learning technologist might be better utilised in any educational setting.

These tips are generic in their nature and are not mutually exclusive. They could or should be combined as needed to drive the engagement of learning technologists across all levels of any university or college. Each tip is expanded upon by some thoughts on how the tip could be put into action, which are intended as prompts only. A starting point for which of the following might have most impact in your setting might be to identify any overlaps between gaps in current practice, strategic objectives, and opportunities to evidence the benefits of a shift-change in practice.

- **Do not assume experience and/or skills from a job title**: get to know and fully understand the skills, interests, and prior experience of any learning technologists within your educational setting. Start a dialogue with them or their managers about what they could do to help you improve the quality of your digitally delivered teaching, the resources needed to achieve this, and any other factors that could be relevant.
- **Play to their strengths, interests, and skillsets, as well as yours**: this follows as a consequence of the preceding point. It can also be useful to identify any skills or experience gaps you might have in your learning technology teams when strategically planning future initiatives and work to recruit, upskill, or retrain as necessary to be better able to meet future support and service needs for teachers and students.
- **Get involved early**: early involvement of learning technologists in any project or change in practice, ideally in partnership with educational developers and others, if they are in post, can lead to a better end result. Revisions or reworking because of technological limitations is made less likely than if you began the project without their input. Learning technologists will gain a holistic understanding of the project from the start and, thus, why specifics are seen as important to success.
- **Hunt out opportunities for collaboration**: opportunities could include project-based secondments, joint working parties, or the co-authoring of conference papers or presentations based upon your practice.
- **Get digital learning on your departmental or School agendas**: invite learning technologists to meetings so they are visible and connected with those they support. Ask that they present regular service updates and hear your views and feedback to improve services and the user experience.
- **Involve the Students' Union (SU)**: establish contacts between the SU and learning technologists to hear the student voice in/formally. The SU can be an effective ally for disseminating information about service improvements to students.
- **Learning technologists' support can be proactive**: don't just get in touch with your learning technologist when you have a problem. Instead, be inquisitive and ask their opinions on your practice and how this could be improved. Grow a culture of regular and frequent proactive contact that links pedagogic improvement with technological use.
- **Draw upon learning technologists' networks to bring the outside in**: learning technologists often network with their peers in other institutions, meaning they can have knowledge of practice within other providers. Knowing what has or has not worked elsewhere is valuable knowledge to be directly applied in your own setting or it can be used to influence the development of bespoke local solutions or support.
- **Delivering extra value for the institution**: particularly relevant in smaller specialist institutions, how can a learning technologist be encouraged, empowered, and upskilled (if necessary) to deliver more for the institution?

For example, might they help deliver aspects of a Postgraduate Certificate or other teaching-focussed programme or mentor/referee Advance HE recognition applications where learning technology forms a significant component? In return, could they be encouraged and supported to gain relevant qualifications and external awards (e.g., S/CMALT) and have CPD time in order to gain them, which would reinforce their professional standing and identity as well as reflect well upon the institution?

Key take-aways

- The role of 'learning technologist' is well established in higher education and offers a valuable contribution to the enhancement of learning and teaching.
- In many cases, learning technologists have a multiplicity of roles and expertise (whatever their job title might imply).
- Colleagues are encouraged to make the most of their local learning technologist(s) and work collaboratively with them and other professional services.

References

Association for Learning Technology (2010). *About Us.* https://www.alt.ac.uk/about-alt

Jobs.ac.uk (2023). *Search for 'learning technologist' job roles.* https://www.jobs.ac.uk/search/?keywords=learning+technologist&location=

Oliver, M. (2002). What Do Learning Technologists Do? *Innovations in Education and Training International,* 39(4), pp. 245–252. DOI:10.1080/13558000210161089

Scott, D. (2019). *What Makes a Learning Technologist?* Part 1 of 4: Job titles. https://altc.alt.ac.uk/blog/2019/09/what-makes-a-learning-technologist-part-1-of-4-job-titles/

Tupper, H. & Ellis, S. (2020). *The Squiggly Career: Ditch the Ladder, Discover Opportunity, Design Your Career.* London: Penguin Business.

Vasant, S. (2014). *What Is a Learning Technologist.* https://blog.jobs.ac.uk/education/teaching-learning/what-is-a-learning-technologist/

Whitchurch, C. (2013). *Reconstructing Identities in Higher Education: The Rise of 'Third Space' Professionals.* New York, NY: Routledge.

Part III

Developing the artistry of teaching

Chapter 11

Developing the artistry of teaching and approaches to learning

What we can learn from those teaching theatre improvisation

Petia Petrova, Shaun Mudd, Imogen Palmer, and Stephen Brown

Introduction: context and reasons for creating the programme

The COVID-19 Pandemic brought many challenges for the University of the West of England, UK (UWE). Like many other universities across the world, we experienced the rapid switch to online teaching. This was then followed by maintaining online teaching for an extended period. Academics had to consider effective means of engaging students online, and later, of re-engaging students in the physical classroom. In some circumstances, academics were engaging students in the physical classroom for the first time – students who up to that point had only experienced online teaching at university level. Post-COVID, attendance rates have dropped down considerably across the sector (Williams, 2022) and academics at UWE frequently reported similar experiences.

The pandemic put a spotlight on areas of teaching practice that have always been important but were now called to attention. It has surfaced the importance of creating open, engaging, and inclusive spaces that enable and encourage students to actively participate in the learning process. Academics quickly realised that they needed to develop and deploy a repertoire of strategies which can work both online and in face-to-face learning.

The pandemic also challenged students' mental health and feelings of connection and belonging. The emotional difficulties experienced by many in the higher education (HE) community throughout the pandemic has led to sustained interest in the emotional impact of teaching. Now there is renewed vigour behind work on "compassionate pedagogies" (Hao, 2011) and "humanising teaching" (Pacansky-Brock et al., 2020). Care and empathy in the classroom have become necessary. Creativity has become inevitable.

At UWE, the Academic Practice Directorate focussed on supporting staff across the institution to deliver effective teaching, learning, and student support. Our key question throughout the pandemic was: "How do we actively

DOI: 10.4324/9781003437826-15

support the development of staff teaching practices so that they are better able to respond to the challenges of the moment?" We were working in an unprecedented environment, facing new problems and challenges. We needed new solutions, both in the classroom and in the way we support those who teach. Many colleagues, including some highly experienced teachers, reported that they struggled with required adaptions to their teaching. Teachers who took a more expertise-based approach to practice and development (aligning to adaptive expertise and progressive problem solving) generally found it easier to move to online teaching at the start of the pandemic (King, 2022d, p. 163; on progressive problem solving: Dreyfus & Dreyfus, 1982; on adaptive expertise: Bale, 2022). This was mirrored by students who needed to employ extensive flexibility in their learning. Flexibility and adaptivity seemed to be key. This resonated with the idea of adopting an improvisational approach to teaching and learning.

This chapter examines the approach to, and impact of, an eight-part programme titled "Improvisation Skills for Teaching" (IST). The programme focuses on UWE staff experiencing, reflecting upon, and incorporating into their own practice a range of teaching tools and techniques from the theatre arts and from teaching improvisation. It was created in April 2021, as a response to the pandemic and the context outlined here, but its success and impact appears set to outlive the pandemic with staff demand for this course and evaluations remaining strong. To date (October 2023), 646 workshop attendances have been registered, reaching 311 staff. The programme initially focussed on online learning, given corresponding adaptions to teaching during the pandemic, and was delivered online to model these activities more authentically. But the activities are easily adapted to in-person, and we have subsequently broadened our scope to focus equally on online and face-to-face formats.

This chapter provides a case study which contributes to the evidence-based discourse on the importance of the artistry of teaching to the development of teaching expertise (King, 2022a). It examines the underlying principles of the design of the IST programme at UWE, and what has been learnt from its implementation to date. Our reflections will be supported by findings of an evaluative study into the impact of this programme on UWE staff.

Overview of the programme

The IST programme focuses on developing staff expertise in learning and teaching by focusing on the artistry of teaching as defined by King's model of expertise in teaching in HE: "artistry relates to aspects of performance such as being authentic to oneself, engaging an audience and improvisation" (King, 2022c, p. 22). Making connections with others, promoting human interaction, authenticity, adaption, and so on; this plethora of intangible elements is what the IST programme is about. It is about guiding HE teachers to focus on their voice, performance, improvisation, and the creation of effective interpersonal relationships in their learning contexts. We offer tangible tools and techniques for participants to take away and adapt.

Our philosophy at the inception of this programme aligned to recent observations in the sector and one of the central themes of this current book: that the artistry of teaching has often been neglected in formal HE educational development initiatives, but it is possible for artistry to be nurtured in this way (King, 2022c). It prominently features explicit considerations of the relational and emotional aspect of teaching. This aligns to the views of Gravett and Winstone (2020), who shortly before the pandemic argued the importance of relational pedagogies in HE and of creating meaningful connections with learners. The programme addresses how to foster two-way interaction and surfaces explicitly the concept of emotions in the classroom. It acknowledges that for students to be open to learning, they need to be taught in emotionally safe environments.

The mantra of the IST programme is articulated well by one of the facilitators (Stephen Brown) in the first session: "We are not here to teach you how to teach. These are just tools for your toolbelt". The workshops are therefore a space to share expertise, ideas, and practice. The facilitators bring with them several key concepts which they explore together with the participants. These key concepts are summarised in Figure 11.1.

The programme comprises three main parts, each addressing a key question.

Workshops 1–3: Creating a Positive Learning Environment			Workshops 4–6: Your Voice, Presence, and Authenticity		
Happy fail	Leap and discover	Resilience	Enthusiasm	Authenticity	Breathing and body language
Creative facilitation	Bravery	Active support	Acceptance	Play	Adaptability
Teacher-learner partnership	Collaborative learning	Active listening	Being present	Being relaxed	Being authentic
	Empathy	Gathering feedback	Caring about what you are talking about	Listening to the audience	
Workshop 7: Coaching Workshop on Applying the above Improvisational Concepts and Tools to Teaching			Workshop 8: Coaching Workshop on Applying the above Improvisational Concepts and Tools to Teaching		

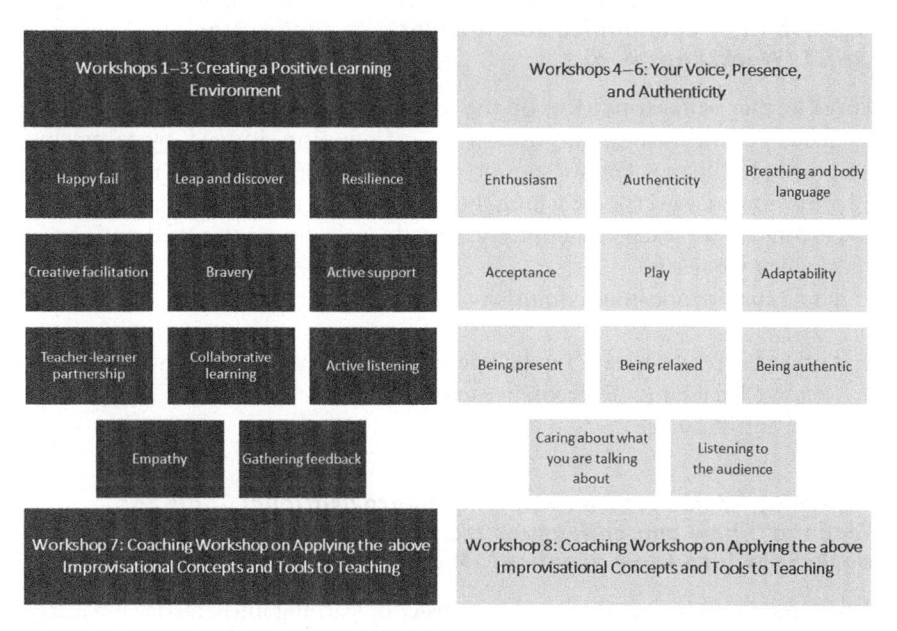

Figure 11.1 Key concepts from improvised theatre featuring in the IST Programme

'Creating a Positive Learning Environment': how can colleagues improve student engagement and participation? (Workshops 1–3)

These first three workshops focus on the student. They centre on creating inclusive emotional space in the HE classroom for both the teacher and the student. We engage staff as learners; they experience and reflect upon the (emotional) impact of classroom activities and consider which activities they may adopt and adapt to their own teaching practice. The activities modelled are designed to create an open, inclusive, and engaging classroom atmosphere, where students are helped to discover what supporting their peers looks and feels like. Perfectionism is actively discouraged and bravery encouraged. These activities emphasise that failure can be a tremendous learning opportunity for all, challenging us to re-examine familiar and long-established approaches to teaching and learning.

These three workshops comprise:

1. Building Rapport (Bravery and Resilience)
2. Collaborative Learning Environments (Acceptance and Support)
3. Facilitating Meaningful Interactions between Learners (Listening and Responding)

'Your Voice, Presence, and Authenticity': how can colleagues apply lessons from improvisation and acting to improve their communication, delivery, or facilitation skills? (Workshops 4–6)

Three further workshops focus on the teacher. They centre on supporting staff to challenge their own predisposition to perfectionism. Instead, by embracing the concept of 'happy fail' we support staff to develop both 'performative' and 'identity'-based aspects of teaching: how do we look after, and strengthen, our voice; how do we teach authentically; how do we cultivate our 'authentic presence' when we teach?

These three workshops comprise:

4. Authentic Teaching and Public Speaking (Authenticity and Enthusiasm)
5. Creative Facilitation (Acceptance and Play)
6. Voice and Presence

'Coaching Workshops on Applying Improvisational Tools to Teaching': how can colleagues transfer learning from these workshops into their practice? (Workshops 7–8)

This programme acknowledges that transfer of learning into practice is a learning process in itself (Eraut, 2009). The programme concludes with two coaching workshops, each aligning to one of the two earlier sections of the programme. They facilitate the transfer of learning from the previous six workshops into each participant's individual context and practice. These coaching workshops therefore enable deeper enhancement of pedagogic content knowledge (Shulman, 1986) within the context of the artistry of teaching.

Evaluation of the programme and its impact

Launching the programme, we were not sure what to expect in terms of staff interest. The programme was immediately successful, and this success has been sustained to date. This is evidenced through sizable appetite and attendance numbers (despite being elective CPD), generating long waiting lists as well as consistently positive participant feedback.

This section outlines key findings from our evaluation of the programme. Participants regularly provided evaluative feedback via surveys after each individual workshop. Three participant focus groups were also conducted in September 2022 to explore in more depth the impact on participants' practice.

Preconceptions

This programme seemed unusual to participants in terms both of focus and style. It appeared to fundamentally challenge their preconceptions of learning, modelling the approaches it proposes, and encouraging critical exploration and deep reflection. Participant feedback repeatedly notes that they felt like they were stepping into the unknown when they signed up to these workshops. Feedback also regularly reports that the workshops opened participants' thinking about what it means to be a 'good' teacher; combatting the pervasive culture of perfectionism, excellence, and inherent competitiveness in the sector where all aim to get the better grade, the higher accolade.

> It was a wonderful light relief and way of learning, as well as I just found it quite empowering as me as a teacher, and making me challenge my preconceptions, potentially. So yeah, just gave me permission, I think, to explore.
> (Participant focus group comment)

King (2022c, p. 16) argues that experts "will have a deeper conceptual understanding based on principles." This programme aims to promote expertise through exploring new and familiar concepts in deeply reflective ways. This allows for meaningful engagement and reflection on participants' own concepts and assumptions about teaching.

An example of this is how in educational development we often focus mechanically on session planning. Yet it can be seen as a pointless, mechanistic requirement for staff, perhaps jettisoned as one becomes more experienced. One experienced HE teacher in the focus groups articulated reflection which juxtaposed planning in teaching with preconceptions on improv, and provided a convincing case for a mode of planning in advance:

> I think what I've learned from the process is that these [improvisational] activities are not really about how I can do things impromptu, but how I can plan them into it [a session]. And so it's been a little bit of a mind shift so that even though it's called improv, it's really planned activities. And so as I'm beginning now with getting ready to deliver the next [subject] sessions, I'm beginning to think: OK, so what could I do to plan in and some of these activities?

Practical tools and techniques

In the authors' own experiences, educational development interventions in UK HE have generally tended to underestimate or underplay the importance of exploring (and training staff on how to use) specific teaching techniques and tools (an exception is around digital tools, which more commonly receive this focus). As a discipline, we have tended to focus more heavily on 'teaching someone to fish' (i.e., developing skills to aid their long-term development, e.g., reflective practice), rather than simply 'giving them a few fish' (i.e., giving them some ready-made activities, tools, and techniques to take and use immediately). Both are, of course, important, but we argue that HE teachers need a significant number of tools in their toolkit to form a foundation of their practice. Staff can then draw on these tools in appropriate contexts that challenge their approach and require higher-order thinking (e.g., to pivot, improvise, respond, etc.). Hence, in terms of expertise, having a good grasp of tools and activities can lead to greater automation of tasks, increased capability to apply them to different contexts, and being able to reflect more deeply on their use. This can facilitate staff engaging more deeply in practices characteristic of the expert teacher, such as adaptive expertise (Bale, 2022), reflection in action (Schön, 1991), and progressive problem solving (Dreyfus & Dreyfus, 1982).

Participants in the focus groups validated this argument by voicing that the IST programme seemed to be filling a gap, both for novice and experienced HE teachers. Several stated they were unaware of other development activities which focussed on practical tools and techniques for teaching in this way. Participants also noted that the practical focus was indeed a key motivating factor for staff to engage with the workshops. For instance, one focus group participant summarised their group's consensus:

> Like most of you, I thought I needed practical knowledge, practical skills. I knew what do to but I didn't know how to do it. So I thought it [the IST programme] was going to be very useful, and indeed it was. It was, in the sense that I learned very specific skills, techniques, how to use them.

Our post-workshop evaluation identified four key themes which participants found especially useful and impactful:

1. The practical tools, ideas, and techniques;
2. The focus on student engagement and building rapport;
3. Techniques to aid voice, presence, and practice;
4. Support for online delivery.

These seemed to be themes with limited focus in other professional development initiatives at UWE (the first three) or (as in the case of online delivery during covid) in high demand. Words such as "techniques", "tools", and "activities" also feature prominently in the feedback (see Figure 11.2).

Educational development initiatives should therefore not shy away from demonstrating (and even 'teaching') key teaching techniques. Indeed, experience on the IST programme shows it is possible to do this whilst also introducing more complex concepts and whilst learners engage in criticality and creativity.

Workbooks

The workshops centre on a series of practical activities that model key concepts which participants might take away to use with their own students or colleagues. To support this, detailed workbooks are given to participants at each workshop. Key details of activities, tools, and techniques are summarised in the workbook for the participant's future reference. The workbooks also double as reflective notebooks. Space is provided against each activity for participants to write their own reflections and to jot down how they may adapt and adopt it in their own practice. An example is captured in Figure 11.3.

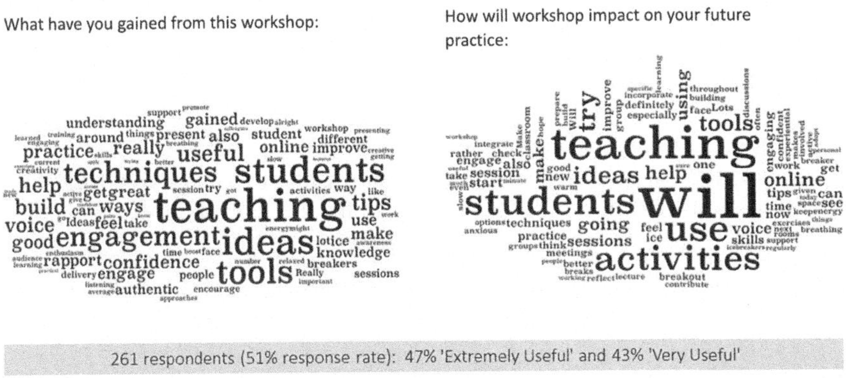

Figure 11.2 Word clouds showing common words from the IST Programme's end-of-workshop participant feedback forms

BRISTOL IMPROV THEATRE WORKBOOK - BUILDING RAPPORT ONLINE

VOLUNTEER

USEFUL FOR...
Building Rapport, Reflecting on personal style

This exercise helps to build empathy, bravery and support around getting involved in learning.

RUNDOWN

- Explain that we are going to demonstrate an exercise. For this demonstration you will need a brave volunteer. Can anyone stick their hand up?
- Wait until someone volunteers. If no one volunteers, pick someone and explain it will be really short and simple.
- Ask the volunteer to introduce themselves and then give a bow and everyone will applaud them
- This process can be repeated a few times
- Ask the group: How did you feel when I asked for a volunteer? What stopped you from getting up? How did you feel when someone volunteered?

PRACTICALITIES

- Recommended for groups of 6+

TIPS

- Can be fun to do at the beginning of a course or with a new cohort of learners

VARIATIONS

- If it is a small group, you can invite each person to 'volunteer' one by one, say their name and receive a round of applause. This helps cultivate a space where we celebrate bravery.

Figure 11.3 Excerpt from the workbook for the IST Programme's Workshop 1 (Building Rapport: Bravery and Resilience)

The workbooks reflect the practical focus of the workshops. They enable staff not only to have a reference point during activities in the workshop, but also in their future practice. The focus groups emphasised how useful participants found these workbooks:

"I'm also a lover of having resources. So, you know, the idea of having a book [of these worksheets] as a toolkit that I can go to and know that I've got, you know, selection of things that I can use as icebreakers ... for me will be invaluable."

"There is a whole, like the book [of workshop worksheets] [...]. They're all listed there brilliantly, so it's a great resource."

Bravery and safe spaces

It is important to think about creating psychologically safe environments for both students and teachers in HE. This requires explicit effort by both parties and interventions to promote bravery and limit judgement. King (2022b, 2022d) highlights the importance of care and empathy and community and collaboration between students and between students and their teachers. This is teaching practice motivated by curiosity, community, and care (King, 2022d, p. 171). It is aided by developing a shared understanding of what it is to support others in this learning context, with teachers supporting students, students supporting each other, and so on.

This is mirrored by the ethos of improvisation. Effective improvisation requires high levels of attention by and towards all present, and this aligns to commonly stated priorities in effective teaching such as active listening. It requires developing and employing new techniques; trying ... and likely failing on occasion. It necessitates a shared space of bravery and safety. Only then can a group be in a place ready to improvise; for each individual to bring others along, and to respond to others.

The IST programme is designed to exemplify this. It shares tools and techniques that can be used and adapted by colleagues to develop psychologically safe spaces for their students. These in effect "train" students how to engage with each other in a manner that supports others to participate. Participants are encouraged to reflect on this and the impact it could have on learners:

> To witness what the two deliverers, you know, they were amazing. I've observed them quite a lot on how they held a space, their attention to detail, and that motivated me to want to experience them more because it really made me think about that. Attention to detail about how you create that psychological safety and then go in and have some quite, quite silly fun. But actually it worked. It helps to loosen people up and they are more receptive.

The programme also seemed to boost the confidence of some participants related to their own practice. One participant highlighted that they found this an especially useful element of the programme:

> Building courage if you want to call it that.... Just getting more courage is pivotal. So I think it's a step by step process of doing this. It's both an inner journey and an outer journey.

The same focus group went on to discuss in more depth the IST programme's role in increasing one's confidence and courage as a teacher. They noted feeling like permission has been given to try something new. One participant commented that it had helped give them the confidence to move away from overpreparing their teaching:

> I like to plan. When I do a lecture, I know exactly what I'm going to say. I've been doing it long enough that I can, you know, obviously respond to different questions and things, but I'm a planner. I like to not be ... caught out, you know, and all of these things which we should be able to do and we

should be much more flexible about. So, when I saw the ad [for the IST programme], it was going to put me straight out of my comfort zone, but I knew it's something I needed to do. I'll be honest, I am a control freak. I don't like getting anything wrong. ... But obviously as a lecturer, I know that I don't know everything and I am constantly learning, especially with teaching .... I wanted to put myself in a position where I might not be able to anticipate [what was going to happen] and I thought that would be really [useful] and also to be OK to get things wrong.

In another focus group, one participant summarised how the programme had encouraged them to take new risks, employing several activities the programme had modelled:

I have attempted several things [from the programme] and I think the course gave me permission to try things out. And it was OK to fail, right? OK, to fail. Failing was OK. ... In my designing of my new course of module that I'm running come September ..., the teachings are all online. I have an engagement piece right at the beginning. So, it may only be the five minute check-in or something, but then maybe I try to do an activity straight away that gets them talking, gets them engaged. ... And I wouldn't have had the confidence to do that if I hadn't done the course, I think.

This programme was instrumental in helping some colleagues pursue expertise, as expertise in teaching is not simply about practiced routines but requires creativity, improvisation and curiosity (King 2022b, p. 9).

These workshops also focussed on practical performing arts skills such as using your voice, breathing, centring, and mindfulness; how to manage nerves; and so on. These had a long-lasting positive impact on some colleagues' and students' mental well-being:

And the other aspect of it which was an unexpected surprise was the 'de-stress', the well-being side of it and that also kept me coming ... it just elevated my mood and perception.

I find the part of this improvisation skill [workshops] with the flexibility exercise which I practice. I shut down my computer, open the windows and, like you know this, this, some stretching exercises ... when I do that for like 5 minutes, I feel better, you know? ... It's therapeutic ... I think that really helped my mental health as a lecturer 'cause I invite some of this practice when I'm overwhelmed. During the lectures ... I do practice some of this with some of my students ... I believe the improvisational skills [workshops] was quite unique and compared to other workshops. It has some flavours of actions to get away from away from [didactic?] lecturing that could help re-boost your mental health.

A new language for talking about teaching

We were particularly excited to hear about where this programme was having an impact on whole teams. King highlights the collaborative nature of expertise development; that community and collaboration are core to development of expertise (King, 2022b; King, 2022c). In one focus group, a short conversation surrounded three colleagues at different stages of employing this learning with their colleagues. One looked to the future and how they could inspire other teachers:

> I'm going to look at how I can incorporate some of this, and in a way it's a role modelling. So, it's role modelling and encouraging others to think about [this].

Another was starting to feed this thinking into collaboration with their team:

> I've had conversations with my team about it and […] how it helps, and yeah, we have had some really useful discussions as a module team about how to bring in some of these things.

A third was further along: they were attending this programme along with their colleagues so that they had shared understanding and language. This provided a springboard for team development and team conversations:

> There's a lot of newbies [in my team], so I encourage all the newbies (as we call ourselves) to go on these courses and to sign up and encourage them to go along. And so, therefore, we have a shared language. So, we've all been there. We've all done it. We've seen how it works and kind of have conversations around how we can use it.

This also reaffirms our argument that educational development initiatives focussed on teaching tools and techniques for teaching can provide an impactful way of encouraging staff to employ critical skills in developing their practice.

Expertise from beyond HE

A key reason for the success of this programme was the expertise of our workshop facilitators. Imogen Palmer and Stephen Brown (Bristol Improv Theatre) are not only experts in improv theatre, but also in teaching improv. Teaching improv requires a very unique set of skills to build a safe environment to support participation in what can be a very alien and vulnerable practice. There's much value just in observing their expert facilitation:

> Imogen and Ste were sort of top, top notch you know. They were the right people to run it and it was like you know they're really good double act.

I just think that it was good 'cause they both complemented each other. And I was just reading about their background on their [web]site yesterday and I mean they just, you could just, when you knew more about them you could just see exactly how so true that was. I think for me, they really made it, and how they made us feel really at ease and just such a, you know, a real fun sort of environment to work with other people.

An important point both facilitators make at the start of each session is to appreciate the expertise in the room. They are not here to teach staff how to teach; most (if not all) colleagues are obviously already doing that. They are here to introduce a few extra tools, techniques, and activities. There's space to discuss and critique, and participants are invited to consider if any may work in their own context. Thus, from the start, they dismantle the expert–student divide, whilst their expertise then speaks for itself.

Conclusion: reflections on how to develop teaching artistry and expertise

The pandemic, and the difficulties of student engagement, require us to think hard and develop deliberate steps to create positive learning environments and attend to the emotions in the classroom. Expertise comes in different shapes and forms, and to respond to the challenges we are facing in HE today requires creative problem solving in more ways than one. There is a lot to learn from the theatre arts and from the teaching of improvisation that can apply to the HE classroom (Bale, 2020). As King (2022c, p. 17) aptly summarises, "high performance also requires support from fields outside one's own domain".

At its most impactful level, improvisation can offer a new but compatible lens through which to view one's own teaching practice. It can offer new and exciting, but relevant, shared language and practices that can lead to developing of innovative team philosophies, practices, and communities. Furthermore, as summarised by Modesto Corderi Novoa in Box 11.1, the use of drama and performance can also be a powerful tool for learning intangible concepts.

Professional development for staff teaching in HE should not shy away from modelling, exposing teachers (as learners) to different tools and techniques and to have these at the centre of a conceptual and practice-based shift to our understanding of what it means to teach in HE. All of the IST programme workshops centre on practical activities which participants can take and use in their own teaching. And all workshops provide multiple points of reflection in and on action that are practical and specific, which are profoundly impactful for staff teaching practices.

Box 11.1 Using performative language teaching to explore intercultural concepts in the Chinese language classroom

Modesto Corderi Novoa

Language teaching is both a form of art and a skill that can be learned and taught. Schewe (2013) first introduced the concept of Performative Language Teaching (PLT) as an umbrella term for all different activities related to theatre and drama that can be used for education and language teaching. More recently, the concept of PLT is also related to the use of embodiment to teach second languages.

From the linguistic and second language acquisition perspective, PLT promotes language learning because it fosters interaction and collaboration among the learners by connecting the interaction hypothesis (Long, 1996) and sociocultural theory (Vygotsky, 1978). When students perform, they are accessing both the cognitive and affective dimensions. By giving them a context, the students interact with an intense focus on meaning. A key advantage of PLT is that participants can simultaneously be actors and audience members. Experiences in the use of drama in the language classroom (DICE, 2010) improve teachers' reflexivity and attention as they craft their own pedagogical practice and reflect on the concept of both artistry of teaching and expertise.

In recent years, there has been a dramatic increase in the number of students of Chinese language. However, there are several problems related to the quality of Chinese language teaching and learning, such as teaching pedagogy that relies heavily on memorization and repetition and lacks communicative language use. Therefore, Chinese teaching needs a more collaborative and engaging methodology that can help students improve their oral proficiency skills and motivation. Corderi Novoa (2019) used qualitative measures to assess PLT's use in a Chinese language experimental open drama summer class at Beijing Language and Culture University.

In Chinese culture there are several intercultural concepts that are difficult to explain only by using traditional teaching methods since those concepts do not have a direct equivalent translation in other languages. Therefore, they are extremely complicated to understand for students from other cultures. One of those concepts is 缘分 (Yuánfèn), which means "serendipity in a relationship" (Hsu & Hwang, 2016).

Language teaching connects cultures with different degrees of context (Hall, 1976) and cultural dimensions (Hofstede, 2001). Glynn and Hadley (2021) argued that "translatability" and "performability" could

> be complementing concepts. Therefore, using PLT could be a significant tool for teachers and students to better understand cultural identities and unique cultural aspects.
>
> The author participated in a creative drama workshop in the summer of 2022 in Ireland as a part of the Lacunae Project (Piazzoli & Ó Breacháin, 2022) with a group of eight expert drama and language teachers. In the workshop, using Practice-as-Research (PaR) methodologies, they applied different dramatic expressions to perform and embody the intercultural concept of Yuánfèn, including exploration, reflection, and evaluation. Much more research is needed in this field on how to use PLT to explore intercultural concepts in the Chinese language classroom.

Key take-aways

- Improvisational theatre has a lot to offer HE teachers. It can provide a variety of tools, techniques, and activities which can aid student engagement and learning (both online and face to face). It can also provide a useful lens through which colleagues can reflect upon their own teaching practice.
- Supporting colleagues to take an improvisational approach to their teaching can also support the well-being of students and staff. It can help with the fostering of bravery, the creation of safe spaces for learning, and can also support staff mental health.
- We argue it is important for educational development initiatives to support academics to explore concrete tools and approaches. These can help HE teachers to develop confidence and provide a foundation for deeper reflection.

References

Bale, R. (2020). *Teaching with Confidence in Higher Education: Applying Strategies from the Performing Arts.* Routledge, London & New York. DOI:10.4324/9780429201929

Bale, R. (2022). Developing adaptive expertise: what can we learn from improvisation and the performing arts? In: King, H. (ed.), *Developing Expertise for Teaching in Higher Education: Practical Ideas for Professional Learning and Development.* Routledge, London & New York, pp. 203–217. DOI:10.4324/9781003198772-19

Corderi Novoa, M. (2019). Improchinese: Using Improv Theater in a Chinese as a foreign language experimental classroom. *Revista de Artes Performativas, Educación y Sociedad,* 1(1), 147–163. https://www.apesrevista.com/_files/ugd/762f4b_32d4fd50773740998ef5060fd3a36c35.pdf

DICE Consortium. (2010). The DICE has been cast. Research findings and recommendations on educational theater and drama. European Union. http://www.dramanetwork.eu

Dreyfus, H. & Dreyfus, S. (1982). *Mind Over Machine.* Free Press, New York.

Eraut, M. (2009). How professionals learn through work. In: Jackson, N. (ed.), *Learning to be Professional through a Higher Education.* E-Book: University of Surrey. http://learningtobeprofessional.pbworks.com

Glynn, D. & Hadley, J. (2021). Theorising (un)performability and (un) translatability. *Perspectives*, 29(1), 20–32. DOI:10.1080/0907676x.2020.1713827

Gravett, K. & Winstone, N.E. (2020). Making connections: authenticity and alienation within students' relationships in higher education, *Higher Education Research & Development*, 41(2), 360–374. DOI:10.1080/07294360.2020.1842335

Hall, E.T. (1976). *Beyond Culture*. Anchor Press/Double day, New York.

Hao, R.N. (2011). Critical compassionate pedagogy and the teacher's role in first-generation student success. *New Directions for Teaching and Learning*, 127, 91–98. DOI:10.1002/tl.460

Hofstede, G. (2001). *Culture's Consequences: Comparing Values, Behaviors, Institutions, and Organizations Across Nations*. Sage, Thousand Oaks, CA. DOI:10.5465/amr.2002.7389951

Hsu, H.P. & Hwang, K.K. (2016). Serendipity in relationship: a tentative theory of the cognitive process of yuanfen and its psychological constructs in Chinese cultural societies. Frontiers in Psychology, 7, 282. DOI:10.3389/fpsyg.2016.00282

Long, M.H. (1996). The role of the linguistic environment in second language acquisition. In: Ritchie, W.C. & Bhatia, T.K. (eds.), *Handbook of Language Acquisition: Vol. 2. Second Language Acquisition*. Academic Press, New York, pp. 413–468 DOI:10.1016/b978-012589042-7/50015-3

King, H. (ed.) (2022a). *Developing Expertise for Teaching in Higher Education: Practical Ideas for Professional Learning and Development*. Routledge, London & New York. DOI:10.4324/9781003198772

King, H. (2022b). introduction: developing expertise for teaching in higher education. In: King, H. (ed.), *Developing Expertise for Teaching in Higher Education: Practical Ideas for Professional Learning and Development*. Routledge, London & New York, 1–12. DOI:10.4324/9781003198772-1

King, H. (2022c). The characteristics of expertise for teaching in higher education. In: King, H. (ed.), *Developing Expertise for Teaching in Higher Education: Practical Ideas for Professional Learning and Development*. Routledge, London & New York, pp. 15–28. DOI:10.4324/9781003198772-3

King, H. (2022d). Professional Learning for Higher Education Teaching: An Expertise Perspective. In King, H. (Ed.), *Developing Expertise for Teaching in Higher Education: Practical Ideas for Professional Learning and Development*. Routledge, London & New York, pp. 157–174. DOI:10.4324/9781003198772-15

Pacansky-Brock, M., Smedshammer, M. & Vincent-Layton, K. (2020). Humanizing online teaching to equitize higher education, *Current Issues in Education*, 21(2), 1–21. DOI:10.13140/RG.2.2.33218.94402

Piazzoli, E. & Ó Breacháin, A. (2022). *Embodying the Untranslatable in the Lacunae Project*. IDEA 9th World Congress. Reykjavik, Iceland.

Schewe, M. (2013). Taking stock and looking ahead: Drama pedagogy as a gateway to a performative teaching and learning culture. Scenario: Journal for Performative Teaching, Learning and Research, 8(1), 5–23. DOI:10.33178/scenario.7.1.2

Schön, D.A. (1991 [1983]). *The Reflective Practitioner: How Professional Think in Action*. Ashgate, London. DOI:10.4324/9781315237473

Shulman, L.S. (1986). Those who understand: Knowledge Growth in Teaching. *Educational Researcher*, 15(4), 4–14. DOI:10.3102/0013189X015002004

Vygotsky, L.S. (1978). *Mind in Society: The Development of Higher Psychological Processes*. Harvard University Press, Cambridge, MA. DOI:10.2307/j.ctvjf9vz4

Williams, T. (2022). Class Attendance Plummets Post-Covid, *Times Higher Education*, 9 June. https://www.timeshighereducation.com/news/class-attendance-plummets-post-covid

Chapter 12

The characteristics of expertise in online teaching in higher education

Sarah Wilson-Medhurst and Mark Childs

Problem: why do we need teachers to engage with online learning?

The evidence for the potential effectiveness of online learning is well established, indicated by the age of many of the examples we are citing in this introduction. Zawacki-Richter and Naidu (2016) characterise the period of 1995–99 as the early stages of research into online learning and the second half of the 2000s as the era of exploration of collaborative learning and online interaction. More recent studies of blended learning (combining online and in-person teaching) show that the combination can enhance learning outcomes, flexibility of access, a sense of community, the effective use of resources, and student satisfaction (Poon, 2013).

For some people, collaboration online may be *more* effective, a factor that has been described in the literature for at least 20 years. Caplan (2003) notes that many people have a preference for communication online as it "entails greater anonymity, greater control over self-presentation, more intense and intimate self-disclosure, less perceived social risk" and "are relatively more depersonalized than FtF (i.e., in-person) activity because of the reduced number of contextual and nonverbal cues" (p. 629). Furthermore, more recently there are the observations that in-person environments privilege participants who are male (Carter et al., 2019), white (Laufer, 2012), and neurotypical (Pasek, 2015) and which challenge the idea that nonverbal cues from audiences are universally understood and desired (Pasek, 2015) or free from bias (Laufer, 2012).

Problem: the issues we have seen some people face with online teaching

The COVID-19 pandemic of 2020–23 and our response to it has highlighted ways in which the teaching and learning experience can be enhanced with the judicious use of technology. Yet some colleagues have (largely) rejected the options technology offers with strong reactions presenting antipathy towards online teaching. At Durham University, for example, analyses of staff experiences of the use of technology were conducted in 2020 and 2021 as part of

DOI: 10.4324/9781003437826-16

the institution's contribution to the Jisc Digital Experience Insights Surveys (Jisc, 2022). These analyses showed many commonalities in the experience of staff, but also quite large discrepancies.

The analysis of the 2022 qualitative survey data from Durham staff took a different approach. Rather than developing a typology of responses, we aimed to develop a typology of *staff*. We did this by conducting a sentiment analysis of the open text responses to questions that asked staff to identify a positive experience of online teaching, a negative one, and the type of support they required to help them with teaching online. From previous surveys it was observed that the dominant answers to these questions was to note the positive aspect of online learning was flexibility and the negative aspect was a reduction in engagement from students. As we were interested in *divergence* from these norms, for our typology we classified these as neutral statements, and tagged statements that differed from these as either more positive or negative. Staff were then grouped according to the combinations of positive, negative, or neutral responses.

The five categories amongst the 117 respondents were:

- Positive-positive – (n = 2, 2%) Within this category, staff identified positive *pedagogical* advantages to teaching online, rather than logistic. They did not consider the negative aspects of importance as they could be resolved over time.
- Positive-neutral – (n = 29, 25%) Within this group, staff identified positive pedagogical advantages to teaching online, primarily the inclusion through chat of students who were normally non-participative. Some identified the reduction in student engagement as an issue, others identified reduced student motivation or their own disconnection from a community of teachers.
- Neutral-neutral – (n = 48, 41%) These staff identified flexibility and accessibility as the chief advantage of online teaching and decreased engagement as the main disadvantage (our two baseline answers identified from previous surveys). In answer to the support question, some saw this as a technical issue (needing help with the technology, or better technology), others requested more support in learning the *pedagogies* of online teaching.
- Neutral-negative – (n = 21, 18%) These staff identified flexibility and accessibility as the chief advantage of online teaching and stated that engagement was *absent* when teaching online, not merely reduced. The support they identified included better equipment, spaces to use the equipment, or training in using the technology; no-one in this category identified support as a *pedagogical* issue.
- Negative-negative – (n = 17, 15%) These staff stated there were *no* advantages to online teaching, not even accepting increased flexibility as a benefit. They stated that there was no interaction – typical statements were "no student engagement", "lack of communication with students to assess understanding", "absence of feedback", and "lack of interaction".

Further to this, the responses of the negative-negative group to questions also included attitude and value judgments about teaching online *per se*. These comments included statements such as:

> Do not keep on pushing online teaching please! It is making life much harder for staff and lowering the quality of education!

> Cease online teaching.

And one longer response summed up the attitudinal opposition thus:

> Teaching online cannot be properly called teaching. It does not allow the possibility of forging connections with individual students. It leads to disengagement of both students and staff. It deprioritises commitment to the pedagogical process. Online instruction is the enemy of learning and investing in it represents an irreversible reputational threat.

There is clearly a very different perspective on teaching online. The previously indicated statements from the negative-negative group make claims that contradict the decades of experience, research, and practice in effective online teaching. Although the numerical values in samples that are self-selected are unreliable, this does indicate a core of staff who are particularly antipathetic to online teaching. This different perspective cannot be explained only by a poor experience of teaching, as the same issues with enacting an effectively engaged online learning experience were indicated by the neutral-negative and neutral-neutral category.

These examples of resistance were reflected in the wider community. For example, Danisch (2021) observes the importance of active learning, but then states that this "feels unlikely in remote learning environments". Similarly, Herman (2020) states that in online learning, "the transition from face-to-face to online removed the opportunity to learn 'from other students', and breaking into smaller groups or commenting on each other's writing was no substitute for the real thing", raising the question about why in-person teaching is "real" and online learning is not.

While trying to understand this degree of antipathy to online teaching from those who have a negative (or negative-negative) experience of it and why it fails to seem "real" to some teachers, we encountered the concept of the *artistry* of teaching as described in King (2022). This raised the possibility that this severe opposition to online teaching could be due to a loss of the opportunity to express an artistry that these teachers experience in in-person settings and that this opposition to online teaching is embedded in attitudes to teaching and colleagues' identity as teachers. To further this proposition we have attempted to create a framework to describe the artistry of teaching *online*, specifically. The aim for this approach is that if we can identify the elements that constitute the artistry of online teaching, then we can more clearly identify the areas in which this experience of loss of artistry could arise, and thereafter create a strategy for addressing this opposition, or even pre-empting it in the first place.

The framework

Defining beliefs, attitudes, and values

Before laying out our framework we clarify some key terms – belief, attitude, and value. Belief is "a principle, etc., accepted as true, especially without proof" (Collins English Dictionary, 2005). Thus, beliefs might be characterised as one's philosophy or viewpoint; the significant point is that "proof" is not necessary for that belief, whereas an attitude is "the way a person views something or tends to behave towards it, often in an evaluative way" (ibid.). Thus, attitudes might be characterised as the way people express beliefs, for example as an approach, outlook, manner, or stance. Values are "the moral principles or accepted standards of a person or group" (ibid.) typically expressed as principles, standards, morals, ethics, ideals, and so forth. The role of values, attitudes, and beliefs and their importance in achieving sustainable change in (higher) educational practice has underpinned approaches in other contexts (e.g., Wilson-Medhurst, 2008). In investigating the emotional dimensions of the change process associated with teacher development, Saunders (2013) highlights the interconnection between emotion, personal belief systems, and identity in professional development that should not be neglected when supporting teachers (and often is).

Overview of the framework

The starting point for our analysis of expertise in online teaching was King's framework (King, 2022). King's model identifies three key aspects of the expertise of teaching in higher education. The first of these draws on Shulman's *pedagogical content knowledge* model (Shulman, 1986 cited in King, 2022) which King highlights thus: "a teacher in any context must weave together skills and knowledge from two domains, that of their subject matter and that of teaching itself (pedagogy)" (King, 2022, p. 20). The second is professional learning, defined as "intentional and purposeful learning that leads to improvement" (ibid., p. 22). The third aspect of King's model is that of the *artistry* of teaching. Artistry is difficult to define, but King's elucidation of the idea includes this description (ibid., p. 22):

> [Artistry] emphasises the relational nature of teaching, that it is fundamentally about human interactions. Artistry relates to aspects of performance such as being authentic to oneself, engaging an audience and improvisation

We have placed artistry last in our account of King's model for emphasis, because for us, it was this conceptualisation of teaching as an *art* that was revelatory and which suggested a new perspective from which to analyse the experience of colleagues. The overview of this framework is shown in Table 12.1.

The knowledge domains of online teaching

As noted earlier, teaching requires the weaving together of two different domains. Online teaching requires a third, that of the knowledge of the *technology* being used for teaching. An existing model that describes this interweaving is TPACK – The Technological Pedagogical Content Knowledge Framework (Mishra & Koehler, 2006), which unpacks its three domains as a series of individual domains and four combinations of these (Figure 12.1). For the purposes of this paper it is the TPK (technological pedagogical knowledge) that we are focussing on, that is, what are the pedagogical techniques specific to using a particular technology, and what modes of engagement do particular technologies offer when using them with students?

An added nuance to this conception of applying a series of different types of knowledge is provided by Oancea and Furlong in their conception of *techne* (2007, pp. 125–6), which they see as not simply technical knowledge but also "the activity of installing order and increasing human control over underdetermined circumstances". *Techne* is not simply understanding the technology;

Table 12.1 The overview of the framework and the relationship to the frameworks it incorporates

Wilson-Medhurst and Childs 2022	TPACK Mishra and Koehler 2006	Attitudes and beliefs Critical reflection Values relating to technology and teaching Identity	Artistry Situated understanding Flow Presence
King 2022	**Pedagogical Content Knowledge** Knowledge of discipline + Knowledge of pedagogical techniques	**Professional Learning** Experience Reflection Intentional learning and development	**Artistry** Pattern recognition, Problem solving Flow
Oancea and Furlong 2007	*Techne* Technical skill and control	*Epistome* What is valid What is proper	*Phronosis* Receptiveness Transformation Situated understanding

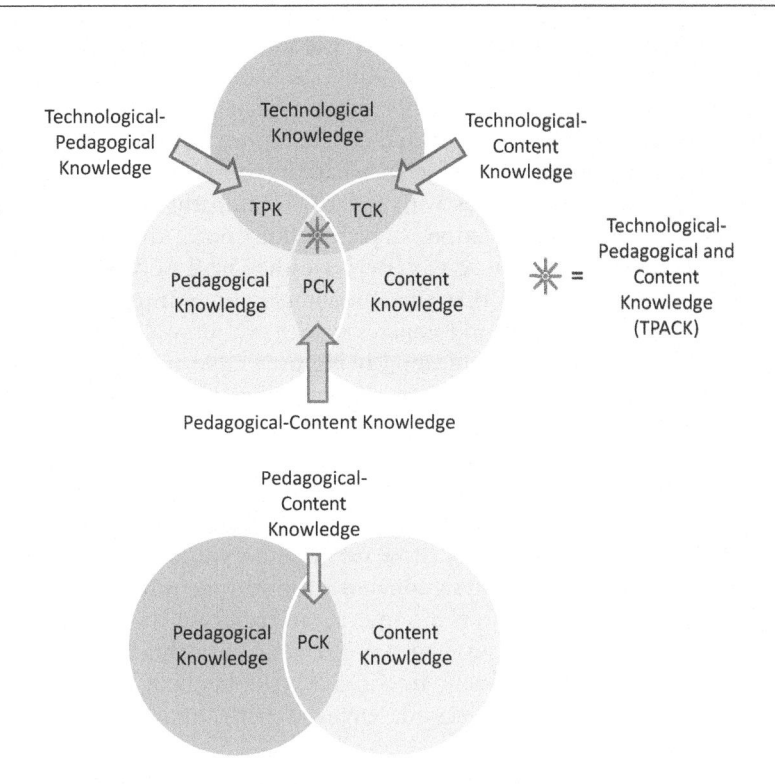

Figure 12.1 The TPACK model compared with the PCK model

it is using that understanding to appropriately interact with and exhibit control over one's environment.

This concept of *techne* forms one of three domains of professional expertise identified by Oancea and Furlong, that of *techne*, *phronesis*, and *episteme*, applied in their initial paper to practice-based research and extended to professional development in a later paper by Winch, Oancea, and Orchard (2015). In developing our framework we found these domains correlate to and augment those of the King framework. The other two aspects we will look at in the following.

Critical reflection, attitudes, and identity

Returning to the second of the King aspects of expertise, a mechanism for how professional learning for teachers can be enacted is through critical reflection on practice (Winch, Oancea & Orchard, 2015). This reflection on practice forms the basis of many postgraduate programmes that provide in-service training in teaching for university lecturers. The process involves evidence-informed reflection on one's own performance and where improvement may be aimed for, but improvement requires a willingness to engage in the associated, intentional professional learning (King, 2022).

The disparity between personal opinions at what online learning *cannot* achieve in regard to communication and collaboration, and the wider evidence that it is effective at supporting these, may have its roots in the personal beliefs and linking attitudes and values with regard to antipathy towards, or even distaste for, online communication. Caplan (2003) notes the preference for online communication for those who perceive they have poor social skills in in-person settings and finds that this encourages more Internet usage but identifies this as problematic and equates it with withdrawal. Pasek critiques the stance of in-person communication being preferable and calls for greater scrutiny of the "corporeal standard" as a "foundational part of being human", finding it ableist in character (2015).

Childs and Peachey (2013) identify a range of reasons that people oppose online engagement, one of which is an attitude towards the lack of authenticity of online experiences, which they relate to Mitcham's concept of "ancient scepticism" (Mitcham, 1994). For those participants whose resistance to technology takes this form, the analysis concludes the attitude is that online activities "lack authenticity, or are even immoral, and appease those members of society who are weakest, because they are relying on technology", and that these opinions are so self-evident to those who hold them that contesting them requires them to be surfaced, engaged with, and then challenged (Childs & Peachey, 2013, p. 32).

In the Oancea and Furlong framework, this category aligns with their concepts of *episteme* in that it is concerned not only with what is valid in the advancement of knowledge, but also with *propriety* (Oancea & Furlong, 2007). The responses to those opposed to online teaching suggest that not only is online teaching ineffective, it is wrong.

Some of this might be explained by the literature on identity development and how we see ourselves, including the possible selves we might like, or definitely do not want, to become (Markus & Nurius, 1986). Ronfeldt and Grossman (2008) highlight the centrality of "practices" and the knowledge and skills embodied within them to our identity construction. This might explain in part why knowledge and skills developed in in-person settings can form such a key part of our identity as teachers and a reluctance to reform what we do. However, arguably, the majority of those involved in teaching and supporting learning faced a similar challenge and not all have expressed the same level of desire to "revert" or certainly the same level of antipathy to online teaching that some express. Beliefs and attitudes to learning and to technology seem to be central here in the willingness to engage in the professional learning that will enable the adaptations in skills and knowledge required to "deliver" effective online teaching and experience it positively. To further examine why this might be the case we turn now to the third element of our framework.

Situated understanding, flow, and artistry

A key part of the ability to employ artistry is the degree to which expertise can become automated, so that more cognitive capacity can be applied to thinking purposefully about what you are doing, rather than consciously applying the content knowledge and technical skills required. King links this to Csíkszentmihályi's concept of flow (Csíkszentmihályi & Rathunde, 1993). Like artistry, "flow" is a concept difficult to define, yet easy to recognise – it is those moments where you feel everything comes together, you are applying your skills to their full extent, but are not being taxed beyond your ability. Järvinen, Heliö, and Mäyrä (2002) applied Csíkszentmihályi's concepts to those of digital environments and identified seven components in flow when online including the "paradox of control" (p. 21). Online, our control is constrained by the technology we are using, but, they argue, when we experience flow we are unconsciously working within these constraints and only aware of our ability to exert control over the aspects we *can* control (ibid.). In our formulation adopted from Oancea and Furlong, it is applying *techne* without being conscious we are.

King also links artistry to "the pattern recognition, problem-solving and adaptive expertise of teaching, therefore, 'require[s] sensibility, imagination, technique, and the ability to make judgements about the feel and significance of the particular'" (Eisner, 2002 cited in King, 2022, p. 22). Again, we find parallels in Oancea and Furlong's framework, where this recalls their third component of expertise, that of "*phronesis*", which is the ability to apply critical reflexivity, deliberation, and receptiveness and hence experience transformation and personal growth (Oancea & Furlong, 2007). In a later paper, these attributes are linked to a prerequisite of *situated understanding* (Winch, Oancea & Orchard, 2015, p. 205) which they define as "a capacity to grasp the salient features of a situation, deliberate imaginatively and holistically". When this situated understanding is diminished, the relational aspects of teaching – the human relations that are at the core of its artistry (King, 2022) – therefore become much more problematic.

Though we have looked at these elements as separate factors, there are undoubtedly overlaps between them: a person experiencing a diminished situated understanding within an environment may do so because of their more limited experience, which may lead to a devaluing of the authenticity of the learning. An antipathy towards technology may lead to a resistance to developing the technical skills or the desire to acquire the control required for online learning. And during a time of crisis, all of these factors will be exacerbated by limited time and extra external pressures such as childcare, lack of space at home to work, finite resources for support at institutions being stretched, and actually catching COVID (Damşa et al., 2021). These inter-relationships will be explored in the next section.

Using the framework to explore resistance to online teaching

Looking through the various findings in the literature and our own observations, we can see how these many different factors can reinforce each other. The move to online learning led to a series of experiences, some of which were the following:

1) Given the suddenness of lockdown and resultant lack of time to prepare, many teachers were (initially) often trying to emulate or replicate the in-person teaching environment online. However, like-for-like replacement was less likely to succeed due to the different affordances of online versus in-person.
2) From research literature dating back to the mid-1990s, online communication has been shown to be social, engaged, and informal – for some people and situations even more so than in-person communication. It is slower to develop, however, so the initial lack of interaction does not indicate that this will hold true over a longer time period. But as Damşa et al. note, their data "show teachers positioning towards trying new teaching methods (or trying new formats in online environments) but not always succeeding or enjoying the situation, as it often placed them in vulnerable positions" (2021, p. 7).
3) As Hofer, Nistor, and Scheibenzuber (2021, p. 5) observe, "Educators who tended to feel threatened by online teaching during the Covid-19 pandemic were more likely to suffer from burnout experiences and seemed to provide learning opportunities of lower quality as assessed by the students", which in turn leads to a less satisfying online engagement.
4) In the results of the survey analysis at Durham University, those teachers who had a negative response to teaching online looked to additional technological support for help; none saw it as a pedagogical issue. The conclusion is that not only were they lacking knowledge of the technological-pedagogical domain, but they were also unaware of its *existence* and so therefore would not have been prompted to seek out help in how to redesign for an online experience.
5) Philosophically, the view of the "corporeal standard" as a "foundational part of being human" (Pasek, 2015) is closely aligned with Mitcham's concept of ancient scepticism of technology as a turning away from social values (1994). Despite it favouring male, white, and neurotypical voices, in-person teaching is seen as a higher standard *morally* by many people.

Our suggestion in applying this framework is that these factors, whether they are technical-pedagogical domain knowledge, beliefs, and attitudes or a sense of situated understanding and flow, mutually reinforce each other (though without stating which is cause and which is effect). That is: someone who is morally opposed to online learning is less likely to research online teaching literature, or even engage with the field enough to identify that there *is* a pedagogy specific to online learning, so not acquire the technology-pedagogy domain knowledge. Someone who is more anxious about online learning experiences burns out more quickly and so does not engage for the longer time required to experience the human connections with others which take longer to emerge. Without the situated understanding that comes with the ability to apply *techne* automatically, teaching can feel alienating and inhuman. And since the converse also holds, this may go some way to explaining the divergence in experience we noted earlier in the chapter.

Our argument is also that these reinforcements are exacerbated by a sense of loss of artistry in the move to online teaching. That flow and situated understanding in an in-person setting are an intrinsic part of the experience of teaching for many people, and for those who lose this in the move online, their sense of loss reinforces their disapproval of online teaching and creates an even bigger barrier to overcome. This might be diagrammatically represented as in Figure 12.2.

This led us to identify four categories of staff experience as depicted in Table 12.2.

Table 12.2 Four categories of staff experience of artistry for the transition from in-person to online teaching

| | | Whether or not staff experience artistry of teaching (flow, feedback, etc.) when **in-person** ||
		Do not experience artistry in-person	Do experience artistry in-person
Whether or not staff experience artistry of teaching (flow, feedback, etc.) **online**	Do not experience artistry online	Teachers in this category did not experience loss of opportunity to enact artistry during lockdown-enforced remote teaching.	The move to online during lockdown-enforced remote teaching had a particularly negative impact on the teachers in this category.
	Do experience artistry online	Although we've not encountered anyone in this category and consider it unlikely, we acknowledge there may be some, e.g., those who have chosen to do online teaching only.	Teachers in this category were able to continue to enact artistry during lockdown-enforced remote teaching.

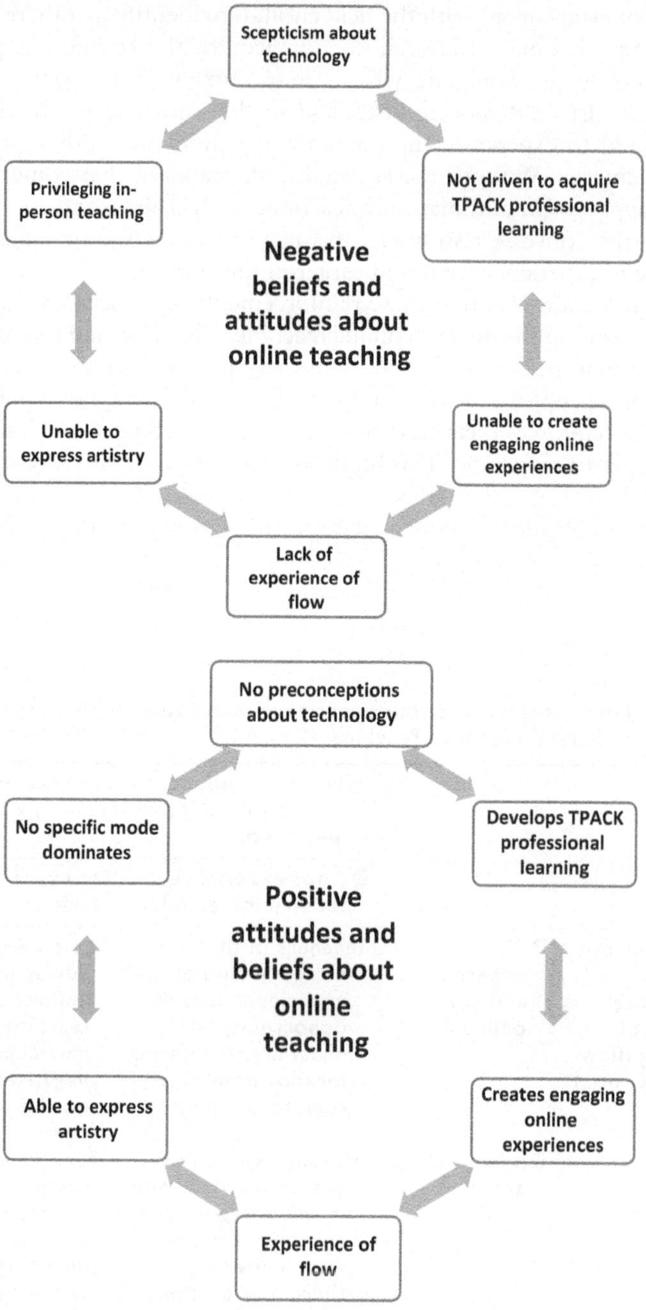

Figure 12.2 The sets of attitudes, beliefs, and experiences that lead to two different patterns of reinforcement

Initial presentation of the model

We introduced our model and the preceding four categories of staff experience of artistry to attendees at an online symposium (Wilson-Medhurst & Childs, 2022). Our intention in making this initial presentation was to see if the model and the categories of staff depicted in Table 12.2 aligned with attendees' experiences and observations and make an initial assessment of the model's viability. We were also interested in attendees' views on its usefulness in making the implicit (some staff do not like or enjoy online teaching), explicit (why they might not like or enjoy it) so that appropriate (development) action might be taken.

One of the initial pieces of feedback we received was that resistance to online teaching as a result of the lack of experience of artistry was something a number of the audience had observed the effects of and had tried to address, for instance by providing relevant development activities or programmes. The model also provoked personal reflections on how individuals had responded to the challenge of moving their teaching online during lockdown periods and this is an encouraging indication of how the model, and the reflections it might prompt, could be used to support educational and academic development. The added difficulty, or certainly complexity, highlighted by the TPACK model was echoed in comments made with some acknowledging this in the form of developing different "muscles" in the online space to enable them to teach effectively in this different environment, or for others being a "translation" of existing in-person practices. Certainly, surfacing the adjustments in knowledge and skill sets required is helpful, but as we have already argued, the challenge is that (some) colleagues' (negative) beliefs and attitudes are resulting in an unwillingness to engage in professional learning and an ongoing lack of experience of artistry as a result, which perpetuates the status quo. Table 12.2 was presented and some of our expert attendees indicated they had experienced working with colleagues whose experience might fall into one of these categories. We concluded such a typology of experiences based on our model might therefore be a useful tool for surfacing such experiences to aid (support for) staff development.

Conclusion: implications for academic development

We preface these concluding remarks by first acknowledging all professional development and educational change take place in a complex and dynamic environment and change is not a linear or mechanistic journey. Our model suggests that any professional development programme or activities related to learning and teaching might usefully include (or enhance) support for staff to appreciate and investigate the beliefs, attitudes, and values that underpin their approach.

We set these recommendations against the new Professional Standards Framework (PSF) 2023, an internationally available professional teaching standards framework which provides a renewed focus on inclusivity, effectiveness, and impact (of teaching) (AdvanceHE, 2023). Given the literature indicates how in-person teaching favours white, male, and neurotypical voices, teachers cannot be inclusive and effective in their support of all students if they are privileging one form of interaction over another, in the mistaken belief that the chosen method is always 'better'.

From the evidence presented here and the associated model, there seems to be an important step that is (largely) missing, in an explicit form, from many current staff development strategies, programmes, and activities. That is, an explicit focus on facilitating staff to be aware that they will have beliefs and associated attitudes and values that will have an impact on their orientation to a particular learning approach, technique, or technology. We are obviously not proposing a (learning) environment in which these beliefs, attitudes, and values are judged. Instead, we propose that the core of professional development includes an actively supported invitation, aided by appropriate pedagogies and tools, to enable teachers to understand their current beliefs, attitudes, and values and how these may impact on the practices they prefer or are willing to invest time and energy to adopt. Our next steps in taking forward the learning from this model include continuing to identify, use, and evaluate such approaches and tools and we invite others to do the same.

Key take-aways

- Opposition to teaching online often takes the form of statement of objective truths rather than as beliefs or attitudes and can arise from a lack of opportunity to exhibit artistry in teaching.
- Beliefs and attitudes that are antipathetic to online teaching lead to reticence to research appropriate pedagogies or seek pedagogical support and add barriers to overcoming reduced engagement online.
- Academic support for online teaching would be enhanced through a discussion of attitudes and beliefs, identity, and artistry in addition to knowledge and skills, and we propose that the Wilson-Medhurst and Childs (2022) framework described in this chapter would be an effective structure for those discussions.

References

AdvanceHE (2023). *Professional Standards Framework*. https://www.advance-he.ac.uk/teaching-and-learning/psf

Caplan, S.E. (2003). Preference for online social interaction. *Communication Research*, 30(6), 625–648. DOI:10.1177/0093650203257842

Carter, A.J., Croft, A., Lukas, D. & Sandstrom, G.M. (2019). Women's visibility in academic seminars: Women ask fewer questions than men. *PLOS ONE*, 14(2), e0212146. DOI:10.1371/journal.pone.0202743

Childs, M. & Peachey, A. (2013). Love it or hate it: Students' responses to the experience of virtual worlds. In: Childs, M. & Withnail, G. (eds.), *Experiential Learning in Virtual Worlds*, Oxford: Interdisciplinary Press, pp. 27–46. DOI:10.1163/9789004372153_003

Collins English Dictionary (2005). *Collins English Dictionary*. Glasgow: Harper Collins Publishers.

Csíkszentmihályi, M. & Rathunde, K. (1993). The measurement of flow in everyday life: Toward a theory of emergent motivation. In Jacobs, J.E. (ed.) *Nebraska Symposium on Motivation, 1992: Developmental Perspectives on Motivation*. Lincoln: University of Nebraska Press, pp. 57–97.

Damşa, C., Langford, M., Uehara, D. & Scherer, R. (2021). Teachers' agency & online education in times of crisis. *Computers in Human Behavior*, 121. DOI:10.1016/j.chb.2021.106793

Danisch, R. (2021). The problem with online learning? It doesn't teach people to think, *The Conversation*, 13 June 2021. https://theconversation.com/amp/the-problem-with-online-learning-it-doesnt-teach-people-to-think-161795

Herman, P.C. (2020). Online learning is not the future. *Inside Higher Ed*, 20 June 2020.https://www.insidehighered.com/digital-learning/views/2020/06/10/online-learning-not-future-higher-education-opinion

Hofer, S.I., Nistor, N. & Scheibenzuber, C. (2021). Online teaching & learning in higher education: Lessons learned in crisis situations, *Computers in Human Behavior*, 121. DOI:10.1016/j.chb.2021.106789

Järvinen, A., Heliö, S. & Mäyrä, F. (2002). *Communication & Community in Digital Entertainment Services: Prestudy Research Report*. Tampere: University of Tampere Hypermedia Laboratory. https://trepo.tuni.fi/bitstream/handle/10024/65663/951-44-5432-4.pdf

Jisc (2022). Digital experience insights. https://www.jisc.ac.uk/digital-experience-insights

King, H. (2022). The characteristics of expertise for teaching in higher education. In: King, H. (ed.) *Developing Expertise for Teaching in Higher Education Practical Ideas for Professional Learning & Development* Abingdon-on-Thames: Routledge, pp. 16–28. DOI:10.4324/9781003198772-3

Laufer, M.A. (2012). *Black Students' Classroom Silence in Predominantly White Institutions of Higher Education*. Masters Thesis. Smith College, Northampton, MA. https://scholarworks.smith.edu/theses/639

Markus, H. R. & Nurius, P. (1986). Possible selves, *American Psychologist*, 41(9), pp. 954–969.

Mishra, P. & Koehler, M. (2006). Technological Pedagogical Content Knowledge: A Framework for Teacher Knowledge, *Teachers College Record*, 108, pp. 1017–1054. DOI:10.1111/j.1467-9620.2006.00684.x

Mitcham, C. (1994). *Thinking Through Technology: the Path Between Engineering & Philosophy*. Chicago: University of Chicago Press.

Oancea, A. & Furlong, J. (2007). Expressions of excellence & the assessment of applied & practice-based research, *Research Papers in Education*, 22(2) 119–137. DOI:10.1080/02671520701296056

Pasek, A. (2015). Errant bodies: relational aesthetics, digital communication, & the autistic analogy. *Disability Studies Quarterly*, 35(4). http://dsq-sds.org/article/view/4656/4111. DOI:10.18061/dsq.v35i4.4656

Poon, J. (2013). blended learning: an institutional approach for enhancing students' learning experiences, *MERLOT Journal of Online Learning & Teaching*, 9(2), 271–288. https://jolt.merlot.org/vol9no2/poon_0613.htm

Ronfeldt, M. & Grossman, P. (2008). Becoming a professional: experimenting with possible selves in professional preparation. *Teacher Education Quarterly*, 35(3), 41–60. https://eric.ed.gov/?id=EJ831708

Saunders, R. (2013). The role of teacher emotions in change: Experiences, patterns & implications for professional development. *Journal of Educational Change*, 14, 303–333. DOI:10.1007/s10833-012-9195-0

Wilson-Medhurst, S. (2008). *The Role of Attitudes, Values & Beliefs in Sustainable Educational Development for Organisational Change.* 13th Annual SEDA conference, Birmingham, 19 November 2008.

Wilson-Medhurst, S. & Childs, M. (2022). The characteristics of expertise for online teaching in higher education. *Developing Expertise for Teaching in Higher Education: The Artistry of Teaching, Symposium,* University of Warwick, 14th October 2022. https://www.youtube.com/watch?v=r39aoEmRmrc&list=PLNUkecXGxdTn_LNDVTmvJQ1otJg2uBnL3&index=15&t=77s

Winch, C., Oancea, A. & Orchard, J. (2015). The contribution of educational research to teachers' professional learning: philosophical understandings. *Oxford Review of Education,* 41(2), 202–216. DOI:10.1080/03054985.2015.1017406

Zawacki-Richter, O. & Naidu, S. (2016). Mapping research trends from 35 years of publications in Distance Education. *Distance Education,* 37(3), 245–269. DOI: 10.1080/01587919.2016.1185079

Chapter 13

Developing the artistry of language teaching through practitioner research

Anna Costantino

Introduction: An enquiry-based approach to navigate the intricacies of higher education contexts

Teaching in higher education (HE) comes with a variety of challenges. The field is constantly changing, becoming increasingly complex, and influenced by local, national, and international policy trends, all of which put demands on teachers. Some of the challenges affecting the professional knowledge and development of HE teachers arise from having to accommodate changes in the student body. The internationalisation of the student population and the widening participation goals in HE social equity policy agendas has called for adapting teaching to students with varying educational backgrounds. Additionally, the growing awareness of diversity – including age, gender, sexual orientation, culture, ethnicity, religious beliefs, disability, work commitments, and family responsibilities – means that teaching must be malleable enough to meet the diverse needs of diverse student populations (King, 2022b; Norton, 2019). Hence teachers need to keep abreast of and innovate in pedagogical approaches mindful of the diverse needs and capabilities of students.

Another set of tensions for universities concerns the imperative of providing *quality education*, the meaning of which is frequently defined by public policies and interests. For example, universities in many countries are compelled to participate in national and global ranking schemes to attract students and increase enrolment numbers. Attaining high rankings in such schemes can lead to implementing performance-based quality standards and inspections, which in turn affects how teaching is understood. Reliance on performance measures can be viewed as a move towards compliance and standardised practices to the detriment of individual creativity and practitioners' autonomy. It restricts the possibility of developing an understanding of contextual differences and engaging more profoundly with the pedagogical matters that arise locally. This tension can conflict with the goals of inclusion and social equity associated with the notion of quality education (Burke et al., 2015; McNay, 2017) as articulated in the Quality Education Sustainable Development Goals (SDGs Goal 4) in the United Nations agenda for global transformation, which aim to

DOI: 10.4324/9781003437826-17

"ensure inclusive and equitable quality education and promote lifelong learning opportunities for all" (UNESCO, 2016).

The UK's Teaching Excellence Framework (TEF) requirements are an example of accountability as a means through which the government monitors and assesses the quality of teaching in universities (Burke et al., 2015; Norton, 2019). The TEF framework also hints at the complex dynamic of constraints and affordances HE teachers must navigate. One of the TEF founding aims was to balance the competing university activities of teaching and research by recognising both of these with equal status, as well as rewarding teaching career paths (Burke et al., 2015; Gunn, 2018; McNay, 2017). To this end, supporting "staff professional development and excellent academic practice" remains a crucial drive in the latest policy criteria (Office for Students, 2022, p. 74).

The challenge for HE teachers is to balance the demands of institutional contexts and standardised practices with local needs to foster high-quality student learning and social equity opportunities. Teachers can develop this expertise through experience and through professional learning. King (2022b) suggests that expertise in teaching is characterised as the attainment of knowledge and skills related to teaching and to the discipline (Pedagogical Content Knowledge: PCK, Shulman, 1986), specific ways of thinking and practising (Artistry), and engagement with professional learning.

This chapter explores engagement with professional learning through practitioner research (PR) as one way of developing PCK. PR also represents an opportunity to reflect on and practise artistry, with artistry being understood here as autonomous professional learning and creative doing. PR nurtures "teachers' capacity for reflective, critical inquiry, and their ability to take responsibility for their own professional learning" (Slimani-Rolls & Kiely, 2019a, p. 34). Therefore, PR complements a holistic view of Continuing Professional Development (CPD) that intertwines PCK and artistry.

Teaching expertise that is mindful of the challenges that teaching staff face in HE contexts is considered by the concept of *personal practical knowledge* (Clandinin, 2013; Connelly & Clandinin, 1985; Golombek, 1998) or *personal practical knowing*. This form of professional learning is informed by teachers' pedagogical content knowing (PCKg) (Cochran et al., 1993) and rests on the acknowledgement that teachers are *worldmakers* (Schön, 1987). This implies that practitioners are capable of developing teaching expertise with agency and autonomy and engaging in transformative practices (Kennedy, 2005, 2014). Individual teachers' thinking, feeling, acting, and knowing are viewed as complex and organically intertwined with their contexts of practice, "the academic", "the organizational context of policy discussion" and "practice itself" (Eraut, 1994, p. 20), whilst also engaged in transforming these. To transform their contexts, teachers need to master practical knowledge that "integrates complex understanding and skills into a partly routinised performance, which has to be deconstructed and deroutinised in order to incorporate something new" (Eraut 1994, p. 20). This view hints of a characterisation of expertise as building on what is known and works and also highlights the need for risk-taking so as to engender spaces for creativity and innovation. PR addresses this characterisation by providing a form of professional learning that feeds on a conceptualisation of teaching expertise that is not "a static point to be reached but a dynamic process [...] of experiencing and experimenting" (King, 2022a, p. 3; see also Bereiter & Scardamalia, 1993; Tsui, 2003).

Developing personal practical knowing from initial to further professional development

In the literature on language teacher education, there has been a broad consensus that teacher professional knowledge and learning are situated and experiential (Block, 2016; Johnson & Golombek, 2002; Golombek, 1998; Richards & Farrell, 2005). Teachers possess capabilities and knowledge "that comes from experience, is learned in context and is expressed in practice" (Connelly & Clandinin, 2007, p. 90). When teachers participate in teacher education programmes and engage in further professional development, they develop a personal practical knowledge (Clandinin, 2013; Connelly & Clandinin, 1985; Golombek, 1998). Their practical experience is supported by knowledge that is continually elaborated, personally and socially, in such a way that past experience and future expectations are considered when addressing present situations and challenges (Swart et al., 2018).

Context is crucial for the acquisition of teachers' professional knowledge, particularly for teachers working in HE, who need a deep awareness and understanding of the institutional policy and local practices in addition to subject matter knowledge (Eraut, 1994). The ability to engage with their context of practice is one factor that is viewed to set experienced teachers apart from novices. However, the difference between them is not seen as deficient, but developmental. The PCKg model (Cochran et al., 1993) depicts the intricate and ever-changing relationships that teachers encounter as they develop professionally and complements the idea of personal practical knowledge. In PCKg, Shulman's (1986) idea of PCK and the constructivist underpinnings of teaching and learning are further elaborated. Indeed, the deployment of the term "knowing" implies an active approach to learning and understanding, as all aspects of learning and teaching are interconnected. Knowing is an active process occurring "in contexts where the goals are focused on *specific* content to *specific* contexts" (Cochran et al., 1993, p. 266; emphasis in the original). Hence, PCKg involves four components of knowledge: subject matter, pedagogy, students, and environmental contexts.

However, the relationships of PCKg's features may vary as language teachers develop from being novices to experienced professionals. Integrating these dimensions is a dynamic process, and teachers with little or no teaching experience are less likely to blend these dimensions. Novice teachers tend to focus more on pedagogy and subject matter and neglect the knowledge of the students and the environmental context. However, the more teachers become experienced the more their knowledge and behaviours present traits encompassing all the PKCg dimensions.

In initial or pre-service teacher education for language teachers, professional development typically entails mastering the core learning and teaching theories, including how an additional language is learnt, while becoming accustomed to applying these learnings during practicum experiences. This application means mastering the content knowledge of the language taught, which in turn entails covering its linguistic components (e.g., lexicon, grammar, cultural and intercultural awareness, pragmatics, proxemics, and so forth). The knowledge base for a language teacher also involves becoming familiar with teaching techniques and learning strategies into which the learning theories and research findings have been incorporated. Procedures are reinforced by the literature that shapes the guidelines of teacher education programmes. Those, in turn, inform the content of published materials, the criteria for assessing effectiveness and performance management procedures, such as classroom observations (Slimani-Rolls & Kiely, 2019b). The mastering of pedagogical materials and activities, which are key in a language classroom and the basic of classroom management are stepping stones that enable teachers to settle into their initial teaching practice.

At this stage of their development, the acquisition of how to handle pedagogical materials and the internalisation of teaching methods is critical. For novice teachers, teaching methods "provide a framework for planning lessons and managing instruction and interaction in the classroom. Thus, methods and their underlying principles can facilitate teaching, and provide information that guides adaptation and innovation" (Slimani-Rolls & Kiely, 2019b, p. 7). Moreover, procedural frameworks such as Present, Practice, Produce (PPP), Engage, Study, Activate (ESA), Authentic, Restricted, Clarification (ARC) (Harmer 2015; Scrivener 2011), or learning-oriented methods, such as Task-Based Language Teaching (Ellis, 2013) represent a common language and shared understanding amongst classroom participants and stakeholders within their language community (Farrell, 2012). Methods therefore allow novice language teachers to develop their PCK, which is not yet a full engagement with PCKg.

The preceding description broadly characterises how novice language teachers learn and what they learn. Cochran et al. (1993) acknowledge evidence that the four components of the PCKg model may not develop evenly at any stage of the teacher's journey. This also means that the four components may not fully integrate throughout a teacher's career development, which is often the case when there is not support for professional learning. Privileging the idea of *knowing* over *knowledge* also effects the understanding of teacher preparation. *Knowing* suggests "autonomous conceptual understanding" (Cochran et al., 1993, p. 266), which paves the way to creative doing. Conversely, *knowledge*, which may be associated with "training", "may lead to the replication of a behavioural response" (p. 266) and the endorsement of mechanistic views of teaching that hinder artistry and innovation.

In language education, there have been criticisms of initial training for being transmissive and the nature of the learning being top-down. Richards and Farrell make a distinction between "teacher training" and "teacher development" (Richards & Farrell, 2005, p. 3), which, at the core of teacher education, tend to be seen as interchangeable in early professional development. There are two types of learning involved, with the main difference being the duration of the programme. *Training* typically involves short, intensive courses like the Certificate in Teaching English to Speakers of Other Languages (CELTA) certificate for English language teaching. *Teacher development* is associated with longer programmes such as the Postgraduate Certificate in Education (PGCE) in Modern Languages, which runs for a full academic year. Training courses are considered top-down activities (Foord, 2009), whereas teacher development has a deeper and broader scope and can be seen as a bottom-up activity giving teachers more agency (Richards & Farrell, 2005).

Teacher training, with short-term goals such as CELTA, aims to provide teachers with a basic understanding of classroom principles and practices. It is designed to prepare teachers for their first teaching position or a new role. The expected goals of short training courses are:

- Learning how to use effective strategies to open a lesson
- Adapting the textbook to match the class
- Learning how to use group activities in a lesson
- Using effective questioning techniques
- Using classroom resources (e.g., video)
- Techniques for giving feedback to learners.

(Richards & Farrell, 2005, p. 3)

Serving a long-term-goal, teacher development "seeks to facilitate growth of teachers' understanding of teaching and of themselves as teachers" (p. 4). Goals for teacher development are:

- Understanding how the process of second language development occurs
- Understanding how teachers' roles change according to the kind of learner
- Understanding the decision making that occurs during lessons
- Reviewing theories and principles of language teaching
- Developing an understanding of different styles of teaching
- Determining learners' perception of classroom activities.

(Richards & Farrell, 2005, p. 3)

Teacher development programmes encourage individuals to create reflective assignments based on feedback received from mentors or peers during classroom observations. However, not everything can be learnt about teaching through self-observation and critical reflections even within teacher development programmes. Aspects such as a thorough subject-matter knowledge, an understanding of the curriculum, how programmes are organised and managed, and importantly, pedagogical expertise are difficult to be grasped at an initial stage. A long-term exposure to practice and attuning to learning experiences are needed.

After their pre-service teacher education programme, teachers begin to gain experience moving "from teaching the language to teaching students, and thus extending their understanding of the social nature of classrooms" (Slimani-Rolls & Kiely, 2019b, p. 15). They move from a more static handling of pedagogical content knowledge to developing a sense of their "environmental contexts" and their students and therefore embracing the dynamic of PCKg.

Experienced teachers need to engage with new learning and teaching theories and methods in their specific context of practice (Richards & Farrel, 2005). This engagement includes familiarizing themselves with teaching methods for additional languages as well as academic subjects. They may also need to become proficient in digital pedagogies or modify their programmes based on new assessment frameworks.

In HE, changes in quality assurance policies or management may depend on national or international policies that require standardisation across institutions. Teachers must learn and relearn how assessment is administered in response to these policies. Language education in HE often relies on the Common European Framework of Reference for Languages (CEFR) (Council of Europe, 2020), which provides proficiency descriptors used across Europe and beyond. Changes in the Council of Europe's language policies may require modifications to assessments and content, affecting learning objectives and pedagogical activities.

Language teachers' knowledge base and developmental dynamics call to be considered in the light of the *personal* dimension in what was earlier introduced as *personal practical knowledge* (Clandinin, 2013; Connelly & Clandinin, 1985; Golombek, 1998). For teachers, becoming aware of and engaging with their context of practice presents different levels of complexity attaining to how they respond to theory and environment. When considering teachers' knowledge, we need also to stretch beyond its cognitive remit and delve into the moral and emotional dimensions of their professional engagement and learning. Indeed, teacher beliefs and attitudes are integral to developing personal practical knowledge as an ever-changing process rather than static acquisition of knowledge, which is essential in developing teachers' personal and professional identities (Borg, 2010; Farrell, 2012; Gallardo, 2019).

The moral and emotional aspects are also relevant to understanding how novice teachers engage in development since they are not a blank slate to be filled with knowledge. For language teachers, the formation of professional identities intermeshes with their ever-changing personal identity trajectory. As highlighted by Gallardo (2019), language teachers' identities are "multiple, plurilingual, pluricultural, and transnational" (Gallardo, 2019, viii). Even if they are often slippery to pin down, they are nevertheless inherently intertwined with teacher development. Gallardo's (2019) work with language practitioner-researchers in UK universities reveals that the sense of personal identity of transnational language teachers is closely tied to their teaching practice and their relationships with students and fellow practitioners. Socially constructed, language teacher identity is part of a "learning trajectory" (p. 3) that emerges from the criss-crossing of local and global practices (Block, 2016). As pluricultural and plurilingual individuals, teachers have the ability to respond and take action in their social environment, while building their identity as members of academic departments and educational institutions. Their sense of agency and resilience in decision-making allows them to develop their full potential and enhance their professional lives. Language teachers are "agents in the formation of their own identity within the social and educational contexts which they inhabit and to which they make a contribution" (Gallardo, 2019, pp. 3–4). This agency has been captured by Schön (1987) in the idea of practitioners as *worldmakers*:

> "Through countless acts of attention and inattention, naming, sensemaking, boundary setting, and control, they make and maintain the worlds matched to their professional knowledge and know-how.... When practitioners respond to the indeterminate zones of practice by holding a reflective conversation with the materials of their situations, they remake a part of their practice world and thereby reveal the usually tacit processes of worldmaking that underlie all of their practice."
>
> (Schön, 1987, p. 36)

Expertise as a mesh of agency and teacher autonomy

Personal practical knowing encompasses the developmental trajectory of both novice and experienced teachers and can be further characterised by considering the difference between the two concepts of expertise and experience.

In their context of practice, expert teachers do not solely rely upon a fixed skill set acquired by accumulation during their learning and professional practice. Nor do they retrieve those skills in classroom at-hand tasks (Connelly & Clandinin, 2007). Rather, expertise is a dynamic and continuous process informed and shaped by the contingencies and events encountered in complex practices. It entails the acquisition of PCKg and involves the mastery of techniques, attained through experience and turned into work routines. To conceptualise the idea of teacher autonomy in language education, Little (1995) draws on Gardner's definition of a learner as "disciplinary expert" to define those learners who can master concepts and skills of a discipline or domain and can then apply those appropriately in new situations. In routinised practices, expertise contemplates elements of automaticity and effortlessness (Tsui 2003). Those attributes are compared to artistry as an ability to improvise, while remaining in vigilant control of the classroom dynamics. Schön (1987) refers to it as "professional artistry" and characterises it as a dimension of practice close to autonomy, as practitioners exhibit this quality in situations of practice that are unique, uncertain, and often conflicted.

Yet, the fine distinction between an experienced performance and expert performance still needs to be drawn. Tsui (2003) argues that there are three crucial dimensions that discriminate between experience and expertise. Expert teachers:

(1) Engage actively in the act of teaching, rather than solely reproducing what they know, e.g., their toolkit of techniques. This construct resonates with the idea of artistry as "reflection-in action" (Schön, 1987); an action that occurs amid the practice and allows practitioners to use it to deal with unique or conflictual events by experimenting with their context of practice and taking risk;
(2) Strive to make sense of their context of practice while perceiving and seeking learning opportunities that are not immediately visible; and
(3) Are able to "theorize the knowledge generated by their personal practical experience as a teacher and [...] 'practicalize' theoretical knowledge."

(Tsui, 2003, p. 247)

Further, Tsui maintains, expertise is *multiple* and *distributed*. Teachers are able to integrate different forms of knowledge, for instance formal or informal, practical and theoretical. In addition, they pool together the expertise of several individuals "because it is only through constant engagement in professional discourse communities that expert knowledge can be developed and maintained" (Tsui, 2003, p. 281).

It is worth considering an additional aspect that differentiates expertise from experience, which provides us with a full-fledged idea of expertise as autonomy and agency. Expert teachers engage in "progressive problem solving" (Bereiter & Scardamalia, 1993, p. 81). On the one hand, they develop the ability to solve problems and create routines that ease their work. They then utilise the time available to investigate novel problems. When they tackle new challenges, they develop abilities that increase their expertise. Consequently, expert teachers always work "at the edge of competence" (Bereiter & Scardamalia, 1993, p. 98). In Box 13.1, Leonardo Morantes-Africano et al. add weight to the argument for teacher autonomy as an underpinning principle of the artistry of teaching.

Box 13.1 Breaking good: a critical interrogation of neoliberal 'common sense' that constrains artistry in education

Leonardo Morantes-Africano, Laura Heels, Lindsay Marshall, and Carys Watts

Traditional definitions of professionalism encompass practitioners' knowledge, expertise, values, and ethics that underpin their professional practice (Taubman, 2015). This requires passion, dedication, and often failure; such as the Japanese call shokunin kishitsu (職人気質), which loosely translates as "artisanal spirit" and encapsulates not just expertise, but also the artistry of the craft. This develops over time, based on the fundamentals of disciplinary knowledge and seeking meaning, combined with an intuitive understanding of how to convey this innovatively and with enthusiasm. Whilst this expertise normally enables autonomy and the exercise of judgement, the neoliberal agendas of performativity and accountability undermine not only teacher professionalism but also reconfigure the meaning and value of education (Hastings, 2019; Read, 2009).

Currently, educators (and students) live a life of high stakes, and thinking about artistry can be lost to worries about value for money, efficiency, and customer satisfaction. We should be creating an environment where students are comfortable with failure; be actively encouraged to question their understanding and why conclusions are drawn and to embrace the meaningful learning that arises. Giving them a voice to question their learning in a sense of development, not questioning the vendor. Standards of practice are important as guiding principles, as are specifications of core content, but if these become the focus of professional practice, this can thwart educators' ability to develop artistry in teaching when applied too rigorously (Winkler-Reid, 2017). Rote teaching is as bad as rote learning and is the enemy of artistry. Favouring a culture of performance and measurability rather than one of problem solving and innovation has tried to turn teachers into technicians. Hargreaves (2000) argues this is driven by metrics and control of narrowly conceived competence frameworks. The scope for teachers to exercise professional autonomy originally felt little intervention from external forces, but with gradual increase in policies, expectations, and stakeholders' competing agendas, this has diminished.

There is a need for further and higher education (HE) to start shaping a future where ensuring financial sustainability does not need us to compromise our values and beliefs. Given that a syllabus is often confirmed before an academic cycle is complete, and may be subject to non-negotiable parameters associated with accreditation, what scope is there to reflect on student learning gain, such as personal growth, or innovations in the curricular content? Fundamentally, we need to re-establish the trust and value in educators that allows their artistry to develop rather than proscribing every detail for an economic or output driven metric (Schroeder, 2021). This quantitative and pre-measured approach to education requires us to adopt what Lyotard (1984, xxiv) called an "incredulity towards metanarratives". We must question neoliberalism and the power of its logic (Foucault, 1980). We suggest that HE needs to start shaping a "preferable future" (Inayatullah, 2013) where ensuring quality and improvement in our practice does not mean forgetting the purpose and value of education, or our values and principles as educators. Thus, we posit teacher autonomy as an underpinning principle for the artistry of teaching. Reintroducing creativity to learning enables value creation, which is in the DNA, coding language, and pedagogy of both discipline and learning journey. Neoliberalism is a human creation, and we have the capacity to change it.

Practitioner research to develop expertise and autonomy in HE

PR is one professional practice that can help HE teachers pursue a holistic view of CPD with the previously outlined characteristics as it has been seen as a powerful tool for professional learning and for professionalising teachers (e.g., AdvanceHE, n.d.; Norton, 2019; Fanghanel et al., 2016; Richards & Farrell, 2005; Trigwell et al., 2000).

PR is an umbrella term (Hanks, 2017) for a broad variety of approaches used by practitioners to investigate their own practices within professional and community contexts. PR relates to action research, educational action research, participatory action research, teacher research, teacher as researcher, reflective practice, and exploratory practice, to name a few. Such terms are often used interchangeably (Cochran-Smith & Lytle, 2009), particularly action research. As one of the most established forms of PR, action research tends to function as the hyponym for the practice per se (Kemmis, 2006).

Several features of PR align with the idea of professional learning as development of artistry and autonomy. PR is an enquiry that is undertaken by practitioners to investigate their own practice at the local level. It develops situated knowing addressing the complex dynamics of pedagogy, broader context, and learners' needs. Practitioners engage in critical instances arising from their practice to make sense of it. In doing so, they work on conceptualising their practice and practicalising theoretical knowledge (Tsui, 2003). PR is reflexive as it calls for practitioners to review and question their values, knowledge, professional and personal experiences, and so to be open to experimentation (Arnold & Norton, 2018). PR is a means to develop expertise as an open-ended process "at the edge of competence" (Bereiter & Scardamalia, 1993). PR is collaborative, as it is conducted with other practitioners constantly participating in communities of practice and learning. Collegial engagement allows for understandings and expertise to be sustained and sustainable (Allwright & Hanks, 2009; Tsui, 2003). PR is intentional and systematic; it is an activity that is planned rather than taking place spontaneously (Cochran-Smith & Lytle, 2009).

Professional development constraints and affordances

In many HE institutions in the UK, becoming involved in CPD is a contractual obligation for teaching staff on a permanent contract. However, these opportunities can contradict the view that teachers have agency and autonomy. In language teacher training, CPD events tend to be offered with scope sometimes limited to updating skills and techniques, enhancing competence, or addressing gaps in performance (Kennedy, 2005; Slimani-Rolls & Kiely, 2019a). Such activities typically adopt a top-down approach and lack opportunities for individual teachers to develop personal practical knowing and leverage their experience and artistry (Schön, 1987).

Reflecting on my personal and professional trajectory, I view PR as playing a crucial role in the development of my personal practical knowledge and knowing, and hence my teaching and personal identity as a transnational professional. Kennedy's framework of CPD is an apt illustration of the journey that led me to PR. Kennedy envisages a three-layered framework of analysis comprising nine major models of development identified across the world and grouped under a threefold classification: transmissive, malleable, and transformative (Kennedy 2005; 2014).

CPD models are based according to their "increasing capacity for professional autonomy and teacher agency" (Kennedy, 2014, p. 693). It is important to note that, as discussed with PCKg, the framework does not imply linearity in the pursuit of transformative practice, which may be considered as an ideal aim rather than a developmental point that can be fully reached.

The majority of CPD opportunities across the language education field could be described as "transmission" models. Transmission models are developmental events to update teachers' skills and knowledge to enhance their competence. Examples include short training courses prompted by local policies or the teaching resources industry, such as publishers organising materials' development sessions to promote new publications. These events are top-down and based on a technocratic view of teaching (Schön, 1987; Slimani-Rolls & Kiely, 2019a). They are typically delivered by external experts, who are often not mindful of the teaching and learning contexts of the attendees and nevertheless expect the latter to develop effective teaching techniques. Even the cascade approach, where teachers disseminate to their peers in activities such as show-and-tell, lacks problematisation and risk-taking.

The "malleable model" encompasses approaches that can be found in HE and potentially can enrich teachers' expertise by helping them maintain and develop it further. However, some of them bear shortcomings. The "standards-based" approach enables teachers to consider their context of practice as fully integrated in their teaching. It also hints that standards are met through accountability and inspection, leaving teacher agency and reflectivity out of the frame of their development (Slimani-Rolls & Kiely, 2019a).

"Transformative" models, including coaching/mentoring and communities of practice, are those that have allowed me to engage in PR and envisage my professional learning as striving towards autonomy. These approaches allow for professional learning to be part of the institutional context (Eraut, 1994) and become entrenched in the activity of communities of practice (Lave & Wenger, 1991; Wenger 1998).

My current professional identity is underpinned by the understandings gained after joining a practitioner research developmental project with five other language teachers, while being mentored by a senior colleague (Slimani-Rolls & Kiely, 2019a, 2019b). I joined the project keen to understand and enhance my own practice, although still adhering to the methodological assumptions internalised in my previous professional development and concerned with the effectiveness of my pedagogy and subject-matter above everything. I was an experienced teacher, and I had enough awareness of the expectations of the academic and policy contexts. Yet I began to question my pedagogical assumptions by interrogating instances of my practice and investigating them through my pedagogical activities, which became my investigative tools. The understandings I gained were also engendered by discussions I had with my mentor and my peers.

The PR research form I engaged with was exploratory practice (Allwright & Hanks, 2009; Hanks, 2017), which uses conventional classroom activities to investigate critical classroom instances. Through my questioning, I "deconstructed" and "deroutinised" my pedagogy (Eraut, 1994), which allowed me to review my assumptions about my teaching and my learners' capabilities. By the end of the project, I felt I had developed my professional identity as a practitioner researcher, and committed to the scholarship of teaching and learning as well as to a more inclusive understanding of the mutual nature of learning where agency and responsibilities are shared with the learners.

In Kennedy's (2014) framework, developing "collaborative professional enquiry" is presented as a transformative activity; one that is conducive to autonomy. Ever since I became engaged in PR, I have further developed my own idea of how to develop teacher autonomy, and I am currently working on how to approach pedagogic activities to engender innovation through PR (Costantino, 2023).

Key take-aways

- **Engage in sustained and sustainable professional development**: I continue to engage in "transmissive" and "malleable" activities. It is important that we continue to develop according to our capabilities and contextual possibility for professional learning to be sustainable and sustained.
- **Work inclusively towards "mutual development"** (Allwright & Hanks, 2009): Working collaboratively is crucial. By involving all stakeholders, learners, researchers, teachers, and managers in communities of practice and learning, we can enhance our practice and also the quality of life in our classroom (Hanks, 2017; Tsui, 2003).
- **Take risk and experiment**: It is by questioning and investigating critical instances of our practice that professional artistry can flourish and lead to innovative practices.

References

AdvanceHE (n.d.). *Defining and Supporting the Scholarship of Teaching and Learning (SoTL): A Sector Wide Study*. https://www.advance-he.ac.uk/knowledge-hub/defining-and-supporting-scholarship-teaching-and-learning-sotl-sector-wide-study

Allwright, D., & Hanks, J. (2009). *The Developing Language Learner: An Introduction to Exploratory Practice*. London: Palgrave Macmillan. DOI:10.1057/9780230233690

Arnold, L. and Norton, L., (2018). *HEA Action Research: Practice Guide*. Higher Education Academy. https://www.advance-he.ac.uk/knowledge-hub/action-research-practice-guide

Bereiter, C., & Scardamalia, M. (1993). *Surpassing Ourselves: An Enquiry into the Nature and Implications of Expertise*. Chicago/La Salle, Illinois: Open Court Publications.

Block, D. (2016). Journey to the center of language teacher identity. In: *Reflections on Language Teacher Identity Research*. New York: Routledge, pp. 39–44. DOI:10.4324/9781315643465-9

Borg, S. (2010). Language teacher research engagement. *Language Teaching*, 43(4), 391–429. DOI:10.1017/S0261444810000170

Burke, P.J., Stevenson, J., & Whelan, P. (2015). Teaching 'Excellence' and pedagogic stratification in higher education. *International Studies in Widening Participation*, 2(2), 29–43. https://shura.shu.ac.uk/id/eprint/11087

Clandinin, D.J. (2013). Chapter 4 Personal practical knowledge: A study of teachers' classroom images. In: Craig, C.J., Meijer, P.C. & Broeckmans, J., (eds.) *From Teacher Thinking to Teachers and Teaching: The Evolution of a Research Community*, 19, pp. 67–95. Bingley: Emerald. DOI:10.1108/S1479-3687(2013)0000019007

Cochran, K.F., DeRuiter, J.A., & King, R.A. (1993). Pedagogical content knowing: An integrative model for teacher preparation. *Journal of Teacher Education*, 44(4), 263–272. DOI:10.1177/0022487193044004004

Cochran-Smith, M., & Lytle, S.L. (2009). *Inquiry as stance: Practitioner research for the Next Generation*. New York/London: Teachers College Press.

Connelly, F.M., & Clandinin, D.J. (1985). Chapter X: Personal practical knowledge and the modes of knowing: relevance for teaching and learning. *Teachers College Record*, 86(6), 174–198. DOI:10.1177/016146818508600610

Connelly, F.M., & Clandinin, D.J. (2007). Teacher education—A question of teacher knowledge. In: Freeman-Moir, J., Scott, A. (eds.), *Shaping the Future*. Brill, pp. 89–105. DOI:10.1163/9789087903565_008

Costantino, A. (2023). Exploring the multimodal affordances of pedagogical materials and activities for an inclusive and transformative language pedagogy. In Dominquez Romero, E., Bobkina, J., Stefanova, S., & Herrero, C., (eds). *Rethinking Multimodal Literacy in Theory and Practice*. Peter Lang, pp. 37–57

Council of Europe (2020). *Common European Framework of Reference for Languages: Learning, teaching, Assessment* – Companion volume. Strasbourg: Council of Europe Publishing. https://rm.coe.int/common-european-framework-of-reference-for-languages-learning-teaching/16809ea0d4

Ellis, R. (2013). *Task-based Language Teaching*. Oxford: Oxford University Press.

Eraut, M. (1994). *Developing Professional Knowledge and Competence*. London: Falmer Press. DOI:10.4324/9780203486016

Fanghanel, J., Pritchard, J., Potter, J., & Wisker, G. (2016). *Defining and Supporting the Scholarship of Teaching and Learning (SoTL): A Sector-Wide Study*. https://www.advance-he.ac.uk/knowledge-hub/defining-and-supporting-scholarship-teaching-and-learning-sotl-sector-wide-study

Farrell, T.S. (2012). Novice-service language teacher development: Bridging the gap between preservice and in-service education and development. *Tesol Quarterly*, 46(3), 435–449. DOI:10.1002/tesq.36

Foord, D. (2009). *The Developing Teacher: Practical Activities for Professional Development*. Peaslake/Essex: Delta Publishing.

Foucault, M. (1980). *Power Knowledge: Selected Interviews and Other Writings 1972–1977*, ed. Colin Gordon. Brighton: Harvester Press.

Gallardo, M. (ed.). (2019). *Negotiating Identity in Modern Foreign Language Teaching*. Cham: Palgrave Macmillan. DOI:10.1007/978-3-030-27709-3

Golombek, P.R. (1998). A study of language teachers' personal practical knowledge. *TESOL Quarterly*, 32(3), 447–464. DOI:10.2307/3588117

Gunn, A. (2018). The UK Teaching Excellence Framework (TEF): The development of a new transparency tool. In: Curaj, A., Deca, L., & Pricopie, R. (eds.) *European Higher Education Area: The Impact of Past and Future Policies*. Cham: Springer. DOI:10.1007/978-3-319-77407-7_31

Hanks, J. (2017). *Exploratory Practice in Language Teaching: Puzzling about Principles and Practices*. London: Palgrave Macmillan. DOI:10.1057/978-1-137-45344-0

Hargreaves, A. (2000). Four ages of professionalism and professional learning. *Teachers and Teaching: History and Practice*, 6, 151–182. DOI:10.1080/713698714

Harmer, J. (2015). *The Practice of English Language Teaching*. Harlow: Pearson Educational Publishing.

Hastings, M. (2019). Neoliberalism and education. *Oxford Research Encyclopedia of Education*. DOI:10.1093/acrefore/9780190264093.013.404

Inayatullah, S. (2013). Futures Studies. Theories and Methods. Metafuture, 1–65. http://www.metafuture.org/library1/FuturesStudies/Futures-Studies-theories-and-methods-published-version-2013-with-pics.pdf

Johnson, K.E., & Golombek, P.R. (2002). *Teachers' Narrative Inquiry as Professional Development*. Cambridge/New York: Cambridge University Press.

Kemmis, S. (2006). Participatory action research and the public sphere. *Educational Action Research*, 14(4), 459–476. DOI:10.1080/09650790600975593

Kennedy, A. (2005). Models of continuing professional development: A framework for analysis. *Journal of In-Service Education*, 31(2), 235–250. DOI:10.1080/13674580500200277

Kennedy, A. (2014). Understanding continuing professional development: the need for theory to impact on policy and practice. *Professional Development in Education*, 40(5), 688–697. DOI:10.1080/19415257.2014.955122

King, H. (2022a). Introduction: Developing expertise for teaching in higher education. In: King, H. (ed.). *Developing Expertise for Teaching in Higher Education*. London: Routledge, pp. 1–12. DOI:10.4324/9781003198772-1

King, H. (2022b). The characteristics of expertise for teaching in higher education. In: King, H. (ed.). *Developing Expertise for Teaching in Higher Education*. London: Routledge, pp. 15–28. DOI:10.4324/9781003198772-3

Lave, J., & Wenger, E. (1991). *Situated Learning: Legitimate Peripheral Participation*. Cambridge university press. DOI:10.1017/CBO9780511815355

Little, D. (1995). Learning as dialogue: The dependence of learner autonomy on teacher autonomy. *System*, 23(2), 175–181. DOI:10.1016/0346-251X(95)00006-6

Lyotard, J.F. (1984). *The Postmodern Condition: A Report on Knowledge*. Manchester University Press. (Original work published 1979)

McNay, I. (2017). TEF: why and how? Ideological and operational imperatives driving policy. *Compass: Journal of Learning and Teaching*, 10(2). DOI:10.21100/compass.v10i2.487

Norton, L. (2019). *Action Research in Teaching and Learning: A Practical Guide to Conducting Pedagogical Research in Universities*, (2nd ed.). Abingdon: Routledge. DOI:10.4324/9781315147581

Read, J. (2009). A genealogy of homo-economicus: neoliberalism and the production of subjectivity. *Foucault Studies*, 6, 25–36. DOI:10.22439/fs.v0i0.2465

Richards, J.C., & Farrell, T.S. (2005). *Professional Development for Language Teachers: Strategies for Teacher Learning*. Cambridge University Press. DOI:10.1017/CBO9780511667237

Schön, D.A. (1987). *Educating the Reflective Practitioner: Toward a New Design for Teaching and Learning in the Professions*. San Francisco: Jossey-Bass.

Schroeder, M. (2021). Value Theory. *The Stanford Encyclopedia of Philosophy*. In: Edward N. Zalta (ed.), https://plato.stanford.edu/archives/fall2021/entries/value-theory/

Scrivener, J. (2011). *Learning Teaching*. London: Macmillan Education.

Shulman, L.S. (1986). Those who understand: Knowledge growth in teaching. *Educational Researcher*, 15, 4–14. DOI:10.2307/1175860

Slimani-Rolls, A., & Kiely, R. (2019a). Exploratory practice as a principled framework for CPD. In: Slimani-Rolls, A. & Kiely, R. (eds.), *Exploratory Practice for Continuing Professional Development*. Cham: Palgrave Macmillan, pp. 29–49. DOI:10.1007/978-3-319-69763-5_2

Slimani-Rolls, A., & Kiely, R. (2019b). Exploratory Practice in language education: How teachers teach and learn. In A. Slimani-Rolls & R. Kiely (eds.), *Exploratory Practice for Continuing Professional Development*. Cham: Palgrave Macmillan, pp. 5–27. DOI:10.1007/978-3-319-69763-5_1

Swart, F., de Graaff, R., Onstenk, J., & Knezic, D. (2018). Teacher educators' personal practical knowledge of language. *Teachers and Teaching*, 24(2), 166–182. DOI:10.1080/13540602.2017.1368477

Office for Students (2022). *Regulatory advice 22 Guidance on the Teaching Excellence Framework (TEF) 2023*. OfS. https://www.officeforstudents.org.uk/publications/regulatory-advice-22-guidance-on-the-teaching-excellence-framework-2023/

Taubman, D. (2015). Reframing professionalism and reclaiming the dance. In: Daley, M., Orr, K., & Petrie, J. (eds.), *Further Education and the Twelve Dancing Princesses*. Institute Of Education Press, pp. 107–119.

Trigwell, K., Martin, E., Benjamin, J., & Prosser, M. (2000). Scholarship of teaching: A model. *Higher Education Research & Development*, 19(2), 155–168. DOI:10.1080/072943600445628

Tsui, A. (2003). *Understanding Expertise in Teaching: Case Studies of Second Language Teachers*. Cambridge University Press. DOI:10.1017/CBO9781139524698

UNESCO. (2016). Unpacking sustainable development goal 4 education 2030 guide. http://unesdoc.unesco.org/images/0024/002463/246300E.pdf

Wenger, E. (1998). Communities of practice: Learning as a social system. *Systems Thinker*, 9(5), 2–3.

Winkler-Reid, S. (2017). "Doing your best" in a London secondary school: valuing, caring and thinking through neoliberalism. *The Sociological Review*, 65, 137–153. DOI:10.1177/0081176917693553

Chapter 14

Facilitating in the moment
Being ready for change

Lucy Nicholson, Ruth Spencer, and Kerstin Wellhöfer

Introduction

November 2022 saw Senior Lecturers from the University of Central Lancashire's UCLanDance team come together in a precious moment of deep reflection, squeezed in between the teaching and administrative commitments of higher education (HE). This oasis moment provided opportunity to capture some of the team's learning and inquiries around teaching as an artistic practice in higher education. All staff on the dance course engage in somatically informed creative dance practices that are heavily rooted within education and community contexts. The recorded conversation started to articulate our collective pedagogical approaches. That conversation is developed here, as we reflect upon what it means to teach and attend to themes of duality, focussing specifically on Self – Other, Part – Whole connections. We discuss how intentionally connecting to our physical moving body before teaching supports us to be fully present and in turn enhances our ability to be critically reflective in action. We propose a reframing of the educator from "expert" to facilitating guide and ask how bringing our whole selves into our teaching spaces can support our decision-making processes and allow us to recognise shifts in presence within our student body and bodies.

Finding authenticity in an HE context

Much is expected of us in the current HE context: our approach to delivery prioritises an open, inquiring, creative and reflection-based practice through person-centred and compassionate relationships between lecturer and student amidst a wider work culture within which time to slow down and connect to our present and authentic selves is ever reducing. As a staff team, we viscerally experience the demands of HE and endeavour to allow kindness and creativity to help us through uncomfortable and clashing needs. A desired arriving to teach with time for attending to bodily presence is often short-changed by

DOI: 10.4324/9781003437826-18

numerous interrupters, such as a student knock on the door just before going to class; a short reflective comment that can quickly turn into an absorbing discussion amongst staff who are only in on that day and only free for those 15 minutes; and the endless emails that demand quick responses. Where is the time, the space, the gap in the to-do list to ensure sufficient preparation and reflection can happen?

For our team, the contained and creatively held environment of our dance studios is challenged with the surrounding structures of HE, where the rush and squeeze of the everyday working, unrealistic workloads, and ever-changing initiatives impacts on pedagogical approaches. Dall'Alba, Honorary Associate Professor with The University of Queensland, explores attuned pedagogical approaches within HE and warns that "attentive tuning-in is incompatible with bustling about in a state of distracted busyness" (Dall'Alba, 2020, p. 30), drawing upon Heidegger to express how the "tempting and tranquilising effect" of "busying ourselves" (Heidegger, 2008, cited in Dall'Alba, 2020, p. 30) allows us to evade the challenges that face us, and how in plunging ourselves into "the groundlessness and nullity of inauthentic everydayness" (ibid) we risk immersing ourselves in busy work with "a sham of authenticity" (ibid.). Recognising a tendency towards this "distracted busyness" (ibid.) in our own working practices, key questions emerge: How does this culture of speed, and not enough time, impact on our pedagogy? What's important in these tricky times? How do we arrive in the studio or classroom ready and able to teach? How does our artistic practice support our pedagogy?

Without the ability to control our environment, and to guard against becoming controlling of others, it becomes critical to, metaphorically, put on our own oxygen mask before attending to the needs of everyone, and everything, else. In reality, some of us experience conflict here in balancing our own well-being with the ever-pressing and urgent student and organisational demands with a person-centred and relational pedagogical approach.

In this chapter, we draw on our embodied dance practice to support us to find presence (being here and now) through a keen sense of bodily awareness and a practice of dwelling (Giddens, Long & Spencer, 2018). This awareness enables full-bodied spaciousness, empowering us to slow down enough to notice our whole selves.

What does our dance training offer us in this context?

As dance artists and movement practitioners, our somatically informed improvisational and choreographic skills support and train our capacities to facilitate inclusively. Postmodern dance practices, such as Contact Improvisation (CI), are founded upon nonverbal, sensory-based communication between two or more bodies, with movement duets unfolding through attentive *physical* "listening to another" whilst allowing oneself to be "witnessed/listened to at the same time" (Dowler, cited in Tufnell, 2017, p. 108). Movement practices like CI finely attune a dancer's relationship not only within the dancing space but also in interactions and relationships in the wider world. International CI performer and teacher Catherine Moccialo speaks of how her dance practice became an extremely important part of how she interacts with the world, emphasising how the practice expanded her awareness and knowledge of herself, impacting on her daily life outside of the dance studio in the way she sees and experiences things (Moccialo, cited in Pini and Deans, 2021, p. 108). This transference of skills learnt through the dance class into our ways of being in the wider world impacts on us as facilitators within HE, developing a capacity in a teaching context for the energy and resonance of the group to be whole bodily sensed and responded to. We may do this through a change of pace, tone, or verbal and other sensory cues, with moments of pausing for the learning to resonate and be absorbed. Where some may focus on exercise as the repetition and refinement of applied movement, dance creatively reflects on perceptions of how movement organises, executes, and feels.

The Discipline of Authentic Movement, as established by Janet Adler, centres the development of embodied witness consciousness through in-depth practice of the form, refining the notion of witness (Adler, 2002, p. 12). Studying this form invites dance practitioners to deepen their capacity for perceiving, and ultimately articulating, experience. Through the form is a wholeness of awareness. Drawing on structures of mover, witness, and meta witness, we may engage in exploring and developing multiple nuances of what it means to notice self and other. The curiosity of the meta-witness is how to situate one individual with the task of attending to their own bodily responses (in movement and sensations, feelings, imaginings and thoughts) in the presence of two other people (the mover and the witness). We help nurture the role of the witness by supporting individuals to remain receptive in movement and open to the emerging sensations, impulses, feelings, and ideas. To be sitting or standing with sufficient support from the ground, so that the spine is free to sway, move in all directions and not be limited, is key. To allow the body to move in response to what it is in the presence of is vital information about the movement itself. To value and honour the responsiveness of the moving body is necessary for understanding our own perceptions. This ownership of *my* body moves when *your* body moves invites parallel experience out of which more than one reality is affirmed as welcome and valid.

These creative movement practices, amongst others, experientially offer us gateways into bodily awareness, being present, knowing ourselves (Body–Mind) *and* ourselves in relation to others. In the remainder of this chapter, we will consider how these learnings inform our pedagogical approaches.

Becoming more aware

Our physically moving body can support us to remain aware through gaining clarity of our own inner terrain. As we move, we touch and are being touched by the world around us and our perception of where and how we are within it is communicated to our brain through our parasympathetic and sympathetic nervous systems. These two divisions of the involuntary (autonomic) nervous system, along with a third division, the enteric system, are involved with maintaining internal homeostasis in the body. Body Mind Centering® founder, Bonnie Bainbridge Cohen, describes how the sympathetic nervous system – often known as the three F's of flight, fright, or freeze – "tracks and directs our internal movement and energetic processes" through an "external mind state", carrying signals for "alertness, which can be both for alarm and for clarity" (Bainbridge Cohen, 2008, p. 176), whilst the parasympathetic nervous system mind state is "inner directed" and provides a base level of nervous tone within the body. When we breathe, meditate, and move from internal sensation, we engage in parasympathetic activity. Bainbridge Cohen asserts that when an individual's involuntary nervous system is "calm" and "functioning clearly" (Bainbridge Cohen, 2008, p. 184), then you are much more able to process and interpret information from a wide range of sources supporting "thoughtful responses" (ibid.). Such "calming" of the nervous system in the transition from office to teaching space seeks to serve and prepare us, as facilitators, to arrive with a clarity and spaciousness that enables us to thoughtfully respond to any emerging teaching environment. It is worth noting here that Bainbridge Cohen describes how these two nervous systems, often stated as antagonistic systems in traditional literature, are, in fact, "mutually complementary and supportive of one another" and that each system "supports and modifies the other at all times on a wide continuum of attention, intention and function" (Bainbridge Cohen, 2008, p. 177). In addition, the invitation to contemplate the nature of mind from an "interdisciplinary consilient" perspective, as offered to us by psychiatrist and author Daniel J. Siegel, reminds us of wholeness; our mind is comprised of what it receives, processes, and responds to, the streams of information both from our own body and from the world around us (Siegel, 2020, p. 2). As embodied facilitators, we attend to integrating awareness of our bodily movement, knowing that the information from the body brings perspectives and valuable information streams to the present moment. The mind is not in the brain alone, our whole Body-Mind is engaged through continuous movement in, and interaction with, the world of inner and outer awareness. Through intentionally connecting to our physically moving body, with imaginative and fluid invitations to move, we reclaim our capacity for whole-bodied awareness. This awareness supports us to be regulated, matching our energy for the needs of the present moment; to make considered choices to be present to the here and now.

An invitation to become more aware:

Taking the time you need, consider ...

How is your body currently organised?
What do you notice?
Where is it easy? Where do you notice effort?
Breathe ...
Hear the sounds
What sits on your horizon and what sits close to you?
What can you see?
Twist the spine to allow your eyes to see the space around.
Here you are in this space ... here you are,
You have weight, feel this in your arms,
Choose somewhere on your body to place your hands ... here you are.
Sense your feet ... let them spread ... feel the ground.
Use the support of gravity to re- arrive in now.

How do you note your presence now?

Defining it, capturing the ephemeral moment, and fixing it into a description that encapsulates this state is complex. Through the somatic lens, examining presence invites us to become aware of the embodied process, to ask: How are we present? Our body, our emotions, the thoughts and imaginations that fill our cells and moving tissues, inform and shape our perception of the world. All this is ever-present as the process of life lives us, the tone of our tissues, the speed of our patterns, the dance of breathing and the aliveness of sensorial feedback. When patiently cultivated through awareness, we can find focus within flux through full-bodied presence in the teaching space between us and the students. It is the capacity to inhabit this presence that we seek to cultivate as lecturers working within HE.

Knowing our whole selves

Previously, we have shared some experiences of bodily awareness supporting us to regulate our nervous system and find presence, reminding us of performer and somatic educator Andrea Olsen, who draws us back to "knowing ourselves" (Olsen and McHose, 2014, p. 11) as the first step towards good teaching.

Knowing ourselves within academic culture is often interpreted as *what we know*. Dall'Alba recognises how western HE has "neglected the development of receptive listening in favour of a capacity to tell or explain what we know" (Dall'Alba, 2020, p. 31), placing emphasis on an accumulation of knowledge and how well we have shared and explained our understanding of that knowledge. We are a brain-orientated academy yet the presence required to facilitate and engage students requires a bodily knowledge that somatic movement therapist Peggy Hackney describes as a "lively interplay of Inner Connectivity ... with Outer Expressivity" (Hackney, 2002, p. 214). We see this tension as an ever-calibrating duet between our internal experience, informing how we engage and resonate within the wider world, and our awareness of this wider world and how it connects with us at a personal, private, and professional level.

The importance of bringing attention to our inner self before the facilitation of others is critical here. The ability to connect to the instinctual, nonverbal aspects of building relationship and to be more present for others in the moment of delivery sits at the heart of our approach. We can *know ourselves* in multiple ways; anatomically, emotionally, sensorily, intellectually, through our habits and personality traits, through connection and over time, through this accumulation of noticing and reflecting on our Whole Selves, we develop our capacity to attune to the present moment – a phenomenological presence that allows us to be more confident in making in-the-moment decisions that are immediately responsive to the needs of the group. This presence is described by researchers Sarah Pini and Catherine Deans as "an increased capacity to interact with the wholeness of the other participant and with the space, just as it is in the moment" (Pini and Deans, 2021, p. 108), an acceptance of what arises, a willingness to flow with change and an awareness of ourselves and others in the space together. A somatic invitation to unlearn, reflect, trust what tissues already know, and embrace uncertainty.

Karen Studd and Laura Cox, master teachers of the Laban–Bartenieff movement system remind us that, as facilitators, we are "always changing and accommodating to the present moment" (Studd and Cox, 2020, p. 99) while Olsen and McHose highlight the need to remain "responsive to change and discovery" (Olsen and McHose, 2014, p. 211). These observations bring us to the importance of Donald Schön's approaches of reflecting in or on action (Schön, 1991) as a mechanism to anchor us in this ever-changing facilitative space.

We would like to take that one step further and connect the bodily presence and improvisation required to make phenomenological decisions with our students to the level of critical reflection that educator Barbara Larrivee refers to. Larrivee proposes that we need to "allow ourselves to experience ... uncertainty". When change and uncertainty raises in us too much trepidation, we tend to return to our old habits and approaches. It is when we are able to "surrender the familiar" (Larrivee, 2000, p. 305) that we are moved to a shift in our way of thinking and sensing. It's worth noting that Larrivee recognises this level of critical reflection as a "personal awareness discovery process" (Larrivee, 2000, p. 296). We propose it is the custom of stilling, of finding presence through bodily awareness, that can support critically reflective teaching practice and enable significant change. As lecturers with students, we become a community of learners, a collective presence; the knowing of self, other, and the material happens in togetherness.

Self-other

Awareness of the relational field remains a central component to our understanding of the act of facilitation. As primates, it is through relationship that we humans seek meaning and affirm our existence. We know our bodies through immediate and further-reach environments which we inhabit and unfurl, alongside an ongoing process of discerning self and other, whether directly in the space with us, or in our thoughts. We are always in relationship. This ever-evolving triad of self, other, environment, is the dance that contributes to our whole experience of something. A change in one of these parts ultimately impacts on the wholeness. This wholeness becomes particularly evident in the facilitative relationship where, for example, one student's shift of focus can derail the whole session; a shift in a room's temperature can change the whole group's ability to concentrate; an acceleration of speed in the facilitator's speech can create confusion for the learners. A change in the parts affects the whole (Studd and Cox, 2020, p. 125). Recognising these sometimes-subtle micro shifts in presence is how we may read a room, gauge the capacity for receiving information, or take the cue that a change of rhythm, tone, and volume is needed.

Responsive attunement: staying present with others

Dall'Alba proposes the importance of attunement being "a care-filled, pedagogical approach"(Dall'Alba, 2020, p. 32) which is responsive to others. She speaks of a reflexive "*tuning in*" and explains that this responsive attunement "extends beyond, 'noticing'... [to] responding" (ibid).

Responsive attunement not only develops the student/lecturer relationship but also resituates the students, and therefore also the lecturer's relationship to the learning by encouraging sensitive enquiry and curious engagement *through* rather than *about* the subject in hand.

Penny Collinson, a somatic movement educator and therapist, parallels this observation in encouraging a shift from "thinking and doing" to "sensing and being" and through this shift invites embodied responsive engagement that in turn enables a reframing of the educator from "expert" to facilitating guide; a co-explorer who has within them enough curiosity, space, and freedom to experience the path anew, teaching afresh and in relationship with each new cohort of learners (Collinson, cited in Tufnell, 2017, p. 209). This curiosity brings us to the "live space" (ibid.) between student and lecturer.

We are interested in this shift between the role of expert to explorer within our facilitation. Dance academic, Jo Butterworth's Didactic-Democratic model (Butterworth, 2017, p. 89), outlines different approaches to choreographic delivery that provide structure and language for us to articulate our pedagogical and facilitative choices. We are interested in how, when, and what we teach impacts upon our students' sense of self. Butterworth's model (2017, p. 90) outlines five different processes for facilitating choreography situated across a continuum; at one end sits didactic, outcome-focussed delivery through which participants observe and learn skills from the teacher, such as in the teaching of a set sequence of movements, to the other end of the continuum where a democratic approach develops shared ownership and negotiation to support joint decision-making across all aspects of work. On the dance course at UCLan we engage with this full continuum. We often find that previous dance training and educational experiences leave our students most comfortable in the didactic space with tutor as expert and student as instrument, which at best provides a space for students to be inspired to learn new skills through detailed replication and at worst enables students to operate as passive, non-critical learners.

Through 'tuning in', we invite and nurture students to find and articulate their own artistic voice as we model these different roles within the continuum. It is in this nurturing that the mid-continuum phase of piloting in Butterworth's model resonated with us. Students are invited to become ever more present, engaged, and invested as an individual within a group-learning process, and the tutor as 'pilot/facilitator' allows space for individual active contributions, using open questioning and opportunity for trial-and-error learning alongside time for individual and group reflection. Students are challenged to move beyond roles of being an 'instrument' to the educator's expertise to becoming present to the value of their contribution and autonomous learners.

As well as a need to be responsively attuned within the learning context, there is also a need to be anticipatory in knowing where we want to go next, pre-empting the potential for challenge or dynamic shift in the group. As Studd and Cox inform us, "the next moment is always emerging" (Studd & Cox, 2020, p. 99). We can make decisions for lesson progression based on our preplanned intention and cognitive understanding of where we (students and staff) are at, but what difference does bringing our whole selves into that decision-making process make? How does attending to each moment with our mind and body also support our ability to see and experience the whole group and each individual within it? How willing are we to then let go of predetermined destinations for learning and instead trust the knowledge that emerges in the room, arising out of the co-created experience, as valid and worthwhile learning?

Choreographer Rosemary Lee speaks of the "expectant waiting that is both static and dynamic" (Lee, 2006, p. 173). She discusses choices she has to make with each individual she works with, "when to comment, when not to, when to coax, when to wait, when to surprise and when to be inevitable and predictable" (Lee, 2006, p. 172), but ultimately, in this place of dwelling, she tells us "all roads lead to presence".

We see this waiting as a step towards building a pedagogical approach that is rooted in care, empathy, and compassion.

How is your body currently organised?
How is your 'here I am'?
Be kind, find your own pace, refresh the map of self once more, reawaken.
Do this from a place of stillness or get up and move around.
Remind yourself:
I am weighted and gravity calls. Space invites me.
Breath is perfectly possible and right for just now.
What do your eyes wish to see? Which soundscapes touch your ears?
Allow the world to touch your senses, anchor in the recall of a memory that makes you smile.
Permission to pause, or move, saying yes to right now and shifting weight, remaining with self, notice the threshold, from self to other. Nearby sounds, your breath, the texture of clothes, the touch of surfaces, the detail of patterns,
Here I am.
The sound of life in the distance,
Here I am.
Play with near and far, follow a desire towards or away, be soft or strong or simply shift, wriggle, move.
Have you had enough time …, or maybe one more breath?
How are you now?
From this place of noticing self, how might you shift to notice others? How do you flow into the presence of yourself and other, the relational field.
Here I am, here you are.

Parts–whole

This chapter, so far, has captured different observations and praxis emerging from our conversations as members of the dance team at UCLan and has explored how increased awareness of one's self within the facilitation experience may support a more sensitive, responsive, and attuned learning environment through which we can support students to become independent learners.

Shaun McNiff, an arts for health specialist, reminds us that "excellent leaders have a gift for being able to perceive the whole field of action without being overly entrenched in singular perspectives" (McNiff, 2015, p. 96). How do we enact the presence required to hold the Whole whilst attending to our individual needs, the Parts, within the group? These Part–Whole dualities are described within the Laban-Bartenieff movement system and by Wahl, a somatic educator as, "seeing the whole of something, the big picture, then narrowing in on specific aspects … and after diving into details, zooming the focus back out, seeing what has changed in the whole" (Wahl, 2019, p. 23). Like a focussing camera on a moving subject, as facilitators we are trying to stay present to these moving (and therefore changing) parts. Relationally situating ourselves, as facilitators, in this ever-changing landscape of our own and other people's experiences and actions can be difficult to remain attentive to and impossible to predict or control.

A level of collective awareness, as well as individual presence, supports us to zoom in and out and to hold space within a duality of stability that is grounded and strong and mobility that is flexible and alive (Studd & Cox, 2020, p. 20). We hold the space, recognising it as a complex act; with it comes the reminders of the multiple elements of power, permission, and the importance of always questioning who is present (or not). Collinson stresses the importance of "balancing attention 50:50 between self and other", highlighting how "it is easy to get lost in another person's state of being and lose vital awareness" (Collinson, cited in Tufnell, 2017, p. 109). Lisa Dowler, the Artistic Director of The Small Things Dance Collective, echoes this, describing the importance of "staying with yourself and your own interest whilst connecting spontaneously with others and the strong pull to lose touch with oneself as one zooms into another" (Dowler, cited in Tufnell, 2017, p. 108). This basic pattern of condensing and expanding awareness, the shifts in focus necessary for following and therefore shaping the direction of a group's learning, is constantly refined and revisited through the act of facilitation. Lee reminds us that "to sense [what needs to happen next] one needs an element of distance coupled with an acute attentiveness" (Lee, 2006, p. 173). In Box 14.1, Charlie Reis expands further on the importance of allowing opportunities for spontaneity for the development of expertise.

Box 14.1 Designing spontaneity in learning and teaching as the practice of expertise

Charlie Reis

On spontaneity

Spontaneity or unpremeditated action is a major indicator and identifying characteristic of expertise. Spontaneity is associated with the ability to improvise in new situations, with creativity and play (Temezhnikova, 2022). Definitions of "spontaneous" often refer to "impulsive" as a synonym; however, they also often include "impromptu" in that same list (HarperCollins, 2016). The argument of this section is that the spontaneity of expertise is better and more clearly thought of as impromptu rather than impulsive, and that learning in higher education ought to be designed to support and offer opportunities for spontaneity as an appropriately levelled model of expert practice.

Spontaneity can also be seen as the utilisation of situated possibilities (Benner, Tanner & Chelsa, 1996) or the taking of action based on deep knowledge and consideration, rather than rashness. So, although spontaneity is a hallmark of expertise, it is the result of a process; from this perspective, the spontaneity of an expert in practice is not spontaneous at all, but exploration of familiar practice.

Learning design for progressive problem solving and spontaneity

Experts engage in progressive problem solving as a purposeful activity for improving their practice. Cognitive space for this activity is made available when they have developed sufficient experience to enable the automation of skills and a sense of flow and spontaneity (Bereiter & Scardamalia, 1993). A focus on learning design to facilitate spontaneous action, developing the work of Vygotsky (1978) and Csekszentmihlyi (1996), is a different perspective on expertise in higher education. The notion of the zone of proximal development (ZPD) and Csikszentmihalyi's work on flow are ubiquitous in educational theory and become richer and more textured when used in the study of expertise, as learning design should be informed by the development of expertise to be more aligned to facilitate the conditions for spontaneous action.

This richness would not necessarily change learning designed to appropriately engage and challenge learners through ZPDs, but the perceived pedagogical value for students of this should highlight self-direction and spontaneity towards expertise as an additional value of learning and thread in the weave of student engagement. A case for self-direction in progressive problem solving could also be presented as a capacity and attitude-based version of education for employability, although employability is a weaker target than expertise. Major issues here are how students can determine which activities are purposeful in being self-directed, the differences largely lying in the self-directed nature of exploration of boundaries in expert practice (King, 2022) and the differences in knowledge (Persky & Robinson, 2017).

To support students' spontaneity, a range of options exist, including:

- Encouragement to take spontaneous action and to reflect on the outcome;
- Progressive problem-solving lists that focus on growth rather than achievement;
- 'Developing expertise' journals;
- Presentations on misconceptions overcome.

> Learning design in higher education should allow for spontaneity with the goal of the development of expertise. The inclusion of opportunities for student exploration without undue instructor limitations (Culbertson et al., 2015; Heutte et al., 2016), but with a focus on developing the thinking associated with expertise, is a path to incorporating spontaneity as and into learning.

Dancing our capacity for change

It is embodied movement practices that provide a playground within which to explore and embrace the dualities we have discussed, Self–Other and Parts–Whole, enabling new insights and capacity to connect with others intercorporeally through moving together (Behnke, 2003, cited in Pini & Deans, 2021, p. 107). These dance practices attend to body sensation, support wellbeing, and embrace uncertainty, nurturing our ability to literally, 'go with the flow' and embrace change through our capacity to attune to the needs and desires of others. This capacity to attune is, for a dancer, a holistic whole-body response relating to the body, space, dynamic, and relational elements present; taking time to refine our ability to be present to the sensations, feelings, and dynamic changes within our teaching spaces, supporting us in developing a relationship with the whole space ... to self, to other, to environment and as necessary, helping us respond to what presents in front of us, leading the group we have, not the one we expected.

We conclude that it is embodying this approach of seeking presence and wholeness that supports our capacity for, and to, change. We propose a simple physical practice that supports preparation, engagement, and reflection in and on a teaching experience. A practice that becomes regularly engaged with, so we are always prepared for the unexpected. It is a physical practice of noticing the body and mind that will not only support our own parasympathetic need, but also allows us to be more attuned to the changing presence of others.

Before you teach

Intentionally attend to the body and its movement before entering the teaching space. Practice observing the body and mind to support the nervous system. Close down your computers, put away phones, leave conversations behind, and attend to your body as you transition to the teaching space: deepen your breath, notice your feet on the floor, ask yourself ... what does your body need right now? Throughout this chapter, we have offered movement meditations that could support you in these moments of transition.

During the teaching experience

When meeting and greeting your group, can you find space to check in with yourself? Keep returning to the fundamentals of your breath, your feet on the ground, and noticing your body; what are you attending to? From this place, consider the choices you have in relation to the group's energy. What changes could you make in response? Might you match their energy, contrast it, take the lead, or follow?

As the teaching session unfolds, full-bodied noticing often helps us sense if change is needed. Let's not be afraid of change. Change is often achieved through movement: moving the group to re-energise them; moving ourselves to reconnect to the lesson content; moving the chairs to bring a group together; giving ourselves permission to let the non-essential within a teaching session fall away and zoom in to the learning environment as it unfolds.

After teaching

As at the beginning of sessions, the time after a lecture can often be a barrage of questions, to-do lists, and quick shifts to the next lecture or meeting. Again, how can we seek a little more out of the physical act of transition, taking this as an opportunity to check in with ourselves, and note how the Body–Mind state compares with the start of the session. Is there anything to learn through this observation?

As a team, we are imperfectly attempting to bring our dance practice into our higher education delivery, challenging the norms of daily operation. We offer this chapter to support an alternative approach to navigating the working environment. In an ever-changing university system, with increasing demands, we as a staff team stay with the belief that "a change is only possible through the process of movement. When something moves, a change occurs. When something has changed, it has moved" (Studd & Cox, 2020, p. 6).

> Here I am.
> Letting words swirl, and settle.
> I Breathe, I change pace.
> I soften the gaze and allow my body to move, just as it wants, right now.

Key take-aways

- Come to yourself before being in relationship with other. Our bodies offer information to support us and attune to others in our teaching spaces.
- Explore the wholeness of the Self–Other and Parts–Whole dualities to enhance decision-making and our abilities to be whole-body critically reflective practitioners.
- Draw upon the Body–Mind to cultivate a practice of presence to support adaptation to an ever-changing teaching landscape.

References

Adler, J. (2002). *Offering from the Conscious Body: The Discipline of Authentic Movement*. Inner Traditions International Limited, Rochester.

Bainbridge Cohen, B. (2008). *Sensing, feeling, and Action: The Experiential Anatomy of Body-Mind Centering*. 2nd edn. Contact Editions, Northampton, MA.

Benner, E., Tanner, C., & Chelsa, C. (1996). *Expertise in Nursing Practice: Caring*. Springer, *Clinical Judgement and Ethics*.

Bereiter, C. & Scardamalia, M. (1993). *Surpassing Ourselves – An Inquiry into the Nature and Implications of Expertise*. Open Court, Illinois.

Butterworth, J. (2017). Too many cooks? A framework for dance making and devising. In: Butterworth, J. & Wildschut, L., (eds.) *Contemporary Choreography: A Critical Reader*. Routledge, Abingdon. pp. 89–106. DOI:10.4324/9781315563596

Csekszentmihlyi, M. (1996). *Flow: The Psychology of Optimal Experience*. Harper and Row, New York.

Culbertson, S.S., Fullagar, C.J., Simmons, M.J. & Zhu, M. (2015). Contagious flow: Antecedents and consequences of optimal experience in the classroom. *Journal of Management Education*, 39(3), 319–349. doi:10.1177/1052562914545336

Dall'Alba, G. (2020). Toward a pedagogy of responsive attunement for Higher Education. *Philosophy and Theory in Higher Education*, 2(2), 21–43. DOI:10.3726/PTIHE022020.0002

Giddens, S., Long, E. & Spencer, R. (2018). Employing dwelling to re-consider individual and collaborative relationships to pedagogical practice. *Journal of Dance & Somatic Practices*, 10(1), 52–64. DOI:10.1386/jdsp.10.1.52_1

Hackney, P. (2002). *Making Connections: Total Body Integration through Bartenieff Fundamentals*. Routledge, New York. DOI:10.4324/9780203214299

HarperCollins (2016). *Synonyms of Spontaneous in British English*. https://www.collinsdictionary.com/dictionary/english-thesaurus/spontaneous

Heutte, J., Fenouillet, F., Kaplan, J., Martin-Krumm, C. & Bachelet, R. (2016). The EduFlow model: A contribution toward the study of optimal learning environments. In: Harmat, L., Andersen, F.Ø., Ullén, F., Wright, J. & Sadlo, G., (eds.) *Flow Experience: Empirical Research and Applications*. Springer, New York, pp. 127–143. DOI:10.1007/978-3-319-28634-1

King, H. (2022). Developing expertise for teaching in higher education. In: King, H., (ed.) *Developing Expertise for Teaching in Higher Education: Practical Ideas for Professional Learning and Development*.: Routledge, London & New York, pp. 1–12. DOI:10.4324/9781003198772

Larrivee, B. (2000). Transforming teaching practice: Becoming the critically reflective teacher. *Reflective Practice*, 1(3), 293–307. DOI:10.1080/7136931

Lee, R. (2006). Expectant waiting. In: Bannerman, C., Sofaer, J. & Watt, J., (eds.) *Navigating the Unknown: The Creative Process in Contemporary Performing Arts*. Middlesex University Press, London, pp. 158 – 185.

McNiff, S. (2015). *Imagination in Action: Secrets for Unleashing Creative Expression*. Shambhala, Boulder, Colorado.

Olsen, A. & McHose, C. (2014). *The Place of Dance: A Somatic Guide to Dancing and Dance Making*. Wesleyan University Press, Middletown, Connecticut.

Persky, A. & Robinson, J. (2017). Moving from novice to expertise and its implications for instruction. *American Journal of Pharmaceutical Education*, 81(9), 6065. DOI:10.5688/ajpe6065

Pini, S. & Deans, C. (2021). Expanding empathic and perceptive awareness: The experience of attunement in contact improvisation and body weather. *Performance Research*, 26(3), 106–113. DOI:10.1080/13528165.2021.1983293

Schön, D.A. (1991). *The Reflective Practitioner: How Professionals Think in Action.* Ashgate Publishing, London, England.
Siegel, D.J. (2020). *The Developing Mind: How Relationships and the Brain Interact to Shape Who We Are.* 3rd edn. The Guilford Press, New York.
Studd, K. & Cox, L.L. (2020). *Everybody is a Body.* 2nd edn. Outskirts Press Inc., Parker, CO.
Temezhnikova, O. (2022). Improvising: a grounded theory investigation of psychology students' level of anxiety, coping, communicative skills, imagination, and spontaneity. *Qualitative Report*, 27(4), 965–996. DOI:10.46743/2160-3715/2022.5128
Tufnell, M. (2017). *When I open my eyes: Dance, health, imagination.* Dance Books, Binsted, Hampshire.
Vygotsky, L.S. (1978). *Mind in Society: The Development of Higher Psychological Processes.* Harvard University Press, Cambridge, Mass.
Wahl, C. (2019). Laban/Bartenieff Movement. Studies: Contemporary applications. Human Kinetics, Champaign, Illinois. DOI:10.5040/9781718212725

Chapter 15

Professional development for artistry in higher education

15.1 To 'toy with', 'think about' and 'experiment with': teacher development programmes as space for developing the artistry of teaching

Emma Kennedy and Martin Compton

Among the development opportunities provided to those with teaching roles in higher education (HE), a PGCert in HE or Academic Practice (henceforth PGCert) is one of the most common. However, despite repeated calls for better training of academics, a lack of formal regulatory requirement means that many teaching in HE either have no qualification at all, a swift institutional induction, or a "recognition" qualification such as Advance HE's Fellowship (FHEA) which tends not to focus on development. The time demands for these pathways are vastly different, and so too is the experience (Botham, 2017; van der Sluis, 2021). Recognition is about what candidates have already done (Fung & Gordon, 2016), so PGCerts must prioritise exploration, discovery, and development.

Many have investigated the experience and impact of taught educational development programmes (Chalmers & Gardiner, 2015; Gibbs & Coffey, 2004; Hanbury, Prosser & Rickinson, 2008). Several studies have attempted to measure the 'impact' of these programmes (Ilie *et al.*, 2020; Fabriz et al., 2021). However, key for us was Bamber and Stefani's distinction between "outputs" – for example, ratings of satisfaction – and "outcomes", which "are not quantitative in educational development" as they constitute changes in mindset and practice over time (Bamber & Stefani, 2016).

Our study drew on semi-structured interviews of PGCert participants to draw out personal accounts and here we present our findings of how the programme impacts mindset and practice. We summarise key elements of participant experience and outcomes – and then, adopting Roxå and Martensson's concept of academic developers as institutional "power holders", ask how we can use this power to mitigate some of the issues that our participants found (Roxå & Mårtensson, 2017).

DOI: 10.4324/9781003437826-19

Mindset

Many participants found the programme's quality exceeded their expectations. One had "struggled to [...] go against [their] own experience", but the programme "completely changed [their] ideas about what it means to teach". For another, the PGCert shifted them out of the mindset of the teacher as font of knowledge: "the biggest influence from the PGCert is that admission of not having to know everything". Contrasting their new self to the didactic model, they said "I won't ... repeatedly just deliver the same information hoping [students] take it in", and "I'm very keen to get them to realize that they are adult learners". The shift in self-perception feeds a shift in perception of the students.

Skills

This was a key difference for one participant between FHEA recognition and taught programmes: in the former "you don't get inspired and stimulated in the same way". Others highlighted specific skills and knowledge they had gained on the programme: "all the theory was really useful [...] different teaching styles, delivery". Many participants noted that the digital aspects of the programme had helped them adapt to online teaching during COVID lockdowns. For one, who "borrowed some activities that you guys did [...] I think it allowed me to transition so much smoother than the other colleagues, because I understand some of the challenges that students face". For this participant it was not just having seen the activities used on the programme that impacted them, but having *been a student* on it.

Flexibility and playfulness

Such attitudinal and practice changes enabled flexibility. One participant described this as the ability "to switch when necessary and have a toolbox". Another gained "that adaptability and the understanding that not everything needs to be delivered in a particular way". One participant phrased this in terms of play, citing "a variety of different approaches that you can toy with and then think about and then experiment with". Here we see flexibility as a key element in how the programme empowers participants to change and feel confident in moving beyond their comfort zone.

Observation

Watching and being watched was a key theme in participants' responses. Participants learned from observing others and from being observed. Many found this a contrast to their usual practice: "We only ever get feedback from the students never from somebody who is a trained educator" and for another it "was really the first time that I actually had feedback [on their teaching]". One participant contrasted the focus of observers within the discipline – on "subject delivery" – with the focus of PGCert-related observers on "teaching delivery". For another, this kind of collaborative activity contrasted with their experience of being a PhD student and then early-career teacher in their discipline.

Notably, participants tended not to identify specific skills or insights that observations had given them but rather to see it as an opportunity to expand their mindset. One participant noted the fascinating outcome that the PGCert had made them not just a better teacher but a better *observer*. Before the course, "I would sometimes see something that I thought: oh that's interesting, oh look at that, you know, but without having the vocabulary to actually really interpret what that person was really doing" but afterwards "[with] the vocabulary to actually interpret what that person is doing, then it's just easier to remember and understand it, and also translate it to something you intend to do".

Time constraints

Most participants cited their key challenge as finding enough time to engage with the programme. For one, "due to my teaching timetable I literally couldn't attend anything" and for others, while they attended some of it, they could not give it the time they wanted. This limited the benefits they could gain from the course: "I struggled to have the time to think about how to put [ideas] into practice [...] some of the ideas I could only understand at a superficial level because I didn't have the time to go deeper". Participants reported having to spend their own time to complete the course: "it was generally accepted in my department that your own study was done outside of your working environment, [...] although it was contractually obliged". One participant noted the equity implications of this: "if I have to write this essay in like two or three evenings, I can, because I don't have anything else [...] care responsibilities for or whatever". For many participants, this time issue signified a lack of real investment by the institution, who "say it's important for you to have this qualification, but at the same time [...] not going to give you the necessary time to do this". Participants were clear that the responsibility for this issue lay with the institution and that this was the most important barrier to their learning.

Moving forward

If time is the main issue, and the responsibility lies with the institution, how can we move forward productively, short of solving the problem of workloads in academia (something at which many have already failed)? Perhaps one answer lies in academic developers, as institutional power-holders, and the contrast between institutions' claim to support staff development and their actions on workload. Our power lies in being seen as "authorities" on learning and teaching, so while we do not have the power to rewrite workload allocations, we can perhaps use our intellectual authority to challenge institutional attempts to claim supportiveness while not matching this with action on workload. Can academic developers – especially as a community – "call in" institutions and hold them to account?

15.2 Developing teaching expertise for disciplinary contexts – building the bridges between institution and discipline perspectives

Jackie Potter and Moira Lafferty

Introduction

For higher education providers in many countries, the function of developing teaching expertise is located within central educational development units. These support all those engaged in the teaching and support of higher education students and provide a core curriculum for initial educator development that is largely discipline agnostic. The canon of what is included in such a core curriculum was investigated and exposed by Kandlbinder and Peseta (2009) and revealed a good deal of commonality in the offer across the institutions and the countries involved in the study. What was apparently absent was the role of disciplinary knowledge as well as the application of the core curriculum to disciplinary contexts. Knight and Trowler (2000) explored the potential for discipline cultures (departments) to improve teaching and learning and recognised the importance of these to promote deep transformation and change to teaching practice. In this chapter we argue that central units and department leaders need to collaborate and construct bridges between the institutional offer of a core curriculum and the disciplinary contexts and cultures that the novice educators work in. The transference of the core curriculum into these disciplinary spaces is a manifestation of artistry as the educator needs to reflexively adapt and improvise. This needs to be acknowledged and nurtured with appropriate scaffolding.

Using the metaphor of the bridge, we explore different ways of spanning the distance between institutional central educational development units (EDUs) and their core curriculum, departments with their subject-specific expectations and the needs of both novice and expert educators. We consider the implications of crossing backwards and forwards, of making meaning from the journeys, of sharing the journey with those that travel and those that do not, and how to showcase the development of expertise and artistry to people on both sides.

The professional learning spaces occupied by those new to teaching in HE

Novice educators, those that join the HE teaching workforce with no prior experience of teaching in higher education, often enrol on a teaching development programme run by a central EDU. In some countries this may be a mandatory requirement rather than an option for those that select it. Our EDU staff author has seen firsthand some of the difficulties that novice educators encounter in evaluating and deconstructing, through reflective insight, the custom and practice of their discipline or subject approaches to teaching and supporting learning, even when located at a distance from it and with scaffolding to support structured analysis from peers and pedagogic experts. Kilgour et al. (2019) proposed that the pedagogic development of new lecturers involves transformative learning as those staff grapple with threshold concepts as they come to develop new ways of thinking about their practice. Turner and Spowart (2022) report on the conceptual challenges staff faced as they developed reflection on practice through dialogue with peers, writing, and working with the pedagogic literature. Our discipline-based author, who manages novice teaching staff, values the CPD opportunities afforded to staff by 'crossing the bridge' to study on a teaching development programme and reports on the importance of authentic support from managers for novice educators and the importance of removing barriers to their engagement with taught programmes and the pedagogic content knowledge. They also were keen to engage in co-creation of the learning space of the teaching development programme that sits across the bridge in part because they were able to recognise the potential for learning and the development of expertise that would come from novice educators able to evaluate and assess local custom and practice in comparison to the wider published work and evidence base of effective or excellent practice.

As we conceptualised the experience of the novice educator moving between two learning spaces – the disciplinary community of practice in the home department and the multidisciplinary community of learners from the institution attending the teaching development programme delivered by the educational development unit – we came to explore the value of the metaphor of a bridge. This helped us conceive of ways to link these two places with a focus on securing safe passage for our novice educators so they could learn, improvise, and develop their expertise and demonstrate a growing ability to enact artistry – a unique personal and professional manifestation of competence. In the next section we explore the features of the bridge between these two learning spaces and how managers and senior peers from the educational development unit and within the disciplines and departments make the bridge safe, secure, and welcoming.

Connecting disciplinary and institutional learning spaces

Bridges connect places and need to be secured and anchored within each before the span between them can be crossed. Within the metaphor of bridge building between the spaces of learning for novice educators, the anchors for the bridge can be imagined as the institutional progression and recognition practices, such as the award of tenure or promotion, on the one hand, and on the other, the disciplinary community valuing of teaching and support for students within their teaching contexts as well as the value of peer collaboration and support, such as through mentorship and role modelling by senior colleagues. The use of contractual requirements to complete teaching development programmes in a growing number of institutions and national states secures the bridge in the EDU. And while Smith and Walker (2022) assert that clarity in promotion criteria is important to enable individuals to work towards career advancement, they found that for staff engaging in scholarship activity (usually related to teaching-related advancement or promotion tracks) the support for individuals to develop their expertise was informal and largely through local (school/department-level) mentoring programmes. This is one manifestation of how the bridge can anchor into departments through supportive, collegiate professional ties.

Bridge crossing to developing expertise and demonstrate artistry

When thinking about those that cross the bridge from the academic department it is crucial not only for the bridge to have firm foundations but also an inviting destination. Those who choose to cross the bridge need to metaphorically step into a CPD environment that is welcoming and attuned to the differing needs of all who enter, from the new professional wishing to develop craft knowledge to the experienced practitioner who wishes to explore in more depth their tacit knowledge and share this with colleagues. To cater for these differing needs the environment and those within must provide a psychological safety net that allows for reflection in and on the practice of teaching (Schön, 1983) and a means of sharing experiences. Through drawing on formal and informal learning opportunities within this community, new academics can develop their artistry and thus over time their authentic teacher identity will emerge. However, it is only through recrossing the bridge to their home department that pedagogical learning can be enacted and reflected upon, and this requires genuine support for pedagogical development by their line manager and peers. The provision of genuine support and indeed the valuing of professional development will ensure that academics at all stages frequently cross the virtual bridge to the EDU. The expert teacher will continue their own personal development through reflecting on improvisation and context-sharing practice with others and continuing development of artistry and their personal teaching identity (Akkerman & Meijer, 2011).

15.3 "What's in it for me?": professional services colleagues and teaching expertise

Sarah Floyd and Fiona Smart

The higher education (HE) Professional Services (PS) community occupies a third space within the academy, which according to Whitchurch (2013) and McIntosh and Nutt (2022), amongst others, blurs the boundaries between academic and professional domains creating, potentially, a collaborative space where artisans might gather to share and celebrate practice. Yet HE has ways of establishing division in shared spaces.

One dis-abler is a Key Performance Indicator (KPI) not uncommonly in place in UK universities. It concerns professional recognition afforded by means of the UKPSF (2011)/PSF (2023) and gathers data in respect of academics, not professional service staff. (Professional recognition is offered by Advance HE against the PSF with the categories of Associate Fellow, Fellow, Senior Fellow and Principal Fellow of the Higher Education Academy: AFHEA, FHEA, SFHEA, and PFHEA respectively). The rationale for separating third-space individuals by virtue of their contract of employment relates to Higher Education Statistics Agency (HESA) data gathering but presents as both artificial and unhelpful. Artificial because the distinction between those who teach *or* support learning is not clear cut; and unhelpful because it risks pushing professional service staff to the margins of the collaborative space, rendering them less visible, less comfortable members of the academy (Akerman, 2020). Not gathering data in respect of professional service staff membership of the Fellowship community also risks stifling both the ambition of the individual staff member and of their institution.

It also suggests a narrowing of the lens as it concerns professional learning (Pilkington & Appleby, 2014) and reflective practice (Schön, 1983), both of which are core to King's model of expertise (King, 2022). Put differently, might it be the case that only academics are perceived to be professional learners? From here, it is easy to suggest that only academics are artists in the domain of learning and teaching. In contrast, findings from Cathcart et al. (2021) highlight the importance of being judged as 'belonging' for nontraditional staff.

> So, in a way it's getting us noticed within an academic community as being part of an academic community, if you like, and hopefully giving us a little bit of kudos which we do have amongst people. I'm not saying we're seen as, you know, not important but I think it brings us up to a level that people can actually see, but if you're getting that and I've got that, brilliant, you know. It offers us opportunities to actually get our points across as well, I think. So professionally it was a good thing to do and raising our profile within the institution.
>
> (Learning Support, AFHEA)

> It helps you appreciate your value more within the organisation, professional services are spoken about as "non-academics" which is quite derogatory, so this qualification shows you as an equal in terms of professional status. I believe we are all equal anyway but it's nice to have.
>
> (Learning Technologist, SFHEA)

At a time when we quite rightly should be focussing on inclusion and the practices which enable it, it is timely to challenge exclusion within key data sets of individuals who do not occupy formal teaching roles, but who play significant roles in the workings of the university and in the positive experiences of its students. We recognise the need for a strategic approach operationalised within the daily practices of HE which adopts a more inclusive narrative of ongoing professional learning, evolving expertise, and recognition that values and includes not only those employed on academic contracts, but also the wider community, each of whom contributes positively as individuals and within the collective to the student learning experience (Floyd, 2021).

To argue our case, we draw on evaluative and research data generated from within two Fellowship schemes which consciously value everyone who has a role in teaching and/or learning irrespective of what that role is. We use these data to posit a key question – why then would someone who doesn't need to gain Fellowship seek to do so? In seeking to answer the question we focus on the issue of expertise and its recognition (or not) from within, that is, the individual and from without, that is, the system within which the individual operates.

Of respondents, 88% told us that gaining Fellowship was a means of being explicitly valued for their contribution to student learning. Through the process of reflection, evidence gathering, and positioning their approaches through the lens of how they make a difference to the student learning experience, respondents provided a legitimisation and validation of their contribution.

> It made me appreciate my role as a leader within the university which I had highly underestimated until I started gathering my evidence and evaluated my impact on both lecturers and students' lives. It really gave me a boost to get testimonials from those I had worked with and give me a renewed drive and confidence going about my work.
> (Learning Technologist, SFHEA)

> It has encouraged a sustained focus on the quality of the student learning environment with a clear commitment to all the Professional Values. I aim to be an active supporter of learning and teaching initiatives within the training restaurant – ensuring that students acquire the right set of employability skills for successful careers as hospitality or culinary professionals.
> (Technician, AFHEA)

> It has made me more aware of how PS staff support and impact the student experience. It has enabled me to encourage members of my team to follow this path for their own development and to know their worth in the HE sector.
> (Administration, AFHEA)

> It made me think in a different way, look at it through a different lens [...] understand better how what I did related to the more academic side of the

university [...] more broadly speaking in terms of that language of academic reflection, I developed it that way.

(Learning Support, AFHEA)

It was clear that formal recognition can impact powerfully on feelings of self-worth and also in PS staff confidence in the ways they contribute to the wider academy.

Who knew we were so valued? Start the process and you may be surprised.
(Learning Technologist, SFHEA)

I am very proud of this recognition and was very grateful for the opportunity to have **my years of supporting student learning recognised**.
(Learning Support, SFHEA)

Achieving formal recognition for my work in developing real world connected learning opportunities for students has helped my work be recognised as a legitimate and valuable learning opportunity for students. It also contributes to the University's impact outside the confines of the institution and recognises the value our staff and students can bring to our University strategy focusing on people, place and partnerships.
(Learning Support, SFHEA)

I think it's probably increased my confidence in the value of what I do and encouraged me to be more confident about that and the contribution that it makes to the university and the importance of building networks across all the different aspects of the university, academic staff, professional staff, facility staff and to acknowledge that really.
(Learning Support, AFHEA)

We have included the voices of our PS colleagues as they capture the importance and value of such processes in supporting them to have confidence in their place within the academy. We argue that continuing to build Fellowship schemes, or indeed other forms of professional development opportunity, without regard for the breadth of experience and expertise in teaching and learning practices which locates in the HE sector is a form of blindness and presents as a form of exclusion that must be challenged.

15.4 Engaging in feedback dialogue to enhance expertise in healthcare teaching

Lucy Spowart and Tristan Price

This project aimed to establish what impact the Review of Educational Practice (REP), undertaken during a PGCert Clinical Education programme, has on teaching practices and conceptual change. We are interested in how the act of both giving and receiving feedback can play a role in enhancing teacher expertise. Feedback is considered one of the key factors in facilitating learning in healthcare environments and can enhance or diminish a learner's motivation to improve (Price et al., 2021). The feedback process aims to effect change; however, in stressful clinical environments, learning opportunities are not always optimised (Telio et al., 2015).

Method

On the PGCert ClinEd participants are observed teaching and then engage in both a verbal and a written dialogue about the process. Participants also observe a colleague teaching and provide carefully constructed verbal and written feedback. To provide a detailed understanding of teacher's concepts, behaviours, and the perceived impacts of the REP on learning, a benchmarking questionnaire was completed at the start (n = 30) followed by semi-structured interviews (n = 8) on completion of a one-year programme of study. All interviewees taught on university healthcare programmes. The project team also had consent to access several written reflective accounts on the process of giving and receiving feedback. The project received ethical approval from the Faculty of Health's Ethics Committee.

Findings

All interviewees reported the benefits of engaging in the REP across all three facets of the feedback process: the act of observing, the process of receiving feedback, and the value of providing feedback to others. Participants valued the opportunity to observe others, gain new ideas, and engage in a dialogue with other trainee teachers about the rationale behind their choice of approach. The time and space to do this was, in many cases, transformational, assisting in the development of both pedagogical content knowledge and teacher artistry, as expressed here:

> "The whole thing has quite profoundly changed the way I practice ..., I was probably very naive before and I didn't really think too hard about the way I was delivering things, the audience I was delivering it to, better ways to do things, and I mean [...] my approach to teaching it's kind of changed quite drastically...."
>
> (Interviewee)

Our learners invariably work in busy clinical settings, where prescriptive feedback models, based on complex acronyms, may be of limited use. Instead, interviewees describe a process of adaptation, where they were able to identify their developing expertise in giving feedback at different levels based on guiding principles: the importance of the relationships with their learner or observer and the role of trust in engendering effective feedback; the setting in which feedback occurs and the need to develop safe environments for feedback conversations; and finally, the format and content of feedback, its specificity, and the importance of feeding forward some specific and realistic points for improvement. Recognising that much of the feedback literature is based upon traditional classroom environments, our interviewees had to adapt their learning for the setting:

> "I was so unsure about how what I had learnt could be applied to the NHS ... but [the REP and associated assignment] has given me ideas and allowed me to reflect."
>
> (Interviewee)

Moreover, for our learners the opportunity to provide feedback to other teachers was equally powerful, providing the time and space to "notice how others organised and engaged with their learners in clinical teaching scenarios, and to then consider explicitly how best to frame feedback in empowering and constructive ways." (Interviewee)

Conclusion

Effective clinical teaching requires both clinical knowledge and skills alongside an understanding of how knowledge and skills are best developed. Shulman (1986) referred to this as Pedagogical Content Knowledge. Given the environmental challenges that clinical teachers face, the authenticity of teacher-student relationships, and the improvisation of clinical teachers to create psychologically safe environments to engage in feedback is of paramount importance. By engaging in the purposeful development activity of giving and receiving teaching-focussed feedback, the participants in this study undertake a journey, gaining greater insights into some of the underlying constructs affecting the ways teachers organise their sessions and engage with their learners.

The relational aspects of feedback embraced by our learners mirrors pedagogical developments in the understanding of how feedback works, moving away from a 'feedback sandwich' model in which an educator seeks to soften the blow of negative feedback by padding it with positives, to one where the learner seeks information on their own performance (Boud & Molloy, 2013), with agency in the process, and where the perspectives of both teacher and learner are valued as part of dialogue more akin to a team debrief (Molloy et al., 2019).

This aids their learning about the importance of building relationships, developing psychological safety, and treating students as individuals. This heightened awareness helps to develop teacher expertise by emphasising the importance of relational pedagogy and developing learner confidence. This more holistic, less prescriptive approach to feedback is particularly pertinent in the clinical setting, where clinical educators will have to be dynamic and adaptive, focussing on key principles rather than specific models (Weallans et al., 2022). The process of observing others teach also helps develop teacher artistry (Schön, 1983) by exposing teachers to a range of different approaches to clinical skill development and enhancing teacher confidence to experiment with new approaches.

15.5 Sketching new horizons: what does evaluation of staff development events tell us about developing expertise?

Charlotte Stevens

Most, if not all educational developers will have been involved in a staff development event at some point, whether a conference or workshop, online or face to face, either as a participant, presenter, or organiser, or possibly in multiple roles. As participants, we may listen to an inspiring keynote who challenges us to rethink our standpoint on a particular topic, or we might engage in a workshop discussion which encourages us to change some aspect of our practice. As presenters, we may reflect on the experience on a personal level, assess our performance, and consider what we might do differently next time. Staff development events, albeit a moment in time, present an opportunity to reflect on practice and gain expertise. Evaluation of events offers a means of capturing moments of reflection and motivation to develop that expertise.

The reasons for evaluating educational development initiatives are well documented, as are the challenges associated with trying to evidence direct impacts. Indirect impacts – to use Bamber's (2013) example, "we run a workshop – academic attends – they feel more confident about particular approach – they believe their students can learn better" – are easier to measure. Indeed, event evaluation can uncover a range of "soft indicators" such as increased confidence, openness to ideas, willingness to try new approaches, and the sharing of learning and teaching strategies with others (2013, p. 13).

In 2019, a subsection of the Open University Associate Lecturer Support and Professional Development (ALSPD) team developed a coordinated approach to the evaluation of large-scale cross-faculty staff development events, delivered online since the COVID-19 pandemic (Stevens, 2022). These are part of a wider staff development offering for associate lecturers who act as tutors for Open University students, delivering tutorials and day schools, marking and giving detailed written feedback on assignments, and providing support via telephone, email, and online forums. The events bring associate lecturers together with colleagues and external speakers for plenaries and workshops focussed on topics as broad as supporting students with dyslexia, developing inclusive online tutorials, sustainable teaching, mental health and well-being, and gaining AdvanceHE fellowship.

A co-evaluation model, comprising two mixed-methods surveys, is used to evaluate events, whereby both associate lecturers and presenters are invited to share feedback on their experiences. Surveys are informed by different models (Kirkpatrick, 2006; Guskey, 2016; Stefani and Baume, 2016) and are designed to focus on learning and potential changes in behaviour in order to evaluate whether the events are useful in helping associate lecturers and presenters develop in their role.

During the 2021–22 period, more than 650 associate lecturers attended events comprised of sessions facilitated by more than 150 presenters. Survey feedback was received from 274 associate lecturers (41%) and from 68 presenters (42%). Within this feedback, there is much evidence of reflective practice, increased knowledge and expertise, and motivation to change practice.

Events provide an opportunity for reflection on action (Schön, 1983). In response to the question: "How do you plan to use what you have learnt in your practice?" one associate lecturer commented: "reflect on my digital learning style and read up on critical digital pedagogy" and another: "reflect on how I might do more to foster student's development of proactive attitudes and sense of empowerment towards key global issues (specifically climate change and inequality)". Respondents are motivated to change their practice in many ways, whether to adapt existing or try new tutoring styles or trial different methods to make tutorials more inclusive, such as polling; engage students more in feedback on their assignments; or signpost the support available for students with disabilities.

The impetus to change practice partly comes from the opportunity to speak to others for, as Pilkington writes, "dialogue is a powerful mechanism in the development of lecturers and as a reflective tool for making learning meaningful" (Pilkington, 2016, p. 64). Of respondents, 42% indicated that interactions had encouraged them to reflect on the way they supported students and 37% on developing tutorial strategies; as one respondent commented: "I will apply practices learnt from other tutors in the way I conduct my tutorials, encouraging more active participation among "quieter" students".

Of the 68 presenters who respondent to the surveys, 90% indicated that presenting a session at an event was useful in contributing to their own professional development. Again, the experience prompted reflection on action. Respondents appreciated the opportunity to hone online presentation skills, inform research, work across faculties and expand their networks, and understand more about the role of the associate lecturer. When presenters were asked how they might change sessions if they were to repeat them, respondents cited providing more instructions, adjusting timings, building in more interactivity into sessions, and using feedback to improve content.

Post-event evaluation goes some way in providing a means of understanding the indirect impacts of staff development events on those who engage in them. However, it is important to remind ourselves that this kind of evaluation presents a snapshot in time and, whilst attendees might communicate intentions to change their practice as a result of attending an event, what happens next does require longitudinal work.

15.6 Building confidence through appreciative self-study

Caitlin Kight

Introduction

When I first became an academic developer, I inherited teaching materials that introduced new educators to reflection using the popular models of Gibbs, Kolb, and Schön (as discussed in Moon, 1999). My own practice, however, was more influenced by other ideas – philosophies of emergence (Osberg and Biesta, 2021), Buddhism, Stoicism, ethics of care, and appreciative inquiry (Cooperrider and Srivastva, 1987). To me, these offered greater comfort and support than the models I was teaching.

While I wanted to share my personal experiences and insights with students, I felt it would be irresponsible to advocate practices I had not yet rigorously scrutinised. Therefore, over the past few years I have piloted a novel self-study intervention with the aim of offering an alternative option for reflective practice.

It centres self-knowledge – not because I suffer from hubris, but because I believe that "without perfect self-understanding, one will never learn to truly understand others" (Novalis, 1798/1997). Because interactions between two people – for instance, teacher and student – are created by the external interplay of their internal selves (Barrett, 2017, p. 53), I hypothesised that greater self-knowledge should lead to improved understandings of, and interactions with, students – resulting in greater self-confidence and, perhaps, greater empathy.

The appreciative self-study intervention

The intervention is best described as self-study – the systematic, reflexive approach to self-knowledge (Kitchen et al., 2020; Mitchell et al., 2005). I have adopted a nested approach, comprising three levels (drawing on the language of Ward and Gale, 2016), to support educators in learning more about some aspect of themselves and then non-judgementally exploring how it impacts teaching.

Level 1 – raising awareness. Teachers engage with any single self-study method; I experimented with several so I could recommend various options (Figure 15.1). This is ideal as a stand-alone activity for short workshops, educators with minimal time, or as a first step in a longer self-study journey.

238 Caitlin Kight

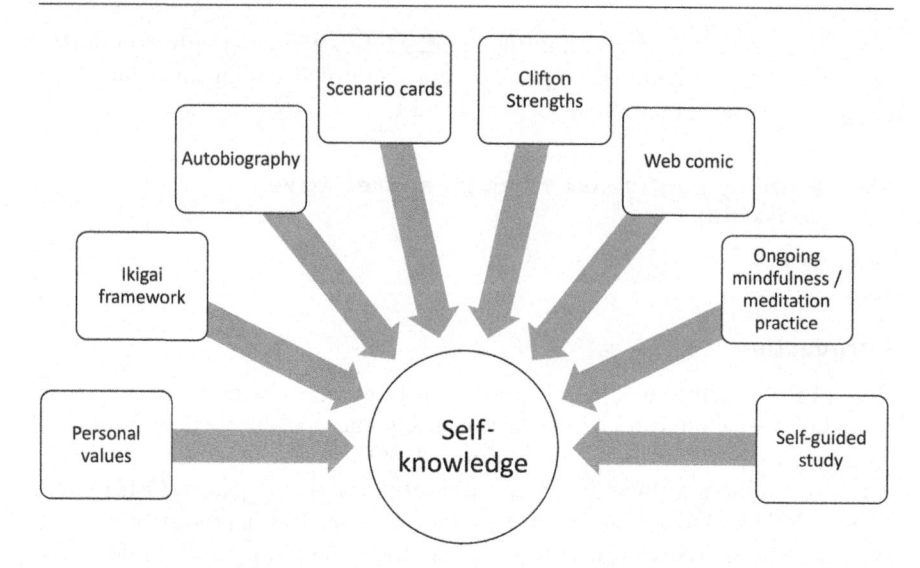

Figure 15.1 Examples of "Level 1" activities. Associated commercial products can be found on https://bestself.co/products/core-values-deck, https://ikigaitribe.com, https://scenariocards.org), and https://www.gallup.com/cliftonstrengths/en/home.aspx

Level 2 – additive approaches. Teachers use a routine (Figure 15.2) to actively apply insights gained from Level 1 before, during, and after teaching. This promotes presence and objectively explores, "what does this trait bring to this context?" This can be done independently or during a longer-term professional development course.

Level 3 – transforming practice. By iterating Levels 1 and 2, educators can take a "meta" reflective approach supporting deeper insights. This facilitates a greater appreciation of and confidence in the power of each educator's unique blend of traits.

Applying the intervention

Engaging with the intervention was transformative. With an attitude of accepting, playful inquisitiveness, I documented who and how I am – and how this influences different people and situations.

I became attuned to each exchange as an "intra-action" (Davies, 2014) emerging between, and forever changing, the participants. This underscored how "self" is connected and collaborative (Baumeister, 2011), which, in turn, offered the opportunity to more deeply engage with the ethics of education and community. For me, this centres on a sense of kinship (Krawec, 2022) between self and other – leading to the flourishing of both. The intervention might lead others to different conclusions; this flexibility is one of its strengths.

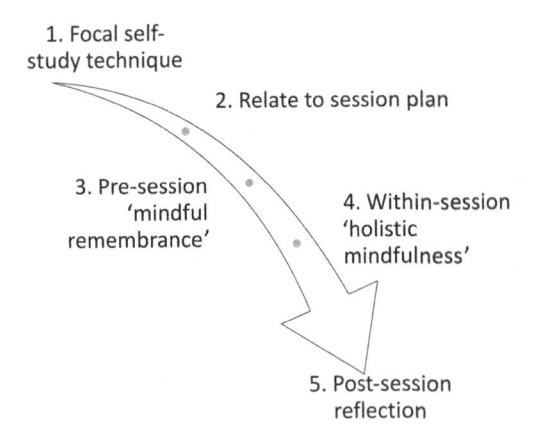

```
      1. Focal self-
      study technique
                      2. Relate to session plan

      3. Pre-session           4. Within-session
         'mindful                 'holistic
       remembrance'              mindfulness'


                              5. Post-session
                                 reflection
```

Figure 15.2 Schematic showing how Level 2 (steps 2–5) builds on Level 1 (first step)

I found daily drawing (Kight and Lemon, in press) and engaging with the concept of *ikigai* (Kemp, 2022) to be particularly impactful Level 1 activities. Forming habits around attention and intention (through Level 2 work) helped me regulate anxiety during stressful teaching moments and make decisions informed by an improved knowledge of my own idiosyncrasies and capabilities.

In thinking more deeply about challenges and triumphs (during Level 3 reflections), I gained greater perspective on how hard it can be to navigate the world with grace. I subsequently felt more compassionate and patient towards the people around me.

Using appreciative self-study in higher education

While my approach draws heavily on previous thinkers, I believe its framing (viewing self-study as a means of appreciating, leaning into, and amplifying strengths) and nested approach (supporting the creation of reflexive habits) are novel.

Together, these support a "radically compassionate" (Brach, 2020) mechanism for building confidence – thereby also fostering well-being. This approach is one manifestation of a "pedagogy of troubled times" (Dallmyr, 2007), which is increasingly called for in an HE environment rife with challenges like imposter syndrome, burnout, and compassion fatigue.

The preceding issues require structural solutions. However, appreciative interventions such as the one described here can be run in parallel, helping educators uncover, understand, and ultimately feel confident in their *self*. This offers the grounding and strength required to face ongoing challenges, both large and small, with equanimity and courage.

References

Akerman, K. (2020). Invisible imposter: identity in institutions. *Perspectives: Policy and Practice in Higher Education*, 24(4), 126–130. DOI:10.1080/13603108.2020.1734683

Akkerman, S.F. & Meijer, P.C. (2011). A dialogical approach to conceptualizing teacher identity. *Teaching and Teacher Education*, 27(2), 308–319. DOI:10.1016/j.tate.2010.08.013

Bamber, V. (ed.) (2013). *Evidencing the Value of Educational Development*. SEDA Special 34, London: SEDA.

Bamber, V. & Stefani, L. (2016). Taking up the challenge of evidencing value in educational development: from theory to practice. *International Journal for Academic Development*, 21(3), 242–254. DOI:10.1080/1360144X.2015.1100112

Barrett, L.F. (2017). *How Emotions are Made: The Secret Life of the Brain*. Picador.

Baumeister, R.F. (2011). Self and identity: a brief overview of what they are, what they do, and how they work. *Annals of the New York Academy of Sciences*, 1234, 48–55. DOI:10.1111/j.1749-6632.2011.06224.x

Botham, K. (2017). The growth of HEA Fellowship – does this impact on an individual's teaching practice and how can we demonstrate a change in the students' experience? *Educational Developments*, 18(3), 4–6.

Boud, D. & Molloy, E. (2013). Rethinking models of feedback for learning: The challenge of design. *Assessment & Evaluation in Higher Education*, 38(6), 698–712. DOI:10.1080/02602938.2012.691462

Brach, T. (2020). *Radical Compassion*. Ebury Digital.

Cathcart, A., Dransfield, M., Floyd, S., Campbell, L., Carkett, R., Davies, V., Duhs, R. & Smart, F. (2021). Tick-box, weasel words, or a transformative experience? Insights into what educators consider the real impact of HEA Fellowships. *International Journal for Academic Development*. DOI:10.1080/1360144X.2021.1938075

Chalmers, D. & Gardiner, D. (2015). An evaluation framework for identifying the effectiveness and impact of academic teacher development programmes. *Studies in Educational Evaluation*. (Evaluating Faculty Development), 46, 81–91. DOI:10.1016/j.stueduc.2015.02.002

Cooperrider, D. & Srivastva, S. (1987). Appreciative inquiry in organizational life. In: Woodman, R.W. & Pasmore, W.A. (eds.), *Research in Organizational Change and Development*, Vol. 1, pp. 129–169. JAI Press.

Dallmyr, F. (2007). *In Search of The Good Life: A Pedagogy for Troubled Times*. The University Press of Kentucky.

Davies, B. (2014). Reading anger in early childhood intra-actions: a diffractive analysis. *Qualitative Inquiry*, 20(6), 734–741. DOI:10.1177/1077800414530256

Fabriz, S., Hansen, M., Heckmann, C., Mordel, J., Mendzheritskaya, J., Stehle, S., Schulze-Vorberg, L., Ulrich, I. & Horz, H. (2021). How a professional development programme for university teachers impacts their teaching-related self-efficacy, self-concept, and subjective knowledge. *Higher Education Research & Development*, 40(4), 738–752. DOI:10.1080/07294360.2020.1787957

Floyd, S. (2021). Transforming educational excellence at an institutional scale. In: Bradley, S. (ed.) *Academic Career Progression: Rethinking Pathways*. Advance HE, https://www.advance-he.ac.uk/knowledge-hub/academic-career-progression-rethinking-pathways

Fung, D. & Gordon, C. (2016). *Rewarding Educators and Education Leaders in Research-Intensive Universities*. Report. York: Higher Education Academy. https://www.heacademy.ac.uk/

Gibbs, G. & Coffey, M. (2004). The impact of training of university teachers on their teaching skills, their approach to teaching and the approach to learning of their students. *Active Learning in Higher Education*, SAGE Publications, 5(1), 87–100. DOI:10.1177/1469787404040463

Guskey, T.R. (2016). *Gauge Impact with 5 Levels of Data*. https://tguskey.com/wp-content/uploads/Professional-Learning-1-Gauge-Impact-with-Five-Levels-of-Data.pdf

Hanbury, A., Prosser, M. & Rickinson, M. (2008). The differential impact of UK accredited teaching development programmes on academics' approaches to teaching. *Studies in Higher Education*, Routledge, 33(4), 469–483. DOI:10.1080/03075070802211844

Ilie, M.D., Maricuțoiu, L.P., Iancu, D.E., Smarandache, I.G., Mladenovici, V., Stoia, D.C.M. & Toth, S.A. (2020). Reviewing the research on instructional development programs for academics. Trying to tell a different story: A meta-analysis. *Educational Research Review*, 30, 100331. DOI:10.1016/j.edurev.2020.100331

Kandlbinder, P. & Peseta, T. (2009). Key concepts in postgraduate certificates in higher education teaching and learning in Australasia and the United Kingdom. *International Journal for Academic Development*, 14(1), 19–31. DOI:10.1080/13601440802659247

Kemp, N. (2022). *Ikigai-Kan: Feel a Life Worth Living*. Self-published. https://ikigaitribe.com/the-ikigai-kan-book/

Kight, C.R. & Lemon, N. (in press) Finding self through acts of creativity. In: Edwards, M., Martin, A. & Ashkanasy, N. (eds.), *Handbook of Academic Mental Health*. Edward Elgar Publisher.

Kilgour, P., Reynaud, D., Northcote, M., McLoughlin, K. & Gosselin, K.P. (2019). Threshold concepts about online pedagogy for novice online teachers in higher education, *Higher Education Research & Development*, 38(7), 1417–1431. DOI:10.1080/07294360.2018.1450360

King, H. (ed.) (2022). *Developing Expertise for Teaching in Higher Education Practical Ideas for Professional Learning and Development*. Abingdon: Routledge/SEDA.

Kirkpatrick, D. (2006). *Evaluating Training Programs: The Four Levels*. Oakland, CA: Berret-Koehler.

Kitchen, J., Berry, A., Bullock, S.M., Crowe, A.R., Taylor, M., Guðjónsdóttir, H. & Thomas, L. (2020). *International Handbook of Self-Study of Teaching and Teacher Education Practices*. Springer.

Knight, P.T. & Trowler P.R. (2000). Department-level cultures and the improvement of learning and teaching. *Studies in Higher Education*, 25(1), 69–83, DOI:10.1080/030750700116028

Krawec, P. (2022). *Becoming Kin: An Indigenous Call to Unforgetting the Past and Reimagining Our Future*. Broadleaf Books.

McIntosh, E. & Nutt, D. (eds.) (2022). *The Impact of the Integrated Practitioner in Higher Education Studies in Third Space Professionalism*. Routledge.

Mitchell, C., O'Reilly-Scanlon, K. & Weber, S. (2005). *Just Who Do We Think We Are?* RoutledgeFalmer.

Molloy, E., Ajjawi, A., Bearman, M., Noble, C., Rudland, J. & Ryan. A. (2019). Challenging feedback myths: Values, learner involvement and promoting effects beyond the immediate task. *Medical Education*, 54(1). DOI:10.1111/medu.13802

Moon, J.A. (1999). *Reflection in Learning & Professional Development: Theory & Practice*. RoutledgeFalmer.

Novalis (1798/1997). *Philosophical Writings*. State University of New York Press.

Osberg, D. & Biesta, G. (2021). Beyond curriculum: groundwork for a non-instrumental theory of education. *Educational Philosophy and Theory*, 53(1), 57–70. DOI:10.1080/00131857.2020.1750362

Pilkington, R. (2016). Supporting continuing professional development (CPD) for lecturers. In: Baume, D. and Popovic, C. (eds.) *Advancing Practice in Academic Development*, London: Routledge, pp. 52–68.

Pilkington, R. & Appleby, Y. (2014). *Developing Critical Professional Practice in Education*. England and Wales: National Institute of Adult Continuing Education.

Price, T., Wong, G., Withers, L., Wanner, A., Cleland, J., Gale, T., Prescott-Clements, L., Archer, J., Bryce, M. & Brennan, N. (2021). Optimising the delivery of remediation programmes for doctors: A realist review. *Medical Education Review*, 55(9), 995–1010. DOI:10.1111/medu.14528

PSF (2023). *Professional Standards Framework* https://www.advance-he.ac.uk/teaching-and-learning/psf

Roxå, T. & Mårtensson, K. (2017). Agency and structure in academic development practices: are we liberating academic teachers or are we part of a machinery supressing them? *International Journal for Academic Development*, 22(2), 95–105. DOI:10.1080/1360144X.2016.1218883

Schön, D.A. (1983). *The Reflective Practitioner: How Professionals Think in Action*. New York: Basic Books.

Shulman, L.S. (1986). Those who understand: Knowledge growth in teaching. *Educational Research*, 15(2), 4–31. DOI:10.2307/1175860

Smith S. & Walker, D. (2022). Scholarship and teaching-focused roles: An exploratory study of academics' experiences and perceptions of support. *Innovations in Education and Teaching International*, 61(1), 193–204. DOI:10.1080/14703297.2022.2132981

Stefani, L. & Baume, D. (2016). "Is it working?": outcomes, monitoring and evaluation. In: Baume, D. and Popovic, C. (eds.) *Advancing Practice in Academic Development*, London: Routledge, pp. 157–173.

Stevens, C. (2022). Get talking about evaluation: Coordinating an approach to evaluating staff development events. *Educational Developments*, 23(2), 1–4.

Telio, S., Ajjawi, R., & Regehr, G. (2015). The "Educational Alliance" as a framework for reconceptualising feedback in medical education. *Academic Medicine*, 90(5), 609–614. DOI:10.1097/acm.0000000000000560

Turner, R. & Spowart, L. (2022). Reflective practice as a threshold concept in the development of pedagogical content knowledge. In: King, H. (ed.) *Developing Expertise for Teaching in Higher Education*. London: SEDA Series. Routledge. DOI:10.4324/9781003198772-12

van der Sluis, H. (2021). "Frankly, as far as I can see, it has very little to do with teaching". Exploring academics' perceptions of the HEA Fellowships. *Professional Development in Education*. Routledge. 49(3), 416–428. DOI:10.1080/19415257.2021.1876153

Ward, N. & Gale, N. (2016). *LGBTQ-Inclusivity in The Higher Education Curriculum: A Best Practice Guide*. University of Birmingham. https://intranet.birmingham.ac.uk/staff/teaching-academy/documents/public/lgbt-best-practice-guide.pdf

Weallans, J., Roberts, C., Hamilton, S. & Parker, S. (2022). Guidance for providing effective feedback in clinical supervision in postgraduate medical education: a systematic review. *Postgraduate Medical Journal*, 98(1156), 138–149. DOI:10.1136/postgradmedj-2020-139566

Whitchurch, C. (2013). *Reconstructing Identities in Higher Education The rise of 'Third Space' professionals*. Routledge.

Index

Pages in *italics* refer to figures and pages in **bold** refer to tables.

academic developers 7, 62, 67, 69, 70–72, 142, 224, 226–227
academic development 63–65, 68–71, 136
academic leadership 137
Academic Practice Directorate 163
adaptive expertise of teaching 185
Adler, J. 211
Advance HE 136, 145, 154, 159, 224, 230
administrative leadership 136–138
agile software development 18
Aitken, V. 108
Almeida, Lucilene 50
Alves, M. 50
ancient scepticism 184, 186
Anderson, J. 122
Arabo, A. 8, 91–104
artistry of teaching 3, 6; adaptive expertise 6; authenticity and professional identity 8; development and enhancement 9–11; embodied thinking 7; flexibility and playfulness 225; in higher education 17; micro-behaviours of educators 7; mindset 225; moving forward 226–227; observation 225–226; self-study intervention 237–239; skills 225; time constraints 226
art theory 23
Ashcroft, Laura 42–43
assessment feedback 74
Associate Lecturer Support and Professional Development (ALSPD) 235

Association for Learning Technology (ALT) 149
Ausubel's Meaningful Learning Theory 50
authentic contextual pedagogy and materials: benefits 100–102; challenges and limitations 102–103; strategies 98–100
authentic educator 94
authenticity: authentic assessment methods 99; create an authentic environment 98; of curriculum design 91, 97; law of ethical hacking 99; in teaching 93–94
Authentic, Restricted, Clarification (ARC) 196
Authentic Teaching and Public Speaking 166

Bainbridge Cohen, B. 212
Bale, Richard 1–12
Bali, M. 76
Bamber, V. 235
Bastos, L. S. 50
Bell, K. 108
Belluigi, D. Z. 33
Biagioli, M. 6, 24–27
Biesta, G. 108
Bingham, C. 108
Bourdieu, P. 7, 63, 65, 68; concept of "*collusio*" 66
Bourriaud, N. 108
Bransford, J. D. 93, 95
Brenton, S. 106
Britton, J. 108

Brown, A. L. 93, 95
Brown, Stephen 163–176, 173
Bryant, M. 6, 17–27
Building Rapport 166
Butterworth, J. 215

Campbell, L. 230
Caplan, S. E. 178, 184
Carkett, R. 230
Carr, Jenni 62–72
Carusetta, E. 95
Cathcart, A. 230
central equilibrium point 51
Certificate in Teaching English to Speakers of Other Languages (CELTA) 197
Challenge Based Learning (CBL) 81–82
Chaplin, Charlie 19
Childs, M. 178–190, **182**, 184
Chinese language classroom 175–176
Chinese language teaching and learning 175
classroom interactions 74
Cochran, K. F. 196
Cocking, R. R. 93, 95
coevolution theory 50
cognitive neuroscience 6, 18
collaborative approach 2, 6
Collaborative Award for Teaching Excellence (CATE) 2
collaborative learning 8, 101, 108, 166, 178
Collaborative Learning Environments 166
collaborative professional enquiry 204
collaged drawing 56; barriers and vulnerabilities 56–58
Collinson, Penny 215
Colman, J. E. 17
communities of practice (CoPs): context 111–113; joint enterprise 111; method 113; mutual engagement 110; results 113–115; shared repertoire 111
community/communities 5, 8, 10–11, 48, 62–63, 66, 69, 71–72, 78, *80*, 84, 95–96, 102, 106–118, 136, 138–140, **140**, 143, 171, 173–175, 179–180, 214, 227–231, 237–238
community collusion 66
compassion 138–139, 143, 145, 216, 239

compassionate 5, 11, 68, 138, 145, 163, 209, 239
competence-based programme leading 136
competency-based pedagogy 6
compliance rewards 65–66
Compton, M. 224–227
Continuing Professional Development (CPD) 194, 203
Corderi Novoa, M. 174–176
coronavirus pandemic 69
corporeal standard 184, 186
Corradini, Erika 1–12
Costantino, Anna 193–205
COVID-19 pandemic 8, 70, 109, 112, 151, 163, 178, 235; lockdown of 2020 117
Cox, L. L. 214
Cranton, P. 95
Creative Facilitation 166
creativity 31–32, 108; creative praxis 44; curiosity 39–40; openness 37–38; perseverance 38–39; proactivity 40–41; role in your day-to-day work 35–37
Csíkszentmihályi, M. 37, 51, 219
cultural capital 63–64, 67, 70
cultural self-awareness 7, 8, 75
Cunningham, Catriona 62–72
cyber security: authenticity and inclusivity 95–97; contextual pedagogy and materials 98; create an authentic environment 98; law of ethical hacking 99; teaching 92–93

Dall'Alba, G. 210, 215
dance training: after teaching 221; awareness of the relational field 215; capacity to attune 220; choreographic skills 210; contact improvisation 210; creative movement practices 211; development of expertise 218–219; ephemeral moment 213; flight, fright, or freeze 212; importance of attunement 215–217; knowing ourselves 213–214; learning design 219–220; moments of transition 220; parts–whole 217–218; teaching experience 221; whole-bodied awareness 212
Danisch, R. 180
data as self-giving 24, 26–27

Davies, V. 230
de Almeida, Lucilene 7
Deans, C. 214
De Bruyckere, P. 95
Delamont, S. 17
DeRuiter, J. A. 196
Dewey, J.: arts of life 19–20; automation of manual labour 21; cinematic celebration 21; idea of occupational artistry 21
Dewsbury, D. 78
Dewsbury's Deep Teaching model 77
Dickerson, Evan 149–159
Didactic-Democratic model 215
Discipline of Authentic Movement 211
doodled hand 55
Dowler, Lisa 218
Dransfield, M. 230
Duhs, R. 230
Duignan, C. 95
Durham University 178, 186

educational developers 9–10, 152, 158, 235
educational development 10, 152, 158, 235
educational development interventions 168
educational development units (EDUs) 227
Education in an Ethics of Hospitality 77
Eisner, E.W. 5
Elkington, S. 7, 31–45
embodied cultural capital 67, 70
embodiment practices: definition 46; drawing for 54–55; drawing programme 48–49; embodied cognition 47; generative drawing 51; habituated thinking 49; mindfulness hand-doodle 54–55; self-regulation 53–54; tools 48; Walsh's embodied intelligence model 47
emotional investment 65
Engage, Study, Activate (ESA) 196
existentialist spontaneity 17
expertise-led approach 3
Expertise Symposium 6

Facilitating Meaningful Interactions between Learners 166
Faculty of Health's Ethics Committee 233

Floyd, S. 229–232, 230
Fossey, Peter 1–12
Fraser, D. 108
Freathy, R. 26
friendship 23, 26–27
Furlong, J. **182**, 183

Gadamer, H.-G.: authentic learning 24; implications of artificial intelligence 24; learning and teaching 23; philosophy of expertise 22; theory of teaching expertise 23; works of art 23
Gage, N. L. 5
Gallardo, M. 199
Gannaway, Deanne 1–12
geographical proximity 110
Gibbs, G. 237
Gibson's ecological psychology 50
Gosselin, K.P. 228
Gourlay, L. 66
Gravett, K. 75, 165
Grossman, P. 184
Groves, Michelle 120–133
Guildhall School of Music & Drama 152, 156

Hackney, P. 214
handwritten letters 7, 64
Hargreaves, A. 201
HE *see* higher education
healthcare teaching: findings 233–234; method 233
Heels, Laura 201–202
Heliö, S. 185
heliotropic effect 54
Herman, P. C. 180
hermeneutics 21; philosophy 22
Higham, R. 26
higher education (HE) 1, 135; appreciative self-study in 239; authenticity in 209–210; challenge for teachers 194; classroom 174; creativity 31–32; developing expertise and demonstrate artistry 229; developing teaching expertise 227; digitisation of 26; educational development initiatives 165; emotional difficulties 163; institutional learning spaces 228–229; interpretive phenomenological analysis 33–35; King's model 181; King's model of expertise in teaching

164; pedagogy 62; productive inquiry 32–33; professional identity formation in 120; professional learning 181; professional learning spaces 227–228; professional services and teaching expertise 229–232; Shulman's *pedagogical content knowledge* model 181; social equity policy 193; teachers and learners in education 42–43; teacher's role 31; teaching and administrative commitments of 209; teaching in 193
Higher Education Academy (HEA) 10, 142
Higher Education Statistics Agency (HESA) 230
Hofer, S. I. 186
Holtham, C. 6, 24–27
Hopper, L.S. 50
hospitality 77
Hulme, J. A. 136
Hutchison, J. N. 108

illusio 64, 70
imaginative co-creation 8, 83
imposter syndrome 7
Improvisation Skills for Teaching (IST) 164; bravery and safe spaces 170–172; coaching workshops 166–167; key concepts *165*; mantra of programme 165; workbook *170*; workshops focus on the student 166; workshops focus on the teacher 166
inclusion 77–78, 84, 96, 179, 193
inclusivity: curriculum design 96; in teaching and learning 92–93
indisciplinary artistry 25–26
Intentionally Equitable Hospitality 77
intercultural development inventory (IDI) 76, *79*
interdisciplinary consilient 212
interpretive phenomenological analysis (IPA): contemporary qualitative methodology 33; creativity in HE teacher practice 34; six distinct stages 34–35

Jacob, Mary 8, 95–96
Järvinen, A. 185
Jisc Digital Experience Insights Surveys 179
journal rejection 65

Kandlbinder, P. 227
Karin, J. 50
Keats, J. 19
Kennedy, A. 204
Kennedy, E. 224–227
Key Performance Indicator (KPI) 120, 230
Kilgour, P. 228
King, H. 1–12, 94, 167, 171, 173, 180, **182**, 194, 196
Kirschner, P. A. 95
Knight, P. T. 227

Lafferty, M. 10, 227–229
Landscape of Life 55
language of artistry 75
Lawrence, J. 135–145
learning centredness 8
Learning Experience Platform (LXP) 106
Learning Management Systems (LMS) 106
learning technologist's 149; auto-ethnography 151; delivering added value 154; educational setting 157–159; pedagogic expertise 152–153; people skills and networking 153; Postgraduate Certificate in Performance Teaching 156–157; problem solving and investigative abilities 153; role and workflow 154–155; roles 150; squiggly career 151; strategic thinking and awareness 153; technological expertise 152; VLE 150
learning trajectory 199
Lee, R. 216
Leigh, J. 46
lesson planning 74
letter writer 65, 66–68, 70
Little, D. 199

Macfarlane, B. 66
malleable model 204
Manifesto for Sustainable Programme Leadership 143
Margonis, F. 108
Marshall, Lindsay 201
Massive Open Online Courses (MOOCs) 107
Materialist/Idealist positioning and Passive/Active agency (MIPA) model

8, 120, 123; annual appraisals 131–132; applications 131; dance teacher educator 130; early career professionals and tutors 131; mapping professional development 132; observation and verbal feedback 131; personality types and decision-making style 127–130; professional identities of dance teachers 121–122; professional identities types 122–125; reflexive thought 125–127
Matisse, Henri 19
Mayo, C. 108
Mäyrä, F. 185
McDaniel, B. L. 108
McGrath, D. 95
McIntosh, E. 229
McLoughlin, K. 228
McNiff, S. 217
Midgley, M. 19
Mills, J. 7, 62–72
MIPA *see* Materialist/Idealist positioning and Passive/Active agency
Moccialo, Catherine 211
models of equity-minded 77
Montero, B. G. 18–19
Moodle 106, 155–157
Morantes-Africano, L. 1–12, 200–202
Mudd, S. 1–12, 9, 163–176

Naidu, S. 178
National Student Survey (NSS) 143
National Teaching Fellowship (NTF) 2
neoliberalism 202
Nicholson, Lucy 209–221
Niiranen, S. 109–101
Nistor, N. 186
Northcote, M. 228
nurturing moral sense 26–27
Nutt, D. 229

Oancea, A. 182, **182**, 183
occupational artistry 21
Oliver, M. 149
Olsen, A. 213
online forum space: joint enterprise 116; mutual engagement 115–116; shared repertoire 116
online teaching: critical reflection, attitudes, and identity 183–184; Csíkszentmihályi's concept of flow 185; explore resistance to 186–187; issues 178–181; King's framework 181–182; knowledge domains of 182–183, *183*; Oancea and Furlong's framework 185; patterns of reinforcement *188*; role of values, attitudes, and beliefs 181; staff experience of artistry 187, 189; TPACK model 189
Open University (OU) 107, 235
Orchard, J. 182

Palmer, Imogen 163–176, 173
pattern recognition 182, 185
Peachey, A. 184
pedagogical content knowing (PCKg) 194; components of knowledge 195; features 195–196; model 195
pedagogical content knowledge (PCK) 3, 20, 234
performances of teaching 52
Performative Language Teaching (PLT) 175
Peseta, T. 227
Petrova, P. 9, 163–176
PGCert Clinical Education programme 232
philosophy of mind 18
Pierson, R. 95
Pijanowski, C. M. 108
Pini, S. 214
political and social relation 110
positive impact of Postgraduate Certificate (PGCert) 10
Postgraduate Certificate (PGCert) 10, 66, 224–226, 232–233
Postgraduate Certificate in Education (PGCE) 197
Postgraduate Certificate in Higher Education (PGCert) 66
Potter, Jackie 1–12, 227–229
Practice-as-Research (PaR) methodology 176
practitioner research (PR) 194; develop expertise and autonomy in HE 202–203
Present, Practice, Produce (PPP) 196
Price, G. 108
Price, T. 232–234
problem-solving 185
professional development: constraints and affordances 203–204; Gallardo,

M. 199; language teacher education 195; PCKg model 195; personal and professional identities 198; procedural frameworks 196; teacher development programmes 197–198; teacher education programmes 195
professional ethics 27
professional identity types: Listener 123; Speaker 123; stage 1: aim 124; stage 2: create 124; stage 3: instigate 124; stage 4: synthesise and analyse 124; stage 5: reflect 125
professional learning 3, 6, 10
Professional Services (PS) community 229
Professional Standards Framework (PSF) 2, 62, 142, 189, 230
Professional, Statutory or Regulatory Body (PSRB) 135
programme evaluation: practical tools and techniques 168–169; preconceptions 167–168; teaching 173; workbooks 169–170; workshop facilitators 173–174
programme leadership: academic artistry and identity 142; artistry 137–138, **138**; competence-based programme leading 139, **140**; complex array of expertise 137; experience 139–140; identity in HE 135–136; knowledge 140–141; method 136; practical and evidence-based ideas 142–144; self-awareness 141–142
project society 20

Quality Education Sustainable Development Goals (SDGs) 193

Reeve, Julia 127–128
Reis, Charlie 10, 218
relational pedagogy 108–110
Review of Educational Practice (REP) 232
Reynaud, D. 228
Richards, R. 33, 44
Romano, R. M. 108
Ronfeldt, M. 184
routine expertise 52
Ruitenberg, C. W. 77
Runco, M. A. 40

Santucci, A. 7, 74–86, 78
Saunders, R. 181

Savage, Jennifer 109
Scheibenzuber, C. 186
Schewe, M. 175
Scholarship of Teaching and Learning (SoTL) 74
Schön, D. A. 20, 77, 121, 199
Schwartz, H. L. 95
Scott, C. 7, 46–59
Scott, D. 149
self-awareness 7–8, 11, 47, 53, 75–78
self-reflection 11, 77–78, 123
Shelley, P. B. 21
Sheridan Center for Teaching & Learning 74
Short, Fay 42–43
Shulman, L. S. 22, 194, 234
Sidorkin, A. M. 108
Siegel, D. J. 212
Smart, F. 229–232, 230
Smith, G. A. 75
Smith, S. 229
social capital 63, 64–65; of academic developers 69–70
Spencer, Ruth 209–221
Spowart, L. 10, 228, 232–234
staff development events 235–237
Stengel, B. S. 108
Stevens, Charlotte 235–237
Stolz, S. A. 46
Studd, K. 214

Tajfel, H. 136
Taylor, Natasha 62–72
teacher artistry: artistic composition 18; art theory of Friedrich Schlegel 18
teacher autonomy: artistry in education 201–202; disciplinary expert 200; expert teachers 200
teacher thinking 4
teaching: artistry of 3–4; model *3*; thinking and practising in 4–6
teaching and learning development 76
Teaching Excellence Framework (TEF) 1, 194
teaching identity, fashioning 128, *129*
Teaching & Learning in Higher Education 74
Technological Pedagogical Content Knowledge Framework (TPACK) 182, *183*, *188*, 189
technological pedagogical knowledge (TPK) 182, *183*

Thayer-Bacon, B. J. 108
Theory and Methods of Foreign Language Teaching 74
Trowler, P. R. 227
Tsui, A. 200
Turner, J. 136
Turner, R. 10, 228
Turner, V. 111, 116

UK higher education institutions (HEIs) 107
University of Central Lancashire 209
University of Queensland 210
University of the West of England (UWE) 163, 169
University of Warwick 6
UN Sustainable Development Goals (SDGs) 81

Vasant, S. 149
Virtual Learning Environment (VLE) 63, 106, 141, 152–153

Voice and Presence 166
Vygotsky, L. S. 219

Walker, D. 229
Watts, Carys 201–202
Wegerif, R. 26
Weidemann, A. 50
Wellhöfer, Kerstin 209–221
Wenger, E. 106, 111, 116, 118
Whitchurch, C. 150, 229
Wilson-Medhurst, S. 178–190, **182**
Winch, C. 19, 182
Winstone, N. E. 75, 165
Woolf, Virginia 19
World Wide Web 106

Yes, And ... Higher Education (YAHE Network) 83
Young, Nia 42–43

Zawacki-Richter, O. 178
zone of proximal development (ZPD) 219

For Product Safety Concerns and Information please contact our EU representative GPSR@taylorandfrancis.com Taylor & Francis Verlag GmbH, Kaufingerstraße 24, 80331 München, Germany

Printed and bound by CPI Group (UK) Ltd, Croydon, CR0 4YY

10/07/2025

01909247-0011